Corporate Governance and Accountability

Corporate Governance and Accountability

What Role for the Regulator, Director, and Auditor?

Dan A. Bavly

Foreword by Roger B. Porter

QUORUM BOOKS
Westport, Connecticut • London

Library of Congress Cataloging-in-Publication Data

Bawley, Dan, 1929–
    Corporate governance and accountability : what role for the
regulator, director, and auditor? / Dan A. Bavly ; foreword by
Roger B. Porter.
        p.   cm.
    Includes bibliographical references and index.
        ISBN 1–56720–280–2 (alk. paper)
    1. Corporate governance—United States.   2. Chief executive
officers—United States   3. Disclosure in accounting—United
States.   I. Title.
    HD2741.B34   1999
    658.4—dc21   98–38314

British Library Cataloguing in Publication Data is available.

Library of Congress Catalog Card Number: 98–38314
ISBN: 1–56720–280–2

First published in 1999

Quorum Books, 88 Post Road West, Westport, CT 06881
An imprint of Greenwood Publishing Group, Inc.

Printed in the United States of America

The paper used in this book complies with the
Permanent Paper Standard issued by the National
Information Standards Organization (Z39.48–1984).

10 9 8 7 6 5 4 3 2

Contents

Foreword

Corporate governance has assumed a higher profile in recent years, and demands for greater accountability are commonplace in the modern age. A heightened awareness of the need for and value of accountability accompany higher expectations for performance and conduct.

In the United States, the search for greater accountability takes many forms—more frequent testing of teachers and students; increased regulatory requirements by all levels of government; a vigilant press seeking ever more information while diminishing the privacy of public officials. At the same time, Americans are committed to the quest for efficiency—in the way we communicate, manufacture, travel, and transact business.

Ours is a restless age, determined to examine and reinvent, to press for more and better. These multiple objectives have led many to reconsider the role of government regulators and corporate management, of directors and shareholders, of internal and outside auditors.

In the field of corporate governance, U.S. practices tend to lead the world. Thus, observers from abroad have a stake in examining American developments. Dan Bavly is such an observer. Having spent a lifetime in the study and practice of business and accounting, he has ventured from his native Israel to the United States to assess and comment on the broad canvas of corporate governance and accountability. The questions he raises are large and timely. Moreover, the subjects to which he addresses himself are rapidly evolving and changing.

Three sets of questions guide his study. First, what levels and types of accountability are desirable? At what cost? For what gain?

Second, in achieving an appropriate level of accountability, what are the appropriate roles for market mechanisms, government regulators, corporate directors, and auditors, both internal and independent?

Third, are the current trends in American corporate governance and account-ability healthy? Should policymakers and corporate executives encourage them, or are they taking us down a path not worth pursuing?

LEVELS AND TYPES OF ACCOUNTABILITY

Greater levels of accountability sound attractive as an abstract proposition, but who will ensure that those overseeing the accountability game are making the correct calls? What remedies are available if there is no instant replay, and the referees miss some infractions and exercise poor judgment in calling others?

The call for greater accountability comes at a time when government and business are both becoming more complicated. Moreover, the costs of under-taking extensive surveillance remain high. The layering of political appointees and management in government, the blurring of staff and line functions, and a rapidly revolving door for key officials all make the challenge of genuine ac-countability more difficult.

We live in an age of information overload, when more is known and proce-dures for handling issues have multiplied. Yet more is not necessarily better, particularly when information overload diverts attention from weightier matters. The things that matter most should not be at the mercy of the things that matter least.

In the United States, at the heart of accountability is the issue of disclosure. Since the early part of this century, the value of disclosure has received much support. As Justice Louis Brandeis reminded: "publicity is justly commended as a remedy for social and industrial diseases. Sunlight is said to be the best of disinfectants."

In considering accountability, one must never lose sight of the objectives of government regulation—to maintain safety and soundness; to ensure that general societal interests are weighed, considered, and protected; and to establish a framework in which private entities can flourish in an environment that en-courages innovation while rewarding integrity.

Creating a regime of regulatory reasonableness, however, is a challenging task. The temptation for regulators is to act as a disciplinary means of gover-nance, to resort to increased rule making and standard setting. Many rules are costly, cumbersome, and counterproductive. The leading alternative—disclo-sure—is less intrusive and often more effective.

APPROPRIATE ROLES FOR GOVERNMENT AND BUSINESS

The roles of regulators, management, directors, and auditors remain in flux. A regime of regulatory reasonableness depends not only on clear standards and understandable rules—it also rests on trust, goodwill, and voluntary behavior.

Dan Bavly raises the question of to what extent governmental regulators need to accept a higher level of responsibility. He is rightly skeptical of provisions that could encourage more litigation, noting that regulatory oversight failures are often ignored and not subject to the same kind of exposure, examination, and discipline that falls on the regulated.

Not surprisingly, directors play a central role in this drama. The continuing transformation of corporate boards of directors is driven by increased sensitivity to their fiduciary responsibilities, the need for engaged and informed directors, and the contribution they can make to shaping strategic decisions.

The picture of directors as disengaged, failing to probe, and willing to play a passive role has given way to a much higher level of activism in many companies. If directors are to play a central role in corporate governance, they need accurate information provided in a timely manner. Moreover, they need to develop an ethos that suggests they are to serve not merely as a sounding board but as a partner with management in guiding company strategy.

TRENDS IN CORPORATE GOVERNANCE

Throughout this volume, Dan Bavly describes a host of developments that impinge on corporate governance—the accelerated turnover of senior management; the growing empowerment of boards of directors; changes in the selection, retention, and rewarding of directors; a decline in the size of boards and an increase in the number of directors with academic and scientific training; the delegation of much oversight to board committees, including audit committees; the shift toward performance-based compensation; the use of stock rather than retirement benefits to compensate outside directors; and a decline in retirement plans for directors, among others.

Two powerful forces have helped transform corporate governance in recent years. The first is the rise in lawsuits, which have heightened the sensitivity of directors and management to their fiduciary responsibilities. The second is the role of institutional investors in holding a spotlight on boards and management. Institutional investors, most notably pension funds, today account for the bulk of equity investments in the United States, and have played a prominent role in the drive for independent directors and tying executive compensation with company performance.

On balance, these forces have probably helped improve governance. As the century draws to a close, most careful observers have concluded that boards function in a much more credible way than several decades ago.

Every book is in part a reflection of the author. This work is no exception. In this volume, Dan Bavly advances "two preliminary hypotheses. First, in complementing a true market economy, it is essential that there be a built-in mechanism of ethics, honesty, and good sense to provide efficient corporate governance. Second, rather than introduce more laws and ordinances, it is probably better to improve governance through education and persuasion of the various actors involved" (p. 126).

A message that comes through repeatedly is the importance of integrity—that character counts and that in the end there is no substitute for ethical behavior. It is a message that regulators, directors, and auditors—the principal audiences for this volume—should consider carefully as they seek to strengthen our system of corporate governance and accountability.

Roger B. Porter
Harvard University

Preface

In the course of many years as a business consultant and executive, I came to realize that although most countries have their own characteristic business procedures, there are general *mores* that embrace the global corporate world. Certainly, this is true of management practices and cultures of governance accountability in the Israeli and the American markets. At the same time, nonetheless, it is also beyond doubt that, with regard to both regulatory laws and the actual conduct of business, the United States is by far the most sophisticated environment in the world.

Some may regard it as presumptuous for a foreigner to write on corporate governance and accountability in the United States. During my decades of CPA practice in Israel, however, I was extensively exposed to American business and spent many professional hours with U.S. peers, directors, and regulators. Many of those I came across were people of charm and intelligence, but they only described what was expected of them in fair weather. I came to believe that there was an unrealized gap between the way they functioned in normal conditions and how they might perform under pressure and stress. It was my impression that they were satisfied with their clients' performance, rather than showing curiosity about what might happen should crisis conditions arise. This was true of my fellow accountants and no less so of directors to whom I talked.

Regulators were another matter. I seemed to see a double standard, with more accountability invariably being expected from the director and auditor than from the regulator. If this premise proves true, it is, I believe, a shortcoming and an impediment to good governance which should be corrected.

In this study I hope to convince the reader that the various organs of corporate governance and accountability are far from being in a fixed state, but, rather, are quite fluid, and that the respective roles of regulators, directors and auditors will continue to evolve as we move into the coming century. The observations made and the conclusions reached are grounded in my many years as an outside, but friendly, observer of corporate practices in the United States.

Although corporate governance and accountability is a popular topic for discussion and study, the subject has been with us for decades, if not centuries.[1] Books on economic history date the beginning of modern governance problems to the Mississippi Scheme and the South Sea Bubble, both of which belong to the second decade of the eighteenth century.

The Mississippi Scheme was conceived by John Law, a Scottish economist[2] who moved to Paris and, in the spring of 1716, obtained patent letters to establish a *Banque generale*. The next year he founded the *Compagnie de la Louisiane ou d'Occident*, in rue Quincampoix.[3] His company obtained extensive powers over the area drained by the Mississippi, the Ohio and the Missouri and secured the title to Louisiana. Its powers were widened in 1718 by the purchase of the tobacco monopoly. In December 1718, the *Banque generale* was converted into the *Banque royale*, with notes guaranteed by the king and John Law as director. The company was granted management of the mint and coin issue for nine years and the farming of the national revenues, on undertaking the payment of the national debt. For a time, Law's projects provoked an outburst of paper money, inflation, and stock speculation, but reaction was not slow to come. The public became alarmed; drastic measures had to be taken to check the drain of coin; but a decree of May 21, 1720, by which the value of the bank notes was to be gradually reduced to one-half, precipitated a panic, and a week later the bank suspended payments. The climax came with the amalgamation of the *Banque royale* and the *Compagnie des Indes*. In June 1720, John Law fled France.

The South Sea Bubble was a different story. The South Sea company was formed in Britain in 1711 and was granted a monopoly of the British trade with South America and the Pacific islands. It was highly successful, and early in 1718 King George I became its governor. The company's directors soon put before the government a scheme whereby, in return for further concessions, it would not only take over the national debt of £51.3 million but even pay £3.5 million for this privilege. Their intention was to persuade the creditors of the State to exchange their annuities for South Sea stock. The stock would be issued at a high premium, and thus a huge amount of annuities would be purchased and extinguished by the issue of a comparatively small amount of stock. In addition, the company would receive some £1.5 million a year from the government in interest. The offer was accepted in 1720. Shortly after, the company persuaded over half the government annuitants to become shareholders of the company. It didn't take long for the company's share price to rise. Within six months it rose by nearly 800 percent, enabling the directors to sell 5 million shares of stock. The speculation involved legitimate companies. A month later, disaster set in. By November it had fallen to 135, and in four months the stock of the Bank of England fell from 263 to 145. Thousands of shareholders were ruined, and many who were committed to heady payments fled the country. A committee of secrecy of the House of Commons reported in February 1721 that the company's books contained fictitious entries, and it was shown that favors secured from the State had been purchased by gifts to ministers, some of whom had also made large sums of money by speculating in the stock, and so it went.[4]

That was close to three centuries ago, and yet, surprisingly, little has changed. Greed remains dominant in the business world. True, many instruments of business governance, laws, rules, regulations, and accounting procedures have been introduced, especially since the Wall Street crash of October 1929. But periodically, not least because the issues that arise are so complex, the economy is shaken by shortcomings in the systems it has developed.

Take the matter of how far regulators should be accountable. Over the past two generations, business laws and regulations, once so simple and short, have become cumbersome and lengthy. The regulatory authorities have increased their supervisory staff and extended their prerogatives until they often give what are in effect operational orders to company executives. If so, are they not accountable for their actions, just like senior executives, directors, and auditors? This is a matter I have thought about for many years, in particular the role of the regulators in various affairs of the last decade, such as the Savings and Loans breakdowns, the debacle of the Bank of Credit and Commerce Internationale, and the crash of the ValuJet plane into the Florida Everglades in May 1996. That both corporate board directors and independent auditors often lack effective tools to fulfill their roles in rough seas has been a concern of mine for many years.

As this book went to press in the late fall of 1998, there were increasing signs that the steady growth enjoyed since early in the decade might have peaked. The extraordinary economic expansion of East Asia had come to a halt. For over a year, the solvency of Far Eastern financial institutions and of industrial complexes in Japan, South Korea, and the other so-called "dragons" were being questioned. Some were going into liquidation. Looking for reasons for the economic difficulties, many observers pointed out that, compared to the United States, the regulatory authorities in the Far East have very little influence. In fact, they are so ineffective that accumulated losses may easily be ignored and not written off, as U.S. standards would require. Why they remain so lax is surely a subject for separate study.

More related to the subject of this book was the near collapse of the Long-Term Capital Management hedge fund which, in October 1998, had to be bailed out by a $3.6 billion cash investment of big brokerage firms and banks. This was another example of how, in the clubby world of high finance, decisions on where to steer vast sums can still be made, with far too few questions asked by regulators, directors, or auditors;[5] how some officials still believe that the governance and accountability regulations and disciplines of the past two generations and more do not necessarily always apply to them. A number of ideas on how to provide more effective remedies are part of the message of this book.

All these seemed to me matters worth studying and on which I believed I could offer insight and ideas. Accordingly, on November 1, 1995, I took up the invitation extended to me a year earlier by Director John White and became a Fellow of the Center for Business and Government at Harvard University's John F. Kennedy School of Government, and the following winter and spring provided a most rewarding experience.

On the advice of Mr. White, I acquainted myself with the facilities of the center before choosing my main topic. Drawing on the superlative assets of the center enabled me to focus clearly and gave me valuable insight as to how I should plan and proceed with my program.

Two professors there were especially valuable in helping define the subject of this book. One was Raymond Vernon, with some of whose writings I had long been acquainted. The location of his office only a few doors away from mine encouraged me to walk over to test ideas and order my thoughts. The other great help was Roger Porter who, when John White left Cambridge to become assistant secretary for defense in Washington, became head of the center. Apart from his ongoing support throughout my stay, it was he who suggested I include government regulators in my study, leading me later to suggest that they be among those who should be accountable in corporate governance. Also very kind was Beverly Raimondo, then executive director of the center, who patiently explained its structure and logistics.

One of the most attractive aspects of life at Harvard in general, and the center in particular, is the accessibility of faculty members. Professor Henry Rosovsky, longtime dean of arts and sciences and always supportive of various projects in which I was involved in Israel, was the first to point this out to me. And, in fact, almost every day I stopped by the office of at least one faculty member for discussions. At the center itself, Robert Glauber, Jack Donahue, F. M. Scherer, Dale Jorgenson, Brian Mandel, Richard Zeckhauser, and Herman (Dutch) Leonard all were generous with their time. Derek Bok, former president of Harvard, was especially gracious, and John Cullinane and Sidney Topol, both alumni of the center, went out of their way to advise me on how to make myself comfortable.

At the Graduate School of Business Administration, Professor Joe Bower (who in 1994 had first suggested that I apply to spend time at the center) and Professor Walter Salmon, both of whom I had first met 20 years earlier when they visited Jerusalem to set up the Jerusalem Institute of Management (JIM), provided friendly guidance. On their advice I met with David F. Hawkins, Joseph Hinsey, William J. Bruns, and Benjamin Esty. Also very kind were Zvi Griliches, economics professor at Harvard, and Don Schon, professor emeritus at MIT, whom I had also known since the JIM days. Dan Carroll of The Carroll Group made written observations on my notes that were of much benefit. Very constructive also was ex-SEC (Securities and Exchange Commission) Commissioner A. A. Sommer, whom I met in Washington, DC.

Then there were helpful contacts in New York, some of whom had been personal friends for many years. Harvey Krueger, general manager at Lehmann Bros., was a young partner at Kuhn Loeb when he first came to Israel in 1961 to make a due diligence study before his firm would underwrite the marketing of Bank Leumi shares, for whom my firm acted as the independent CPAs. Arthur Bettauer, then a partner in Price Waterhouse, accompanied him. Both were invaluable in their observations on my project, as was Walter P. Stern of Capital Resources. Also helpful were Josephine Chaus of the clothing industry, Ludwig Bravmann of Oppenheimer & Co. and Jim Kohlberg.

Dana Edelmann of the New England–Israel Chamber of Commerce introduced me to a number of impressive businesspeople in Boston, including Charles Housen, Paul Rosenbaum, Gil Fishman, and Jacob Levy. Practicing or retired American CPAs who were cooperative included Arthur Aeder, who had been a senior partner with Oppenheim Dixon and Appel; Ray Groves, a retired managing partner of Ernst and Young; Larry Weinbach and Eugene Friedman, who had been managing partners at Arthur Andersen and Coopers & Lybrand, respectively; Paul Neubelt and Lorin Luchs, both still very active with BDO Seidman; Marty Mertz, who had been with KPMG for many years; and Ben Rosenthal, who had been with Deloitte. In the United Kingdom, Peter Chidgey, Stephen Greene, and Paul Hipps—all of BDO Stoy Hayward—over the years afforded me interesting insights into the subject of governance; and Sven Erik Johannson, managing partner of the Tonnervik Group until it merged with Ernst & Young, was a partner and friend with whom I spent many days theorizing and making notes on matters concerning governance and accountability.

When I was about to complete the manuscript, Marco Bongiovanni of Horwath Italia in Rome contributed a number of finely discerning observations concerning the future of the auditing profession.

In the early summer of 1996 I returned home to a small village in the Galilee called Harashim, to work on my manuscript. For the fact that it has reached the form of a printed book, much of the credit goes to Eugene R. Bailey of Westborough, Massachusetts, whose long-distance editing services were exceptional. Working with me throughout this venture, as she has done during more than 25 years, was Penina Barkai, who edited, typed, and often retyped the manuscript and whose patience remains extraordinary.

Finally, although this book addresses the subject of governance and accountability in the United States, an Israeli friend and associate in many of my nonprofessional activities, Eliahu Salpeter, showed a keen interest in the manuscript. I often sought his advice and his comments were always readily given and gratefully received.

To all of the above for their input, support, and help, I am thankful.

NOTES

1. See, for instance, Herbert Heaton, *Economic History of Europe* (Harper & Bros., 1948).

2. "Law, John," *Encyclopedia Brittanica, vol. 13* (1945): 779–780.

3. In the vicinity of the Centre Pompidou (3rd arrondissement).

4. "South Sea Bubble," *Encyclopedia Brittanica, vol. 21* (1945): 94.

5. Timothy L. O'Brien and Laura M. Holson, "A hedge fund's stars didn't tell, and savvy financiers didn't ask," *The New York Times on the Web* (October 23, 1998).

Introduction

The purpose of this book is to reassess some commonly accepted premises of governance and accountability as practiced in corporations today, to describe some of the shortcomings of the system, and propose some basic changes. This venture is not the result of a broad-based call for change. On the contrary, most active participants in the system seem satisfied with the way their companies operate—an understandable sense of well-being, in the climate of economic growth and generally bullish securities' trading experienced since the early 1990s. Indeed, almost all written and oral discussion of the subject indicates contentment with the system, usually addressing only particular management practices and sometimes making modest suggestions relevant to certain boards of directors or senior management. It is especially interesting that most business publications assume continued corporate fair weather, and although some mention is made of the need for greater accountability on the part of participants in governance, attention to this topic is modest.

Endorsing James Madison, who wrote in Federalist Number Ten that "No man is allowed to be judge in his own case, because his interest would certainly bias his judgment, and, not improbably corrupt his integrity,"[1] most observers would contend that society has produced the tools to ensure proper governance and accountability. It is my intention to examine whether this is indeed so.

In conducting research for this book, I was surprised at how little concern is shown about the readiness of officers and directors to deal with sudden, unforeseen crises. Like jaded car drivers, unfazed by the large number of traffic accidents, most directors seem to assume that the problems experienced by other companies will not occur in theirs. Unlike scheduled airline flights, where at take-off passengers are asked to devote a minute to understanding air safety measures, corporate governance seldom mandates routine cautionary procedures in governance. Because of this ingrained complacency, it is rare for a company—particularly one confident in its growth—to conduct preventive exercises that will suggest appropriate responses to possible future threats. This mind-set ignores the fact that corporate crisis and collapse are inevitable in business in good times and bad, although there are, of course, more in periods of economic stagnation or recession. In recent decades, for example, there was the breakdown of Penn Central and Equity Funding in the early 1970s. The following decade saw a series of Latin American sovereign debt moratoria and other incidents of mismanagement. At the end of the 1980s came the debacle of the savings and loan institutions, soon followed by the substantial losses encountered by blue chip firms such as American Express, GM, IBM, and Westinghouse.

Except for the savings and loan institutions (S&Ls), where signs of trouble were ignored and wrong policies pursued, almost all of these collapses came suddenly, without prior warning. Understandably, these events contributed to the growth of public concern about corporate governance. Much attention focused on the chief executive officer's (CEO's) management style and his relations with the board of directors, and in time accountability became a complementary subject of governance. While not presuming to prophesy who will be faced with failure, it is a basic assumption of this book that the business world will continue to witness corporate failures in the future.

Although the fundamental concepts of good corporate governance are simple and straightforward, implementing them is a complex matter. Not surprisingly, then, governance is a subject of interest to many, including business people and academics, and books and articles on this topic fill a growing niche in the wide range of popular publications on economics, business, and management. Part of the explanation for this boom in publications lies in the cyclical behavior of the economy, but it is also a result of what may be called the professionalization of senior company officers. Powerful but not always secure in their functions, they have become partners in the search for a clear definition of the skills and knowledge required for fulfillment of their responsibilities.

One of the more serious aspects of modern governance, hardly touched upon in current literature, is the accountability of regulatory authorities. In many of the corporate collapses of the past 20 years, the regulator's inadequacy was a contributing factor. But, whereas directors or accountants were often sued for negligence in the aftermath of a debacle, the regulator—who, possibly inadvertently, contributed to the breakdown—carried on with impunity. Most mortals are held accountable at some level. Why is it that regulators and related government officials are absolved of accountability as if they resided in another sphere? Captive of a brief established many years ago, regulators lack the self-discipline to assess the validity of the traditional separation of standards for civil servants from those for others.

In fact, the regulator should be aware of his accountability, as should his clients, the public, shareholders, and officers and directors of the corporation. Until regulators are made legally accountable for corporate problems in which they play a part, the public will not be assured that an important—sometimes crucial—step toward better governance has been achieved. Some ideas of how regulators can be made more accountable and why this step is important to enhancing public trust in the system are addressed in this book (see Chapter 2).

THE MAKINGS OF PROPER CORPORATE GOVERNANCE

Until now, probably the two most important basic ingredients of proper corporate governance have been (1) "full disclosure" and (2) the presence of well-informed, independent directors and auditors who each have their own ways to confirm that the data presented by the corporation are true and fairly stated. Most people will agree that an important factor in recognition of the United States as the business leader of the world is the existence of high standards of its corporate governance and the integrity of its economic leaders—sound reasons for the trust of investors and traders in the system. Much of this preeminence is due to the effective use of the two above-mentioned instruments of governance.

The elements of full disclosure are set out in regulatory demands and professional pronouncements, and companies are expected to comply fully. The independence of the outside director or independent auditor, however, is more difficult to define. Possibly because of the many compromises in the system, this subject is more controversial. For example, has the demand of regulators for full and detailed disclosure become exaggerated and counterproductive—this is to say, is the additional information required making corporate accounts harder, rather than easier, to understand?

The question of whether the director and auditor are sufficiently independent is also important to pursue. The approach of regulators including that of the Securities and Exchange Commission (SEC) to this subject seems to indicate that they are captive to the concepts of independence that were enunciated many years ago. Except for slightly fine-tuning the rules, they see no need for restructuring. It is the premise of this book, however, that the traditional view of how the independence of outside directors and auditors can be ensured is untenable and, accordingly, that outside directors and auditors will have to distance themselves considerably further than even the most radical pundits demand, in order to assure shareholders that they have carried out their tasks.

There are two aspects of auditor and director independence in which present practice is especially unsatisfactory. The first is who determines their fees and pays them; the second is the amount of time they are expected to devote to the company's affairs in order to obtain enough knowledge to form independent opinions. The fees of auditors and directors are usually approved by the CEO, who is supported in a variety of ways by the board or one of its committees, usually composed of outside directors. Even when such outside directors are formally not dependent on the CEO, discussion and approval of the annual fee in the cozy boardroom environment ensures more comfort than independence to the recipients, be they CPAs or directors. Even if, technically, the decision is taken by the outside directors, the fees are, in fact, approved or greatly influenced by those who are reviewed, thus impairing the concept of independence normally applied in the corporate world, which is synonymous with impartiality.

The optimal amount of time to be invested by the directors of a company is difficult to establish. The available compiled data show that directors spend an average of twelve to sixteen days annually on company affairs. Among others, Arthur Levitt, Jr., chairman of the SEC, suggests that directors increase their involvement to two days a month. But it is my aim to prove that even this amount of time would be far from satisfactory. To comprehend the business of a company involved in hi-tech research and marketing, or of a multinational providing services in different countries and addressing diverse cultures, for example, a director would have to invest substantially more than 20 days a year. A newly appointed CEO is usually given a hundred days of grace before being expected to master the intricacies of corporate affairs. In the two-days-a-month format proposed by Levitt, it would take directors a full five years to acquire the knowledge that the CEO is expected to gain in just over three months.

HOW IMPARTIALITY CAN BE ENSURED

Other questions concerning impartiality result from the fact that directors and auditors may be asked to provide additional services, usually consulting in one form or other. The question of whether counseling and advising can undermine independence has been addressed repeatedly by both theorists and practitioners. Possibly, more attention should be devoted to the independence-eroding intimacy that develops over time between senior corporate officers and their consultants, be they directors or auditors.

Many CEOs regard consultants as essential, whether they are well-known public figures who can be helpful with the administration, experienced lawyers who can advise on complex business transactions and structures or other specialists. CEOs rely on such support, for consultants can contribute significantly to the company's earnings. Directors should, however, feel uncomfortable in acting also as the shareholders' independent agents. When, as sometimes happens, they are asked to perform as consultants, they might better advise the company to establish what has become known as an advisory board and suggest that they join such a forum (see Chapter 10). Over time, outside directors will find it difficult to fulfill their governance duties objectively if they are also consultants to the same company; and it will be only human if the outside auditors, also asked to provide consulting services on an ongoing basis, find that their auditing objectivity is marred by this additional engagement.

What can be done to resolve these possible conflicts of interest and ensure that we have truly independent directors and auditors? Although many in the corporate world would at first regard the following proposal as totally out of order, one way would be for the directors and the auditors of all companies that intend to go public or in which the public has an interest (such as banks, insurance companies and utilities) to be paid not by the retaining company but by some independent public body similar in structure to the stock exchange on which their equity is traded. This body might also appoint—and, when called for, reappoint—the independent company directors. Basically, this proposal would create a new instrument of governance. This public body, in which all traded companies would be members, would have a budget of its own, supported by fees paid by the members, and a board of governors elected by them. Although some form of monitoring by the regulatory agencies would be appropriate, as with the stock exchange or the Financial Accounting Standards Board (FASB), this activity would be totally independent from the regulators as well as from the traded companies.

It is not, of course, proposed that companies become totally dependent on the decisions taken by this body. A way could be found to provide them with the means for recourse and a voice in the appointment and reappointment of directors and auditors. This new public body, with a management board of senior (possibly recently retired) business people, would be expected to monitor the relationships between companies and their directors and auditors. Paying for its services would be one way to ensure its independence.

BOARD SIZE AND COMPOSITION: THE NEED FOR CHANGE

Directors should also be enabled to perform effectively. To this end, they should be as well-informed as senior corporate officers about the company's activities. To reach this level of competence, they would have to spend from one-third to one-half their working time on company matters. Rather than being restricted to board meetings, their activities would include individual study of the company's activities. They would have open access to company locations and communicate freely with corporate staff (although being careful not to interfere in business operations). The company's organization chart would make it clear that both the internal audit group and the independent auditors report to the directors and that it is the directors' responsibility to set the auditors' remuneration, either themselves or via the outside body proposed above.

Some worry that such involvement might threaten the authority of the CEO, but that will not happen if directors' tasks are clearly and properly defined. It should be explicitly stated that they have no executive authority, and the CEO must be able to call on the public body that chose them to remove them from office. Such a removal, however, should not be effected without the director being given a hearing by the public body.

Because these experienced executives would be devoting much more time to the company, their retainers would be considerably higher. Their number, however, could be reduced from the present average of 9–15 to 3–5. They should also have a limited term of office, possibly being elected to a fixed term of three to five years, with the possibility of one additional term of office. In order to ensure continuity in the board's performance, members' election should be staggered over the period of tenure. Such contraction in the number of board members and far greater knowledge on the part of directors about the company's operations would change both their relationship with the CEO and the format of board activities.

The function of the outside auditors also would change. Possibly, their assignments would be incorporated into those of the company's now far more independent international audit division (see Chapter 13). They would be paid by either the outside body mentioned above or the new, smaller, more specialized board, and they would spend more time on the company's affairs, serving and reporting directly to the board.

In the following pages, doubt will be cast on the ability of the present system to stand up to crisis—or even severe hardship. I will also try to explain why it is not reasonable to expect regulators, directors, and auditors, given the limited amount of time they now devote to the company, to be truly accountable agents to their principals. To improve governance, the radical changes proposed are overdue, and they are well within the realm of practical implementation. And it should be noted that we live in a time of rapid change. Corporate governance and its major components, like other social and economic structures, should be periodically—say, every five to ten years—examined and their efficacy reassessed.

NOTE

1. James Madison, "Federalist Number Ten," continued from Number Nine by Alexander Hamilton on the same subject, "The Union as a Safeguard against Domestic Faction and Insurrection," the *New York Packet*, November 23, 1987.

Chapter 1

Why Accountability?

ON GOVERNANCE AND ACCOUNTABILITY

Just as every social structure has its own accountability system, in the classic market economy a company is held responsible in the marketplace. In the same vein, corporate governance is based on the premise that corporate officers operate best when they are held to account for what they do.[1] Today, business activities are growing continuously in range, diversity, and magnitude. When management assumes operating responsibility for production, thereby overseeing the money of other (often anonymous) people, it must accept being measured by yardsticks designed to indicate performance.

An important consequent obligation of corporate governance is to provide information that enables the company's shareholders to verify that the capital they have entrusted to their agents (the corporate management) is, indeed, well looked after. Society at large, through establishment of regulatory procedures and business standards, has over the years created a set of tools for proper corporate governance. Some of these instruments can be used to hold management, directors, auditors and, for that matter, regulators, accountable to the principals and the public in accordance with the terms they accepted when they assumed their responsibilities.

Inherently linked to corporate governance, business accountability means holding the management of an organization responsible for its performance, and it entails making judgments on the proper use of executive power. Such judgment, of course, can be exercised only when the relevant information is available. Not least, accountability ensures that behavior is consistent with the purpose of the company's undertaking, and that it complies operationally with the stipulations that guide the company's program.[2] In a way complementing the effect of the open market, which establishes prices and measures real profits, a system of accountability provides objective yardsticks for executive and consulting performance. Accountable individuals know that they must be prepared to defend their decisions—that they have accepted responsibility and will have to take the blame for any bad choices they make.[3]

Governance Defined

The *Shorter Oxford Dictionary* defines governance simply as "the office, function or power of governing." *Webster's Dictionary* regards it as the "exercise of authority; control; management; power of government." The *Oxford Dictionary* is somewhat cautious in defining accountability: when one is "accountable," one is "obliged to give reckoning for one's actions."[4] In everyday practice, Canada's province of Alberta states that "accountability is an obligation to answer for the execution of one's assigned responsibilities" and recommends that it is useful "to consider accountability in context of the relationship between the people or organizations involved."[5] In short, accountability provides a way of measuring performance in any and all segments of society, from political organizations and government institutions to social and business communities.

It is but a short step from these definitions to the action and matter of exercising corporate restraint. In this connection, the commercial world has begun to take seriously the importance of integrity and accountability in its business conduct.[6] Those who advocate firm discipline describe governance as a system of control and regulation. Others, responding to business's exciting sense of growth, expect it merely to provide checks and balances. Still others regard the use of the idea of corporate governance as a passing fad. This study views corporate governance as a dynamic concept, one that will take on different shapes in the years to come.

Individual Accountability

There are various ways—some of them complementary—of ensuring proper governance. Whether it is the CEO, the individual director, the whole board, the outside auditors, or the regulatory authority and its officers being evaluated, the execution of individual responsibilities should be assessed periodically. In this regard, the tools of accountability should themselves be measured and updated at regular intervals, in view of the fact that directors, independent auditors, internal auditors, and quite possibly senior and middle-management staff of regulatory agencies are now accountable in ways little considered even a generation ago.

In the short run, companies can survive without applying adequate instruments of corporate governance, but they will get into deep trouble in the longer term. It is the responsibility of the regulator to guide the system of governance and devise its tools. It is up to the shareholders, the CEO, the outside directors, the independent auditors, and the internal audit division to ensure, with the support of the regulator, that the firm applies them and is managed accordingly.

There probably still is a consensus that the single most important way to make the management of publicly owned companies accountable is by requiring full disclosure. The functions of outside director and independent auditor were defined and the tools at their disposal were designed to ensure that the necessary relevant facts become available. In recent years, however, skepticism has arisen as to whether this system as practiced meets today's needs.

As the business world has become more complex and accounting requirements more diversified, those delegated to monitor proper governance—that is, the outside directors and the independent auditors—have become burdened by the need to be acquainted with a continuously increasing stream of statutes, laws, and regulations. They are expected to be knowledgeable in a wide range of business activities, but many observers doubt whether they are up to the task.[7] That is one consequence of there being such a close relationship between corporate governance and accountability.

Accountability in Government

In the bureaucracies we live in, "it is not easy nowadays to remember anything so contrary to all appearances as that officials are servants of the public."[8] Limiting bureaucratic discretion by requiring compliance with tightly drawn rules and regulations has been the basic definition of accountability in government for over 50 years. Whereas in the past, government assigned tasks rather than goals, it now focuses on results and empowers organizations such as regulating agencies to monitor their achievement. In the full-service society, it is no mean task for government to incorporate a healthy accountability framework into these modern complex structures (see note 5). Paul C. Light writes that accountability is not an absolute. Quoting Frederick Mosher, he suggests that "accountability is associated . . . with carrying out assignments, more or less specifically defined, honestly, efficiently, effectively, and at minimal cost."[9] He then distinguishes between two forms of accountability: one relating to performance and the other to compliance. Performance accountability has to do with the evaluation of effectiveness and bench marking; compliance accountability demands detection of violations and enforcement of sanctions. The regulator evaluates accountability through monitoring rather than through execution, looking and recommending rather than acting and implementing. And it follows that in the territory of the regulator, accountability is the responsibility of those who make the rules and then monitor their implementation.

Although there is an increased volume of literature on the importance of accountability and how it is implemented, little has been written about the accountability of regulators when their services are less than satisfactory. Clearly, sanctions are sometimes called for. When, for example, Medicare providers violate the rules, they can be disbarred from the program. Similarly, when Federal Aviation Administration (FAA) staff carry out substandard inspections, when Federal Deposit Insurance Corporation (FDIC) personnel make errors of judgment, or when the SEC hides relevant information from a trading company, punitive action is in order.

When regulatory accountability is discussed, the thrust usually is more in relation to the superior officials in government, with little attention to practical applications for the regulated public. In the coming years, this perspective should change. When a regulator falls short in carrying out assignments, there should be recourse for the damage caused.

The Proliferation of Rules

When the securities laws were enacted in the early 1930s, Congress and the SEC wisely laid down a limited number of regulations, concentrating on the need for full disclosure. They understood that rules tend to procreate, and that too many demands could impair the judgment and effectiveness of those expected to provide corporate governance. In short, they believed that too many regulations would become a hindrance and a deterrent to entrepreneurship, initiative, innovation, and corporate growth.

For decades, regulatory restraint was the order of the day, but two developments, unconnected, have changed that policy. One is the continuing diversification of business; the other is the proliferation of instances of corporate collapse and roguery, with ensuing negative publicity. To address both of these factors, the SEC—and, even more so, the FASB and the AICPA (American Institute of Chartered Public Accountants)—have been introducing rules on a continuing basis, under the banner of "enhancing corporate governance." Sadly, not all the additions are helpful or improve governance. Indeed, some are cumbersome and costly and could even turn out to be counterproductive.[10]

Accountability of the Civil Service

As mentioned above, the concept of accountability has, until recently, been applied only to the private sector. Members of the civil service have not regarded themselves as accountable.[11] When their performance did not come up to expectations, the only recourse for the voters was to wait for the next election, when they could throw their bosses out of office. What many failed to realize (and some still do) is that public administrators are fiduciaries of the citizenry. Although, in theory, the concept of the citizen as customer has been preached ever since the United States came into being, in practice it has only recently come to be thought of as involving a right: Whatever services the state provides, the public has the right to expect them to be worth their cost, in taxes or direct charges. There are increased indications that the public is beginning to understand this right and to expect better services from government staff.[12]

In senior government circles there is increased awareness of this right. According to vice president Al Gore, much of what is wrong with government is caused by excessive red tape. In his presentation of the National Performance Review, the vice president spoke of the "small business owner who has to spend hours and hours filling out a completely useless form." He called "to decentralize authority, empowering those on the front lines to make more of their own decisions, but holding them strictly accountable for results." Gore called for a "shift to a system where you are accountable for achieving results."[13] Apparently, however, the general public still does not expect government agency staff to be accountable in the way that business executives are, and only recently has it begun to dawn on people that government staff should be measured as individuals in their specific roles rather than by the criteria by which politicians are held accountable.

Accepting the need to be accountable is not common in government today. Possibly the last American leader who recognized this duty was President Harry S Truman. His well-publicized dictum that "the buck stops here" was placed prominently on his working table. But neither the president nor members of Congress today have the capability or the time to manage and control the masses of staff working under their authority. Layers of staff and multiple rungs in the government organization make it close to impossible to know who is responsible for any decision. Indeed, such a large number of layers may lead to a cumbersome bureaucracy in which one cannot tell where responsibility lies.[14]

Numerous professional staff are chosen to serve because of their specific knowledge and expertise. Should not such government officials be accountable according to standards similar to those employed in the private sector? The answer is certainly affirmative in the case of executive staff of the various regulatory authorities, ranging from the FAA to the SEC to the FDIC. People employed in such agencies, including those who liaise with the public, should be held accountable. The duties and responsibilities of each agency and staff member should be defined. The areas in which they are accountable and the penalties for less than satisfactory performance should be made clear.[15]

THE CONCEPT OF ACCOUNTABILITY

Accountability implies acceptance of responsibility, without which there is no basis upon which an injured party can initiate a tort action to redress grievances.[16] It is applicable wherever an individual is injured, not least in economic matters. Anyone who serves as agent or leader should be willing to be held accountable.

Companies—their officers and boards and, separately, their outside auditors—routinely accept this general rule, but it has not been spelled out how it should apply to civil servants, staff officers of regulatory agencies, or federal administration employees. To what extent are they accountable for implicit or explicit action that can damage the citizen? This question has not been considered in the past, but regulators and their staff are inevitably going to become legally accountable, just like individuals in the private sector.

There are a variety of reasons why the concept of civil service staff accountability has not yet gained recognition. For one thing, even in democracies there has been a perception of the civil servant as someone set apart from the rest of the people. More specifically, there have been no clear definitions of civil servants' responsibilities or, when they are believed to have been the partial cause of injuries, provisions for quantifying the damage. This, even though the administrator and the regulator who are provided with instruments to govern and thereby given power, can cause harm in carrying out their duties. But having a license to govern implies that they are authorized to make choices, which in turn should make them accountable.[17] Just how they can be made accountable, and how their failure can be measured, are matters to be pursued.

A pertinent question related to the business world is whether the civil servant has a responsibility to share information that could be vital to those charged with providing full corporate disclosure. Different regulatory bodies have different missions according to law and procedures. Thus, for example, various tax authorities may choose not to divulge to other agencies or to the general public information gathered by their staff. But what about regulators who are responsible for proper governance? Should they not share with those whom they regulate information that is considered vital to company operations, and which they have reason to believe may not have come to the notice of the company? And if they choose not to, deliberately or by misjudgment, and significant losses occur, should they then not be regarded accountable for such a decision?

There is an obvious gap between principle and the practice in these matters. Generally Accepted Government Auditing Standards (GAGAS) call for government officials (particularly those employed by the regulators) to render an account of their activities to the public. While not always specified by law, this accountability concept is inherent in the nation's governing process.[18] Among the premises that underlie the standards mentioned is that public officials and others entrusted with public resources are accountable and that audit of government reporting is an essential element of public control and accountability.[19] The practice of accountability in this sense, however, is still in its early stages, and it probably relates more to a general concept of accountability to the public rather than sharing information directly with a specific company to help it avoid losses.

Arthur Levitt, Jr., chairman of the SEC since 1993, believes that ''openness, disclosure, and communication are just as important in the relationship between a regulated entity and a regulator as they are between a customer and a salesman.''[20] He urges corporate executives to work with their regulators, being frank and candid rather than avoiding them. He adds that the system will not work unless the regulated and the regulator have an open and ongoing dialogue and there is a measure of mutual trust and confidence. It is unclear, however, whether even he has recognized that sharing information is a reciprocal process, for he does not say whether the corporate executive or director can expect the regulator to share pertinent information he assumes or knows the company does not have. And he has not yet acknowledged that the relationship he calls for will be greatly enhanced by having his staff as accountable as are those they regulate. Real confidence can be established only if the exchange of information is a two-way process. When that process evolves, another important step will have been taken toward defining the regulator's accountability. Until then, the necessary sense of openness, trust, and confidence will be lacking.

WHY ACCOUNTABILITY IS ESSENTIAL

In today's complex world, we are so dependent on teamwork that it is sometimes difficult to define where one individual's responsibility ends and another's begins; hence, the need for clear lines of accountability is stronger than ever. Indeed, accountability should extend to all who serve in any sphere of public activities, including government officials and, as addressed in this study, members of the regulatory staff.

Since ancient times, scholars have been aware of the importance of accountability. Aristotle, in *The Politics*, wrote that "to protect the treasurer from being defaulted, let all public money be issued openly in front of the whole city, and let copies of the accounts be deposited in the various wards," while Demosthenes is quoted as having said, "I claim that throughout my career I have been subject to the public audit in all the posts I have held."[21] Historians note that accountability was practiced not only by the early Athenian government but also in different instances by governments of nations of the Nile region, early Rome, and medieval Europe. John Stuart Mill stated in 1859 "for such actions as are prejudicial to the interests of others, the individual is accountable, and may be subjected either to social or to legal punishment, if society is of opinion that the one or the other is requisite for its protection."[22] Decades before national administrations grew to their present size, Max Weber recognized that "every bureaucracy seeks to increase the superiority of the professional informed by keeping their knowledge and intentions secret."[23] And lacking pressure from without, it may be expected that they shall continue to do so until they learn that they, like other mortals, should be held accountable; otherwise, government officers have a tendency to become tyrannical, arbitrary, and arrogant. Civil servants, including public administrators and regulators, are fiduciaries of the citizenry of the country. The same is true of anyone active in the armed forces, anyone providing educational, medical, or other services and anyone active as a corporate executive. When this maxim is disregarded or forgotten, the unfettered exercise of authority often leads to a loss of contact with reality, and the autocrat begins to ignore unwanted news and to make insensitive, irresponsible judgments.

A corporation or a regulatory authority has no morality of its own separate from that of the individuals who make it up. It is the individual executive and director or civil servant who must personally decide whether a certain action is ethical. While the need to ensure accountability should be both understood and accepted throughout society, there is little public awareness of the importance of this axiom regarding services rendered the public by government. Even though government has become in most places a huge and complex organization that affects everybody in daily life, there have been few calls for measures to make government employees accountable to the citizenry.

Hidden by the complexity of modern policymaking processes, the power of some bureaucracies is not always noticed, even in the most alert democracies. The elected representatives of the people often lose control, not least because they passively accept the fact that they do not have the detailed knowledge, skills, or time to fully control or monitor the machinations of the civil service. This problem was not always so acute, because at first government staff performed as instructed by the legislators. Gradually, however, in large part because of the wide range of their assignments and commitments, proper monitoring of civil servants came to require more time than elected officials were able to devote to it, and the civil service evolved independent practices of its own. In the second half of the century, the president and Congress first lost full control of, and later failed to attempt to curtail the workings of, an increasingly powerful bureaucracy.[24]

Although the White House and Congress may have believed that they were delegating responsibility, what often happened was that they abandoned their task of supervising how policies were being carried out. At times they were aware of the difficulties and tried to maintain some form of control, but with little success. A bureaucracy with life and dynamics of its own came into being, so vast and complex that elected officials and, at times, senior officers of the administration, had little influence on the activities of the staff in the faraway parts of the country or hidden corners in the bureaus. In 1978, Congress passed the Inspector General Act, in the hope that accountability in government could be strengthened through compliance monitoring, promoting personal incentives in the bureaucracy, and revamping organizational methods to improve performance. But success has so far been limited.

Nearly two decades ago, Harold Williams[25] asked whether the public had access to enough information to discern where corporate power is being abused and how often. Like his peers, he believed in the policy of full disclosure, but he made no effort to emphasize the accountability of those in office. Indeed, he seemed unsure about whether or not the concept should apply also to government bodies and staff. But he did warn that no activity can flourish for long if the public takes a dim view of it, and that no activity can continue unaltered in the long term if public apathy turns into active antagonism.

Another area of concern is the terrain on which the taxpayer and business person encounter the civil servant. With government staff having the power it does, the compliance demanded by, at times, contradictory mandates of different agencies consumes citizens' time and energy and can be costly. And when, as a result, resources have to be spent by them in an unproductive way, it can be irritating, if not downright painful to entrepreneurs and business people as well as to the consumer and the labor force, causing them to wonder whether need for regulation still exists or whether the rules should be updated or revised. In these instances, both the economic actions and judgment of the bureaucrats are tested, and they will be accepted only if regarded as fair. When it becomes clear to all that the bureaucrat responsible for implementation of the rules is accountable, the source of much antagonism will be greatly reduced.

ON APPLYING ACCOUNTABILITY

While the need for responsible corporate governance is discussed almost daily in current business literature and speeches, accountability is addressed far less often, even though one is directly linked to the other. Governance involves service "for whom," while accountability relates to service "by whom." Corporate governance is concerned with the structures and processes associated with production, decision making, and controls within an organization, while accountability systems not only consider the company's operating procedures but also recognize the shareholders' right to know.[26]

"Accountability is the product of a process," Leon Lessinger stated in 1971. He meant that a public or private agency and the individuals working within it enter a contractual understanding with the public they serve and should be held responsible for performing according to the terms agreed upon. In the realm of corporate governance, there is wide acceptance of accountability as applying to corporate officers, to the board of directors, and to the outside auditors. In theory, accountability should apply also to government officers chosen to supervise corporate activities—that is, those employed by the relevant regulatory authorities—but in practice the question of their accountability rarely arises.

Traditionally, accountability focuses on efficiency and productivity; it focuses on justifying, reporting, and explaining, "proving" that the results claimed were actually accomplished. It also implies a subordinate–superior relationship, with corporate officers accountable to the board, the board in turn accountable to the shareholders. Regulators traditionally are accountable to their superiors in the administration and to Congress. But they should also be regarded as accountable to the stakeholders, on whose behalf they were appointed. In fact, insofar as it refers to regulatory officers, the concept of accountability is rather blurred. If they were made aware, through legislation or from a "bully pulpit," that they are just as accountable as company officers in the business world, their performance might well improve. Certainly, increased confidence in them on the part of the regulated public would follow.[27]

A system of accountability places a burden of responsibility on an agency, a regulator, or an institution, as well as on corporate officers or individuals. It mandates full reporting of the results of that responsibility and it defines where "the buck stops." A. Friedman in 1973 suggested three basic reasons why an

agency, institution, or individual should account to the public or the stakeholders. According to him, agencies are accountable for their management practices.
They must show the public and stakeholders that they are fulfilling their mission.
They must be able to prove their efficiency and productivity; and, not least, they
must be able to demonstrate their honesty and integrity.[28]

In the open market, where defining operating results is simple, most yardsticks
of accountability can easily be explained. But we live in a complex society and
have an imperfect market in which it is difficult to compare or to quantify results
and, hence, to measure accountability. It is no accident that the call for accountability is most often raised where objective criteria are not quite clear, as in the
field of education at both public school and university levels, where attempts
are being made to measure the effectiveness of teachers in promoting students'
academic progress. It is to be expected that in not-for-profit establishments,
including branches of government and their agencies, different accountability
yardsticks should be designed, although what or how has not yet been clearly
established.[29]

NOTES

1. "Watching the boss: A survey of corporate governance," *The Economist* (January
29, 1994): 18.

2. Rosella Lavazzi, "Accountability and the internal market," *Financial Accountability and Management* (November 1995): 283–296.

3. Kimberly A. Taylor, "Choices under ambiguity," *Organizational Behavior and
Human Decision Processes* (November 1995): 128–137.

4. Another such term is "ethics" in "business ethics," a term often used in the
modern sense in the business world. These terms are not a central subject in this study
and deserve a detailed and learned separate study. How did it happen that what once
were straightforward terms later became so woolly?

5. "Introduction to accountability": http://www.assembly.ab.ca:80/auditor.gen/in-
troacc.htm#1100.

6. Ian Percy, "Who holds the reins?" *Accountancy* (February 1996): 58–60.

7. Roy A. Chandler, "They're paid too much?!" *Accountancy* (February 1996): 106–
107.

8. Sir Ernest Gowers, *The Complete Plain Words*, 2nd ed., rev. ed. by Sir Bruce
Fraser (Her Majesty's Stationery Office, 1973): 11.

9. Paul. C. Light, *Monitoring Government: Inspectors General and the Search for
Accountability* (The Brookings Institute, 1993).

10. Tim Melville-Ross, "Better behavior in the board room," *Accountancy* (February
1996): 54.

11. Willa M. Bruce, Rejoinder to Terry Cooper's response to the review of *The Responsible Administrator: An Approach to Ethics for the Administrative Role, Public Administration Review* (May–June 1992): 313–314.

12. Van R. Johnston, "Caveat emptor: Customers vs. citizens," *Public Manager* (Fall
1995): 11.

13. Remarks by the president and vice president in presenting the National Performance Review (September 7, 1993): http://sunsite.unc.edu/npr/rermarks.html.

14. Paul. C. Light, *Thickening Government: Federal Hierarchy and the Diffusion of Accountability* (published jointly by the Brookings Institute and the Governance Institute, 1995): 86–87.

15. Clive Brault, Andrew Haldane, and Mervyn Kink, "Central bank independence and accountability: Theory and evidence," *Bank of England Quarterly Bulletin* (February 1991): 63–68.

16. Anne Wells Branscomb, "Anonymity, autonomy and accountability: Challenges to the first amendment in cyberspaces," *Yale Law Journal* (May 1995): 1645.

17. "The talk of the town—Notes and comment," *New Yorker* (December 30, 1985): 15.

18. The Inspector General Act of 1978, as amended, 5 U.S.C. App. (1982), available in: http://www.osa.state.us/ybchap1.htm.

19. The Single Audit Act, 31 U.S.C. 7502 (f), available in: http://www.osa.state.us/ybchap1.htm.

20. Interview with David A. Andelman, "Arthur Levitt, Jr.: The market's top cop," *Management Review* (June 1995): 33.

21. "The accountability of government departments (1995)," quoted in Background: http://hammock.ufl.edu.80/txt/fairs/.13729.

22. John Stuart Mill, *On Liberty* (A Gateway Edition, chapter 5): 119.

23. M. Weber, "Bureaucracy," in *Essays in Sociology*, ed. and trans. H. H. Gerth and C. Wright Mills (Oxford University Press, 1958).

24. Much of what is noted in this chapter was influenced by "Designing bureacratic accountability," by Arthur Lupia and Mathew D. Cubbings, in *Law and Contemporary Problems* (Winter 1994): 92–126. Also, Kathleen Bawn, "Bureaucratic accountability for regulatory decisions: Comment on Lupia and McCubbings," ibid., 139–142.

25. Harold M. Williams, chairman of the SEC, "Power and accountability—The changing role of corporate boards of directors," The 1979 Benjamin F. Fairless Memorial Lectures: 12.

26. Hsin-ling Hsieh, Commentary on corporate governance and accountability: http://weatherhead cwru.edu/board/comment/account.htm.

27. Meaning of accountability, LYCOS on the Internet: http://hammock.ifas.ufl.edu/txt/fairs/pd/13574.html.

28. Purpose of accountability, LYCOS on the Internet: http://hammock.ifas.ufl.edu/txt/fairs/pd/13690.html.

29. Ted Marchese, "Accountability" (editorial), *Change* (November–December 1994): 4.

Chapter 2

Regulators and Accountability

ACCOUNTABILITY IN GOVERNMENT

"It is not easy nowadays to remember anything so contrary to all appearances as that officials are servants of the public"[1] wrote a British savant a generation ago. But views are changing and something is being done. Despite increasing pressure throughout the rest of the world for the civil servant to be accountable, there has been only modest support for this concept in the United States. More attention has been devoted to it, for example, in Canada, the United Kingdom, Australia, the Scandinavian countries, and the Netherlands. Partially acknowledged by the introduction of the office of ombudsman, first in Sweden and then in Denmark, in 1953, this idea was defined in Stockholm as being necessary to "protect the individual against abuse of administrative powers and other forms of maladministration."[2] Derived from this concern, and possibly no less important, was the requirement that the ombudsman identify "*who* is responsible for doing *what.*"

With similar terms of reference, the office of ombudsman was soon adopted by different countries. In 1990, Dennis Pearce, who had retired as Australia's ombudsman, wrote that the objectives of the ombudsman were "to improve the quality of administration and to provide a mechanism for individuals to obtain redress by:

- identifying instances of defective administration through independent investigation;
- encouraging agencies to provide remedies for members of the public affected by defective administration;
- identifying legislative, policy, and procedural deficiencies and encouraging systematic improvements to overcome these deficiencies; and

• contributing advice to the government on the adequacy, effectiveness, and efficiency of the various means of review of administrative action."[3]

Over the years, international concepts of public accountability have changed substantially, and they are continuing to change. There is, for example, increased emphasis on the development of professionalism, and there is closer scrutiny of the policies underlying expenditures. Not less important, there is recognition of a need to protect powerless individuals from poor service by an unhelpful bureaucracy. Especially on those occasions when a citizen encounters an administrator face-to-face, clearly defined accountability, high standards of service that are independently monitored, and the opportunity to file a complaint and obtain redress are called for. As William Reid says, "Such ideas are in the course of elaboration and will occupy much political and administrative time to come."[4]

As in other parts of Canada, accountability is an increasingly discussed topic in Nova Scotia. Following the Nova Scotia Auditor General's Report in 1995, the House of Assembly received a detailed statement on the subject early in 1996. Some of its statements are especially noteworthy:

• *Paragraph 2.7*: "In its simplest terms, accountability means the obligation to answer for an assigned responsibility."

   And the authors made clear who is accountable when they add that the "accountability relationship involves at least two parties, one who allocates or assigns responsibility, and one who accepts it."

• *Paragraph 2.2*: "For Government to hold departments and agencies accountable, there must be an adequate standard framework in place that requires the reporting of sufficient, appropriate, understandable, and timely information. [Without] such a standard ... the effectiveness of efforts to hold Government, departments, and agencies accountable was impaired."

• *Paragraph 2.9*: "The need to improve accountability is a significant issue in the public sector virtually everywhere."[5]

The report takes the position that better modes of accountability will result in increased public confidence in the system (Paragraph 2.18).

The United States has yet to begin on the course that the Canadians have found it advisable to pursue. Clearly, here as well as elsewhere, full disclosure, fiduciary responsibility, and sound corporate governance are concepts that will apply not only to publicly quoted companies but to government as well in the world of tomorrow.

GOVERNMENT BUREAUCRACY AND THE COST OF GOVERNANCE

President Bill Clinton may have exaggerated somewhat when, in his 1996 State of the Union speech, he announced that the "end of big government" had arrived. Indeed, in the following months it became apparent that this was a declaration more easily made than implemented. Turning a large, fat, static, often producer-oriented bureaucracy into a vital, lean, efficient, consumer-directed organism has rarely been easy or fully successful; and, in the absence of effective means of measurement, it is difficult to establish parameters for efficiency and accountability.

There is clear evidence that the president was unhappy with the size of the administration he inherited in Washington. The issue was reflected not only in the body of the civil service but also in the upper rungs of the bureaucracy. In 1960, 451 senior executives and presidential appointees sat at the top levels of federal government agencies. By 1992 there were 2,393 such employees, an increase of 530 percent. Not only has this increase caused an ever more burdensome bureaucracy, it has impaired efforts to achieve accountability as well. The problem, according to Paul Light, is not so much the sheer number of leaders as it is the way these positions have added layer upon layer of management, increasing the communicating distance between the president and the front lines of government and thereby making it difficult to keep track of who is, in fact, accountable.[6]

Light argues that this thickening bureaucracy is both detrimental and dangerous because of the loss of accountability that accompanies it. Information becomes distorted as it travels up and down the bureaucratic ladder, administrative inertia sets in, opportunities to innovate are lost, and employees are discouraged from becoming involved. It becomes close to impossible to hold anyone accountable for what went right or wrong. Light suggests that a ''flatter government would likely deliver better, faster, more responsive services.''

In the context of making government services more efficient, privatization is a so-called ''buzz'' term. The concept has been applied to industries and services in countries ranging from Margaret Thatcher's Britain to the budding democracies of the former Communist bloc. But there are some government services, such as the police or defense forces, that it would not be realistic or practical to privatize. Regarding other services, such as health care, there is an apparent popular resistance to privatization. And among those services that are privatized, some are permitted (often mistakenly) to retain their monopolistic position and, thus, are not necessarily motivated to be more efficient or competitive or to improve standards of service. Government participates in the marketplace, not only through ownership but also through the legal power and control vested in its various regulatory authorities. This fact of life is expressed in various ways. One is the cumbersome, time-consuming paperwork explicitly or implicitly required by regulators of anyone applying for a license to operate. Another is the complex maze of tax and other laws to which business people and corporations are subject. The entrepreneur is faced with a bureaucratic labyrinth to negotiate—often at considerable cost—even as the enterprise contributes at both state and national levels by providing employment and, often, expanding imports, thereby improving the nation's balance of payments.

However committed legislatures may be to containing, if not reducing, the size of government, they have at best slowed its growth. Even in the 1980s, in the age of President Reagan, in an era of deregulation, technological advance, and global integration, government spending as compared with the total gross national product increased from 31.8 percent to 33 percent.[7]

In the realm of business, federal and state regulatory authorities such as the SEC and the various banking regulators continue to consider new ways to improve the dissemination of information, not always bearing in mind the additional paperwork and costs with which they burden corporate America. Not to be left behind, the AICPA, the FASB, and other public bodies compete in their demand for ever more disclosure. All of these requirements contribute to an "information overload" that adds up to waste of time, delay in making important decisions, and considerable senior management stress, according to the 1995 study made on behalf of Reuter's Business Information and covering 1,300 managers in the United States, Britain, Australia, Singapore, and Hong Kong. A striking—and certainly discouraging—fact emerging from the study was that 94 percent of the managers did not believe that the situation would improve.[8]

The cost, however, extends beyond stress and waste: There is a direct cost too. It would not be practical to attempt to measure comprehensively the cost of regulation, even though some data related to such a calculation, such as the gross revenues of the Big Five and the second-tier accounting firms, are public knowledge. There are signs that this might be changing—for instance, the Small Business Regulatory Enforcement Fairness Act of March 1996. Basing themselves on a study that showed that the cost of federal regulations was roughly $5,400 for firms with less than 500 employees compared with $3,000 for larger ones, small business advocates felt that regulators tend to disregard these costs to small firms, believing that they would be better served with this new act.[9] But generally known costs are probably only a fraction of the total cost caused by the bureaucratic machinations of the federal government. More complicated to collect, for example, is information concerning the aggregate remuneration of outside board members of publicly traded companies.

It would be even harder to unearth the cost of the data required by directors, auditors, and regulators or to identify the budget allocations of the various government agencies and the cost of the regulators delegated to oversee these regulatory and reporting activities. Were they all added up, it would probably be found that this sum both raises the aggregate cost of the end product and lowers the profits of the corporations. If research were carried out to assess the need for all this reporting, some of it would no doubt be found wasteful and redundant.

The need to simplify paperwork is discussed periodically, but there have been no genuine attempts to do so; neither has anyone in government or public service made a significant breakthrough in reducing the volume of the various regulatory demands. More surprising is the apparent equanimity with which the public has accepted the present mode of reporting prescribed by those responsible for corporate governance. There has been no call for reexamination of the process;

indeed, it is rare for anyone to ask whether it is time to reassess, reevaluate, or restructure corporate practice and governance. But the shortcomings of the present system should be addressed in order to find ways to reduce the size of the various bureaucracies that relate to the business world and to suggest more efficient management practices.

ACCOUNTABILITY OF THE REGULATOR'S STAFF

Even the strongest proponents of better accountability, who want to see those who do not adhere to proper business practices removed from office and, in extreme cases, brought to trial, also know how unrealistic it has been—so far— to expect similar accountability among the regulators. How to measure the accountability of regulatory agency staff is a complex and as yet open question. This is so not least because the public is never quite sure of the regulator's role in economic monitoring. Accordingly, after every big financial mishap, the regulators may call for more rules to prevent similar situations but no one raises the question of underperformance of the regulators. A better perspective on the mission of the regulator is revealed by defining the goal of business regulation as ensuring that when companies fail, they do not undermine the soundness of the system.[10] With the staff person's responsibility so defined, of course, some of them will argue that they should not be held equally accountable.

Given the American litigation experience, it makes sense to be cautious about starting proceedings against a regulatory authority.[11] In *FDIC v. Meyer*, a unanimous Supreme Court ruling specifically sheltered the government from potentially costly and time-consuming lawsuits arising from the cleanup of the savings and loan industry. Although the case centered on the FDIC, its reasoning will protect all U.S. agencies, until there is a change of mind. In deciding for the FDIC, the Court noted that, as a practical matter, permitting suits directly against agencies would create "a potentially enormous financial burden on the federal government" and that it was up to Congress, not the judiciary, to expand federal liability in this area.

It is difficult to believe that this ruling differentiating the accountability of the civil servant from that of the rest of the population will survive for long. The question remains as to how and to what extent such information should be shared without infringing on civil rights or turning the country into a police state. Still, according to the Court's ruling, regulatory staff can act with impunity in withholding intelligence that reaches them, rather than forwarding it to officers, directors, or auditors in the interest of sound corporate decisions. Surely, for example, there were instances in the Bank of Credit and Commerce International scandal, in some of the savings and loan debacles, and certainly in the moratoria of the Latin American sovereign debt when information reached the regulators that could have had a material influence on corporate decisions if it had been forwarded to management in good time. The current policy should be reexamined.

In the fall of 1997, Congress was debating some of the shortcomings of the Internal Revenue Service (IRS). Proposals were being discussed to shift control over the IRS from the Treasury Department to a board that would include private citizens, and House Ways and Means Committee Chairman William Archer also put forward 20 new protections, such as the right to sue the IRS. His declaration that "we will make it easier for taxpayers who are wrongly accused by the IRS to recover their legal costs . . ." and that too often "the defenseless and the weak become targets for the IRS audits," was an important step toward greater public recognition not only that the regulator and the civil servant are accountable in theory but that damages caused by them are quantifiable and can actually be reclaimed.[12]

The free, full flow of reliably reported news has made an important contribution to the health of the American market. As repeatedly mentioned, the most significant single emphasis of the SEC is on the importance of having all pertinent information available to all currently or potentially interested parties, by means of all the instruments of full disclosure. In our widely diversified society, collecting and disseminating all relevant data can be costly, and as corporate activities have become more specialized, the facts needed for full disclosure are not always readily accessible within the company. Although intelligence can, in theory, be obtained from beyond, sometimes management cannot reach out for it. As previously mentioned, intelligence often arrives at the gates of the regulatory authorities and other government agencies first. When this happens, it is rarely—if at all—divulged to the company concerned. Because the understanding and judgment of those who oversee corporate governance depend on accessibility to such intelligence, withholding it can cause a company immeasurable damage.

In modern society, social and business life are interwoven. There is no such thing as a detached, isolated entity. An audit cannot be carried out as if the company operated alone in a remote, isolated bunker. Rather, it must be implemented with curiosity, close scrutiny, and wide-ranging collection of information. In today's spread-out, diversified economy, in which the operations of the typical company are more sophisticated than ever before (and often internationally diffused) and the cost of controls is a serious consideration, the exchange of relevant information by the various organs of government is crucial to the success of any audit or other form of regulatory supervision. In short, regulators should be regarded as active participants in such matters.

Reaching out for more comprehensive intelligence is going to become more important. The gathering of corporate intelligence and its dissemination in cooperation with government agencies (without infringing on civil rights) is an important objective. Today regulators assess the soundness of an institution by monitoring reports of performance and financial condition and by conducting on-site examinations. They receive and review numerous periodic reports intended to provide information useful for broad regulatory or economic policymaking, and they measure compliance with specific requirements and report on conformance with specific laws.[13]

Until now, however, there has been no evidence that regulators even consider sharing information available to their bureau with those being regulated. The heads of the regulatory authorities invariably deny any shortcomings on the part of their employees and reject any insinuation that the staff lacks courage or judgment. When there are public queries about possible failure on their part and when there is any suggestion that they, too, should be accountable, they invariably exert their political power to lobby for more detailed regulatory guidelines. A challenge for Congress and the regulators is to define how and when agency officers should be held accountable just like corporate officers, directors, and auditors. Until this challenge is met, significant improvement in the quality of corporate governance will be delayed.

THE FAA AND VALUJET: A CASE STUDY

Regulators, being part of the staff of government agencies, are guided by the laws that established their offices, and they function according to rules developed and interpretations made by their seniors and predecessors. When they use their own judgment, it is to interpret the laws that guide their institutions, some of which were enacted many years ago. Possibly most renowned among these laws is the act that established the SEC in the early 1930s. Today, as a result of the many volumes of regulations, decrees, instructions, and explanations that have grown up around the basic laws that established this commission, there are sometimes contradictory policies within the agency. For example, the decision to withhold information about a quoted company may conflict with the more general regulatory expectation for full disclosure.

A major objective of regulators is to ensure that precautionary steps be taken to prevent embarrassment of the subjects within their domain, crisis, or collapse. At present, it is unclear whether their tools for doing so are reviewed periodically or even whether budgets exist for this purpose. Indeed, there is little evidence that regulators' practices are ever reevaluated or that the contradictions in their working procedures examined. This lack of action can be explained in part by the fact that the shared interests of the regulatory agencies, and sometimes those within an agency itself, vary. Undertaking more and more chores, some regulators even appear to have conflicting missions and targets.

Possibly because agencies usually do not have a long-term strategic team, it is difficult for a regulator to assess trends that might guide the bureau, or to decide when changes in the market are such that policy decisions should be updated. Certainly, as in the business environment they regulate, timing can be crucial. A regulator's actions are usually based on available information that has reached the office. This information is part of the agency staff's intangible assets, and it is used to form guidelines and working procedures. When first received, it can be regarded as "raw material" to be weighed, evaluated, and disseminated.

The topics of this discussion are relevant to all regulators, and the conduct of the FAA should provide a clear example of how regulators typically handle information and perform necessary follow-up.

Surely, the FAA should have had a massive dossier on ValuJet Airlines well before the low-cost carrier's plane crashed into the Florida Everglades on May 11, 1996, yet it took the agency almost six weeks to ground the airline.[14] When the order to do so was given on June 17, following a routine inspection, the FAA gave as its reason a series of maintenance and operations problems. But even before the crash there had been plenty of warning signals that the carrier was taking risks beyond the safety levels prescribed by the agency. At a public hearing in November 1996, evidence was produced to show that the FAA had suppressed an internal report, carried out three months before the crash, recognizing that there were serious problems in the company's maintenance procedures and urging a review of ValuJet.[15] Various regulator shortcomings were described at the hearings, including the inability to keep up with inspections and paperwork during the carrier's rapid growth, because of staff shortages.

The questions are obvious: Should not the agency officers have been held accountable? Which employees of the FAA were responsible for the decisions concerning the carrier's performance prior to the crash? Should not these decisions have been examined again after the tragedy? In view of the numerous other cases of government officers responsible for serious mistakes being allowed to continue in office with impunity, should not steps be taken to prevent such lapses in the future?

The discomfort of the agency was evident in the aftermath of the ValuJet crash. Although staff members showed no sign of accepting even part of the responsibility for the tragedy, their behavior made it clear that more preventive action would be taken in the future. In a written statement published on December 19, the FAA stated: "Currently the Department of Transportation is reviewing ValuJet's charter arrangement to ensure full compliance with FAA safety standards," adding that approval would be granted only when the FAA was completely satisfied.[16]

Beginning in February 1997, a wide variety of new airline safety information was made compulsory. The thrust of it was to communicate with the public far more than previously concerning airline safety measures. Oregon Senator Ron Wyden, who supported these measures, explained that, whereas before people had to wade through red tape to get safety information, now "the flying public will be able to conveniently determine if their airline has major safety problems."[17] But these measures, the administration felt, were still insufficient. When a White House commission had its final meeting on February 12, 1997, more recommendations were made, including one supporting the airline industry initiative, in the aftermath of the ValuJet crash, to equip cargo holds of passenger aircraft with smoke detectors. FAA commissioner Victoria Cummock dissented on the grounds that the provision did not go far enough and set no timetable, saying that it "does nothing to protect the flying public" from smoke and fumes in the cabin.[18]

Like other regulatory agencies, the FAA is struggling to keep pace with the increasing complexity of the business it oversees. A recent self-study revealed that there is "no systematic difference" in the way it monitors established airlines, on the one hand, and high-risk start-ups on the other. *The Economist* noted another built-in contradiction of the FAA: Because its job has always been both to police and to promote the airline industry, support of the carriers could have come at the expense of airline safety.[19]

Two examples given by the *Wall Street Journal* state that "the aging DC-9 had a flight-data recorder that tracked only 11 factors because the FAA decided against requiring carriers to go to the expense of retrofitting older aircraft . . . with modern devices capable of tracking about 100 variables." And on a different matter, "the FAA [did not require] child-safety seats [that] would be too costly for airlines." It comes as no surprise that only as a result of the ValuJet crash will Congress be asked to change the FAA charter to make airline safety its sole responsibility. Shortly after the crash, the Transportation Department's inspector general, Mary Schiavo, and other critics were reported to have observed that the agency's dual agenda may have led the FAA to become too cozy with the airlines it regulates. Also, an audit early in 1996 noted that FAA staff abused a program that let carriers shuttle them free as part of their job; employees used their free flight tickets, under pretense of doing work, to fly to London, Munich, Las Vegas, and other exotic destinations.[20]

In a book published after her retirement, entitled *Flying Blind, Flying Safe*, Schiavo reiterated that the FAA is beset by sloppy inspections, lax airport security, and disregard for bogus airplane parts.[21] She also said that some three months before the crash she had warned the FAA about ValuJet's flawed safety record, and she suggested that the agency suppressed important data, not least "sloppy inspections of planes, perfunctory reviews of pilots, lax oversight of airline procedures . . . antiquated air-traffic control systems," that should be part of public knowledge.[22]

In the official report of the National Transportation Safety Board, published on August 19, 1997, board chairman Jim Hall wrote that "The ValueJet accident resulted from failures all up and down the line—from federal regulators to airline executives to workers on the shop room floor." The report pinned the blame on the FAA, which had not carried out a National Transportation Safety Board (NTSB) recommendation to require airlines to install smoke alarms and fire suppression systems in cargo holds.[23] Although there is still no consensus on what should be done to improve air safety, all agree that no one in government has explained why these measures were not activated before the ValuJet tragedy. These questions remain unanswered: Why were none of the agency officers taken to account? Was no FAA employee responsible for decisions taken, or not taken, concerning the carrier prior to the crash? And should not the decisions taken have been reviewed after the crash?

Other regulatory agencies suffer from the same blurred vision, and there have been (possibly numerous) other cases of government officers responsible for serious mistakes not being held accountable. How might this situation be changed? The apparent shortcomings of the FAA in the ValuJet tragedy are a vivid example of a lack of accountability on the part of regulatory staff. Similarly, many in the corporate business world have questioned the roles of the various regulatory officers in the savings and loan debacles, in the collapse of the BCCI group, or in the debt moratoria declared by a number of Latin American governments in the early 1980s.

Assuming that the FAA procedures and controls were not fully satisfactory, would they have been recognized as such without the Everglades crash? In other words, do procedures exist whereby regulators periodically reexamine their policies in order to ensure that their agency maintains high standards? Do they, for example, simulate crises, threats, or other obstacles in order to assess how well they can deal with such occurrences? Although most regulators realize that there is a need to update and fine-tune their requirements, few are willing to assume responsibility for their mistakes or those of their staff. SEC chairman Arthur Levitt, Jr., described a case in which the government required Amoco Oil Company to install benzene filters in refinery waste pipes. Amoco complied, at a cost of $31 million.[24] Some time later, when the regulators revisited the Amoco plant, they discovered that the source of the problem was not the waste pipes but the pumping of fuel into barges. The solution to that problem was relatively easy and inexpensive, but meanwhile $31 million had been wasted. The company had no recourse against the government and regulators were not held accountable. This instance is also an example of the fact that the expectations of the SEC regarding blue chip companies with a long and proud track record are no higher than those they have for high-flying, high-risk, and inadequately capitalized companies.

Sometimes the responsibilities of regulators conflict with those of their free market agents—that is, boards of directors. This conflict is usually perceived only after a well-publicized debacle, when there is an outcry to establish the identity of a villain. The embarrassment of the regulator who plays dual roles is similar to that of the corporate board member who also acts as the company's consultant. There is, however, a difference: Whereas the director is aware that he is accountable, as indeed the law stipulates, the accountability of the regulator has not been clearly defined. Arthur Levitt, Jr., recognizes the need to improve the services provided by the SEC, but there is no evidence that he or his peers are willing to assume accountability when, through errors of fault of their staff, something goes wrong.

THE REGULATORS AND THE S&LS: ANOTHER CASE STUDY

In carrying out their assignments, regulators interpret laws. Some of their actions are clearly spelled out in the law itself or by the regulations that explain the intentions of the lawmakers. Periodically, however, they come across situations that call for action not specifically prescribed by the codes. An example is the instructions given by the FDIC at the height of the savings and loan crisis in the late 1980s. Despite their broad guidelines and in contrast to the basic rules of diligence usually observed, the federal regulators of the time cut some corners, with the help of "supervisory goodwill."[25] This accounting device permitted some of the S&Ls to delay the write-off of debts that, in hindsight, had already become uncollectible. In the early stages of the S&L crisis, regulators, in effect, concealed the scope of the problem from the public. They also did so when they encouraged healthy institutions to acquire failed or failing S&Ls. In their eagerness to pawn off the troubled thrifts, the government allowed numerous institutions to book and then to count "supervisory goodwill" for the purpose of determining capital adequacy. What was, in fact, taking place, was that this use of goodwill accounting resulted in a substantial overleveraging of the industry. It later turned out that this leveraging was nearly equivalent to the excess of acquired liabilities over acquired assets.

With the independent auditors raising hardly any questions, the regulators then encouraged buyers of sick thrifts to record the negative net worth as supervisory goodwill and to amortize it over periods as long as 40 years. A few years later, when the crisis mushroomed, it was realized that the regulators had increased the losses by approving the idea of presenting this intangible as an asset.

The above is just one example of the administration's carelessness in the matter of the S&Ls. Far more damaging was the policy of guaranteeing the deposit debt, which ignored the rapid growth of what effectively were insolvent institutions. The regulators skewed client risk-taking in ways that created singularly escalating losses. Rather than cleaning them up efficiently, a succession of top federal officials labored to hide much of the losses and pushed off the growing deficiency for their successors to resolve.[26] Although more and more serious warnings were sounded in the early 1980s, it was only after the 1989 Financial Institutions Reform, Recovery and Enforcement Act (the so-called bailout law), whereby the thrifts were forced to write off goodwill over five years instead of the 40 allowed previously, that Congress and the public at large realized that the approach of the regulators had often worsened the problem of thrift losses and accelerated institutions' demise.

The owners of Glendale Federal Savings Bank of California appealed this law, arguing that they had suffered damages as a result of the changes in federal regulations. They requested the U.S. court of Federal Claims to rule that in abrogating the right to the 40-year write-off, the government had breached a contract, and they claimed damages.[27] In July 1992 the court found that the government had violated a 1981 contract permitting Glendale to write off over 40 years the $734 million in losses of a thrift it had acquired sometime earlier.[28] Late in December 1997, ruling in a case brought by American Life and Casualty, which had bought four ailing savings institutions in 1988 and claimed to have lost more than $100 million because of the rule change, Chief Judge Loren Smith of the U.S. Court of Federal Claims wrote that "because the dollars at stake appear to be so large, the government has raised legal and factual arguments that have little or no basis in law, fact or logic." There was added suspicion that the government was trying to relitigate issues resolved in the Supreme Court in July 1996 when Justice David Souter said that the government's argument was "fundamentally implausible."[29] It was estimated that as many as 120 failed or weakened thrift institutions were in a somewhat similar position. In all, it was projected that resolution of such claims could cost the government $20 billion, in addition to the other costs of possibly $120 billion incurred by the S&L collapses.

There were other shortcomings that, had they been corrected in time, might have averted or at least reduced the extensive damage caused to the economy. One, related to accounting treatment, was that prior to 1993, securities were often carried on balance sheets at their historical cost, regardless of their current value. The assets of S&Ls, which showed a positive net worth of $36.2 billion in 1980, actually consisted more of bad loans than devalued securities. Had those assets been marked down to market value, the real net worth of the S&Ls would have been evident—somewhere between minus $78 billion and minus $118 billion.[30]

To what extent were the regulators participants in the collapse? In the opinion of Bert Ely, a noted financial expert who foretold the impending crisis in 1985, "while many factors contributed to the S&L debacle, ill-conceived and irrational federal policies must bear the brunt of the responsibility." He added that "surviving S&Ls and banks . . . are suffering heavily from past policy mistakes that have forced policymakers and regulators to impose still new regulations—regulations that don't address the underlying reasons for this problem."[31] Indeed, it was no secret to the regulators or to the accounting profession that this treatment was substandard, but it was only in 1992 that the FASB came to grips with the situation and issued the relevant opinion. Meanwhile, no regulator warned of the prospect of deregulation or other risks involved in the discrepancies of presentation in the financial statements, and no regulator was ever called to account for this or other decisions taken at the Resolution Trust Corporation (RTC) or the FDIC.

The various government agencies involved with the thrifts, however, did pursue the one source of indemnification they could: the almost fully insured Big Six and lesser accounting firms that had conducted the audits of the failed S&Ls. A typical instance was the suit of RTC, the federal agency responsible for disposing of the assets of insolvent thrifts. In November 1994, it sued the accounting firm of Coopers & Lybrand for having conducted a "grossly negligent audit" of Caprock Savings and Loan Association, which failed in 1990. RTC sought damages from Coopers & Lybrand in connection with the 1987 audit that had shown Caprock to have a positive financial situation, when in reality it was hopelessly insolvent. Another example involved KPMG. In August 1994, that company announced it had reached an agreement with the federal government to settle charges of having inadequately audited several ailing and failed S&L institutions in the 1980s. KPMG agreed to pay $186.5 million to settle all pending and future federal claims concerning thrifts.[32]

Three of the other Big Six and some of the smaller audit firms had earlier settled government claims of thrift-related negligence.[33] But few voices were raised to ask whether these service firms were, in fact, accountable, and by the mid-1990s it was clear that the S&L debacle was coming to a close. A small number of senior officers were sentenced to jail. The large auditing firms which, with a small number of law firms, were the only bodies which had insurance coverage to pay damages, did so—usually out of court. Altogether, the auditors had to spend many millions of dollars on legal fees in their defense and even more in damages. The directors—the most notorious of whom was Neil Bush, son of the then president of the United States—were strongly criticized in the media and some spent time in prison. Certain law firms connected with the thrifts suffered embarrassment similar to that of the auditors.

But how did the regulators, who ignored so many early warnings and who clearly could have done more to contain the collapses, escape accountability? Did they not have any responsibility for the breakdown of the system? To what extent did the policies of the RTC or the FDIC contribute to the debacle? Should the law not be amended to define the regulators' accountability far more sharply? There is no evidence that these questions were ever seriously discussed in a public forum. In the end, the American people—by way of the government, which carried the brunt of the cost—paid for the S&L debacle. It was as if the regulators had no responsibility for the collapse and were in no way accountable for the largest financial loss in America in modern times.

A report of the Group of Thirty noted that, as a result of the S&L scandal, "confidence in supervision and financial reporting was badly eroded." It emphasized that "everyone must understand the roles of the respective participants in the process and cooperation among them must be encouraged." Although these developments would seem to argue for closer cooperation, not all the damage had been mended even by the mid-1990s. On the contrary, as a result of this and other shocks, the working relationships among regulators, bank managers, and external auditors had become increasingly contentious.[34]

NOTES

1. Sir Ernest Gowers, *The Complete Plain Words*, 2nd ed., rev. ed. by Sir Bruce Fraser (Her Majesty's Stationery Office, 1973): 11.

2. L. N. Nielsen (Danish Ombudsman), "Parliament and administration: The role of the Ombudsman," lecture to Parliamentary Conference (June 1982).

3. Dennis Pearce (Australian Commonwealth and Defense Force Ombudsman), annual report 1989–1990. Both articles are quoted in William K. Reid, "The changing notions of public accountability," *Public Administration* 70 (Spring 1992): 81.

4. Reid, op cit., 85.

5. "Accountability information and reporting to the House": http://gopher.nlc. bnc.ca:70/0gopher $root% . . . ov-gouv.province.nova-sco.ag]nsagch02.txt.

6. Paul C. Light, *Thickening Government: Federal Hierarchy and the Diffusion of Accountability* (published jointly by the Brookings Institute and the Governance Institute, 1995).

7. "The visible hand," *The Economist* (September 20, 1997): 17. Also, "The world economy survey," in ibid., 11.

8. Robert Woodward, "Managers complain of information overload, stress," Reuters in *The Jerusalem Post* (October 15, 1996). Also "Strangled from the top: How too many layers of managers are stifling government": http://www/brook.edu/pa press/light.htm.

9. Karen Kerrigan, "Fed agencies need watching concerning fairness act," *Business First: The Weekly Business Newspaper of Greater Louisville* (October 21, 1996): http://www.amcity.com/louisville/stories/102196/smallb5.html.

10. "Hooked on financial red-tape," *The Economist* (July 22, 1995): 73–79.

11. Paul M. Barret describes the case of the *FDIC v. Meyer* in the *Wall Street Journal* (February 24, 1994): A5.

12. "Let taxpayers sue IRS—House tax chief," Reuters (October 11, 1997).

13. *Defining the Roles of Accountants, Bankers and Regulators in the United States: A Study Group Report*, by the Group of Thirty (1994).

14. "U.S. authorizes ValuJet to resume flying," Reuters (September 26, 1996).

15. "FAA suppressed report on ValuJet problems," Reuters (November 22, 1996).

16. "FAA rejects ValuJet's planned expansion," Reuters (December 19, 1996).

17. "FAA makes airline safety data available," Reuters (January 29, 1997).

18. "White House panel urges air safety measures," Reuters (February 12, 1997).

19. "A devalued airline," *The Economist* (June 22, 1996): 71.

20. Asra Q. Nomani and Brucer Ingersoll, "FAA's dual role of protecting public, promoting air travel draws criticism," *Wall Street Journal* (May 17, 1996): A4.

21. "Schiavo lashes FAA 'sloppy practices,' " Reuters (March 22, 1997).

22. Excerpts of *Flying Blind, Flying Safe*, quoted in *Time* (March 31, 1997).

23. Joanne Kelley, "Federal probe spreads blame for ValuJet crash," Reuters (August 19, 1997).

24. "Common sense and sacred cows: SEC self-assessment today," remarks by Chairman Arthur Levitt, Jr., of the U.S. Securities and Exchange Commission at the 34th annual meeting of the Corporate Counsel Institute in Chicago, Illinois, alluding to a case he had read in Philip Howard's book, *The Death of Common Sense* (October 19, 1995): http://www.sec.gov/speeches/spch057.txt.

25. "Supervisory goodwill may create U.S. thrift mini-crisis," editorial in *World Accounting Report* (November 1995).

26. Edward J. Kane, "Principal–agent problems in the S&L salvage," *Journal of Finance* (July 1990): 755–764.

27. Paulette Thomas, "Economy: the U.S. is liable for S&L losses in rule change;

judge says '89 bailout law broke prior contracts, entitling restitution,' " *Wall Street Journal* (February 25, 1992): A2.

28. Mark Sell, "Government hit again for thrift rule change," *Miami Review* (July 30, 1992): A1.

29. Neil A. Lewis, "Judge Rejects U.S. Bid to Escape S&L Penalties," *The New York Times on the Web*, Business Section (December 24, 1997): http://www.nytimes.com.yr/mo/ . . . news/financial/sl-rules.html.

30. Remarks by Chairman Arthur Levitt, Jr., United States Securities and Exchange Commission and financial Reporting Institute, University of Southern California (June 6, 1996), Pasadena, Calif.: http://www/sec/gov/news/speeches/spch106.txt.

31. David Hobbs, "Policy errors precipitated and compounded S&L debacle: Can deposit insurance reform prevent another costly bailout?" *Business Wire* (February 7, 1991).

32. "KPMG settles negligence charges," *Facts on File* (November 17, 1994): 860.

33. "RTC sues Coopers & Lybrand," *Facts on File* (December 15, 1994): 941.

34. *Defining the Roles of Accountants, Bankers and Regulators in the United States: A Study Group Report*, by the Group of Thirty (1994).

Chapter 3

When Greed Overwhelms
Good Governance

ON MANIPULATION AND ACCOUNTABILITY

Large corporations, periodically and often quite suddenly, turn insolvent. In the early 1970s came the shock caused by the collapse of Penn Central and Equity Funding. Later in the decade, there was the crisis concerning the viability of Continental Illinois, then one of the largest banks in the United States. In August 1982, the government of Mexico, with no advance notice, requested a debt moratorium from its creditors, mainly American banks. This move was accompanied by the apparition of other cash flow difficulties, which, in turn, cast doubts on the ability of certain Latin American states, such as Brazil, Argentina, and Peru, to repay their sovereign debt. (The total debt of these four countries came close to $200 billion.) The crisis was handled most dismally by the creditors. Although it was never discussed in public, a serious question arose concerning the high-handedness of the U.S. administration and its various regulatory agencies.

The behavior of the regulators was especially significant. Far better information and intelligence resources were available to them than to bank staff, directors, and auditors, with which to assess the condition of the Latin American economies and the ability of the debtors to repay. By failing to advise anyone of the facts or warn that collection would, at best, be delayed, they implicitly supported the decision to show the inflated, misleading operating results reported by the major financial institutions.

The role played by the directors was indicative of how meager their independent sources of knowledge were. If there were individual directors or auditors who queried the collectibility of the Latin American sovereign debt in 1982, 1983, or 1984, they were quite honestly told by management that the regulators, who should know, had made no suggestion to set up reserves against bad debts. Later that decade, some of the largest American blue chip corporations, such as GM, IBM, American Express, Westinghouse, and Eastman Kodak, also suffered serious hemorrhages. Their boards of directors were not as critical as they should have been of the data presented to them, and they addressed the crisis only at an advanced stage, thus inadvertently causing losses that could have been avoided had they acted earlier.

Although managerial carelessness probably delayed the realization that losses were threatening viability in the cases mentioned above, there was no element of criminal negligence in any of them. The following two instances, however, did have some criminal aspects. First, in the breakdown of the savings and loan institutions, some individuals, including regulatory authorities, knew in varying degrees of certainty several years prior to their collapse that these institutions were in dire straits. The FDIC had substantial information about problems with the thrifts' mode of operations and how risky their business had become, yet it did not act to prevent the decline or introduce measures that might have averted the collapse. The ultimate damage, estimated at $1.8 billion, was significantly greater than it would have been if the regulators had intervened several years earlier. Second, there were plenty of warning signals of laundering practices, manipulative international cross-country devices, and other suspicious move-ments of currency via the Bank of Credit and Commerce International (the BCCI group). There was ample intelligence that BCCI was being used as a conduit for the proceeds of the drug trade and other illegal activities at least a decade before the British government issued its "stop trade" order in the summer of 1991.

For years, different regulatory agencies were being fed a considerable amount of intelligence and information concerning the shenanigans of the BCCI group. There is, however, no evidence that, severally or individually, they tried to assess the data or draw conclusions as to the damage caused by its transactions. Worse, it has been alleged that various American and British agencies were close to colluding with various members of the group, yet the group continued to operate with impunity. If anything, its officers felt encouraged by the fact that BCCI had been able to retain such public figures as Clark Clifford and Bert Lance as front men in the United States and Britain. There is still no fully satisfactory answer to how BCCI managed to acquire the largest bank in the nation's capital, as well as banks in at least six other states.[1]

A specific example of failure to transmit information from one agency to another was published in a report of October 24, 1991, in which the CIA ad-mitted that it had failed to notify the Federal Reserve Board about BCCI's secret control of America First bank shares and other matters.[2] Then-acting director of the CIA Richard Kerr declared that the agency had learned of the secret 1981 takeover in 1985. There was no apparent follow-up on why the CIA had with-held this information, even though Executive Order 12333, issued by President Ronald Reagan on December 4, 1981, setting forth the duties and responsibilities of intelligence agencies, presumably requires that such information be shared with the relevant government agency.[3] Just one week earlier, on October 17, the *New York Times* had published an item to the effect that an internal review of the CIA's involvement with BCCI had found no evidence of wrongdoing.

Later, a congressional analysis showed that for more than ten years preceding the BCCI collapse in the summer of 1991, the FBI, the DEA, the CIA, the Customs Service, and the Department of Justice all failed to act on hundreds of tips about the illegality of BCCI's international activities.[4] An elementary working procedure of comparing notes among the various regulators throughout the 1980s would probably have materially reduced the embarrassment they faced with the collapse of the group. As it was, in the various congressional investigations that began at the end of that year into how the BCCI collapsed, many witnesses described in considerable detail the administration obstacle course that those who were suspicious had to navigate before the group's thin facade could be penetrated.

It must be said that shortcomings of regulators are not unique to the United States. BCCI-linked scandals and similar affairs have occurred also in the United Kingdom. For example, a U.S. Senate report published early in October 1992 charged that the Bank of England regulatory oversight of BCCI was ''wholly inadequate to protect BCCI's depositors and creditors'' and added that the bank had ''withheld information about BCCI's frauds from public knowledge for 15 months before closing the bank.''[5] There was also substantial criticism in Parliament of the Bank of England's handling of the BCCI affair. A public enquiry, headed by Lord Justice Bingham, was launched to examine supervisory practices related to the role of the external auditors. It recommended that they be placed under statutory *duty* (as opposed to the earlier *right*) to communicate directly with the Bank of England where necessary. In these reports and later observations, however, there was no clear conclusion that the impact of the BCCI fraud would have been lessened had the Bank of England paid more attention to the repeated early warning signs of serious irregularities.[6]

At no time, even after the liquidators of BCCI sued Price Waterhouse and Ernst & Young for $8.5 billion in connection with the 1985 audit of the bank (additional claims filed in 1994 in connection with the 1986 and 1987 audits were expected to total $5 billion),[7] was a staff member of the Bank of England or any other regulator called to task.[8] Somewhat later, in an editorial, the *Wall Street Journal* opined that Britain's penchant for keeping important affairs behind a veil of secrecy created the conditions that allowed BCCI to run out of control and that this practice will remain unchanged.[9]

The behavior of the American regulators was hardly better. True, the investigation, headed by Senator John Kerry, was more penetrating and the regulators' shortcomings were described in various hearings and publications—but they all walked away. None was sued or fired for negligence.

In another instance on the British scene, the 1971 report of a British Department of Trade and Industry investigation into the management and operations of Pergamon Press concluded that Robert Maxwell was "unfit to exercise proper stewardship" of a publicly quoted company. This study was called for after the collapse of the sale of the company to Saul Steinberg of the New York-based Leasco Data Processing Equipment Corporation, later known as the Reliable Group. In view of the inflated figures he had provided for the intended sale, Maxwell was accused of having "reckless and unjustified optimism."[10] This order was later rescinded, although Maxwell was still perceived as a high-flying adventurer. Despite his image, no British authority took any step in the following two decades to prevent him from structuring his empire the way he did and invading his employees' pension funds. It also became apparent after Maxwell's demise that there were directors of repute who had reason to know what was happening but did nothing. Ernie Burrington, then managing director of the Mirror Group, presumed that "they thought it was for someone else to sort out."[11]

In still another instance, the Bank of England had more than enough information to know that Barings Bank was not only past its prime but actually incapable of managing or controlling many of its activities, including its Far East derivative operations out of Singapore. Against this background, the news that Nick Leeson had brought about its downfall should have surprised nobody.

GOVERNANCE AND GREED

The phrase "corporate governance" has become a catchall. It is used to describe proper business management, but it is also cited when trying to explain any real or perceived shortfall or other disappointment with corporate performance. What does the term really mean? What is wrong with corporate governance as it is practiced today? How can it be improved to avoid some of the recent corporate disasters?

There are a number of basic components to all well-run companies. A corporation, however, is not a scientifically engineered artifact but, rather, a nonlinear social creation that evolves in a sensitive environment. Minuscule variations at the outset of operations of two similar companies can, as both mature, lead to major differences in their performance. Clearly, one important ingredient is the quality of a company's leadership—the good sense and integrity of its officers and directors, who should have keen and inquisitive minds and be able and willing to spend time in mastering the essentials of their brief. But even in well-run organizations, a creative and intelligent crook can succeed in outsmarting control and governance systems—for a time. A certain aura of success or invincibility often surrounds such a crook. When managers and board members are greedy and/or lethargic and choose uncritically to enjoy the fruits of the rascal's activities, and when the auditing systems do not include proper controls and do not provide for the application of judgment, a swindler can have a field day.

A case in point: For close to a decade, Yasuo Hamanaka, chief copper trader for Sumitomo Corporation, occupied a preeminent position and cultivated a risk management expertise that was uncritically attributed to high-level professionalism.[12] In hindsight, it was suspected that Sumitomo was inadvertently party to the trader's machinations, at least by virtue of its silence on some of his trading activities. One of these, code-named "Radr," took place in 1993; it involved up to 20 percent of the world's annual production of copper. Ultimately drawn into the investigation were not only U.S. financial regulators and the FBI but also the British Securities and Investments Board (SIB), the London Metal Exchange (LME), and the Serious Fraud Office (SFO).[13] How much simpler life would have been if the instruments of good governance had been in place before Hamanaka set out on his greedy adventure.

Similarly, Nick Leeson acted for three years or thereabouts without management taking any steps to prevent him from both trading and running a back-office operation.[14] Judge and jury of his own operations, he managed to convince his seniors at Barings, the oldest British merchant bank, that he had discovered financial paradise. Leeson was not called to account by his employers, partly because they were just as busy totting up their fat bonuses from his Far Eastern exploits as he was embezzling. Indeed, most such escapades occur when those whose job it is to ask questions prefer to enjoy some of the profits related to the crookery—which is just how Michael I. Monus, then president of Phar-Mor, of Youngstown, Ohio, managed to delude his company's board of directors, the investors, and the auditors, Coopers & Lybrand.

Leeson also made a mockery of the Singapore International Monetary Exchange (SIMEX) in its role as a regulator. Too ready to accept the explanations provided by the rogue's seniors, SIMEX relied on regulators in other markets and on officials at the Bank of England who, in turn, were totally unprepared to handle or regulate the huge but far from sophisticated fictitious trade he carried on.[15] When the matter was investigated, Barings management admitted that on several occasions they had waited for months for a response from the bank's officials to questions seeking guidance on reporting and accounting issues related to their Asian business. The Bank of England had other signals, if somewhat blurred, that should have made them sit up and take notice.[16] Later it was recommended that supervisory practices could be improved and that there should be closer cooperation between the Bank of England and other regulators in England and abroad.

The collapse of Barings was not just one more episode of slipshod management. Like some of the S&L collapses, it was an indictment of all those self-satisfied, uncritical institutions that let market activities outpace the regulators.[17] The case of Nick Leeson involved huge sums and received corresponding national and international exposure. In view of the gravity of this and other frauds, it is surprising that regulators are so rarely held to account, but their conduct has rarely been questioned. In the aftermath of a collapse, the regulators' reactions are invariably to form a committee that will later, with fanfare, issue new regulations, followed by publicized reassurances that those who should be responsible are investing in more people and equipment to control their risks.[18]

Accordingly, and subsequent to the Barings collapse, the British Securities and Investment Board announced that 50 exchanges around the world agreed to establish a new international framework to identify similar rogue traders by creating a series of "warning levels."[19] (Similar new rules were introduced after the S&L collapses.) It is plain that such additional regulations increase the burden on those companies honestly committed to keeping the law, but will they deter tomorrow's high-flying speculators and criminals?

As the skeptics might have known, it was not long before another major bank and its regulators goofed. Early in 1997, a week after it published its results for 1996, the major British NatWest Bank announced that a 30-year-old derivatives trader employee, Kyriacos Papouis, had blown a hole of at least $135 million in its subsidiary, NatWest Markets. A year later the Union Bank of Switzerland lost something like $700 million in the trading of derivatives.[20] The investigations that followed indicated that management, staff, auditors, and regulators alike had all performed as if little had been learned from previous collapses.[21]

None of the above cases sprang up overnight. All evolved over years out of a series of conscious and devious machinations. A well-oiled team of regulators, corporate directors, and independent auditors, comprised of inquiring individuals free to compare notes, could have raised pertinent questions and sounded the alarm in good time, preventing a substantial part of the losses that occurred. The regulatory authorities (with few exceptions) should have been involved in the above affairs, as should the boards of directors and the auditors. They failed, however, to take preventive steps and their conduct in the aftermath of the debacles was defensive and often not relevant. Also, there is no record of any serious postmortems conducted to find out why the instruments of governance did not function, nor is there any indication that convincing measures have been taken to prevent similar breakdowns in the future. Assurance that the regulators have become more accountable and will take precautions not to perform so inadequately again is essential to the credibility of the agencies.

WHERE *WERE* THE REGULATORS?

Most businesses are law-abiding, disciplined corporations, and their practical honesty is enforced by the potent sampling system of the regulators. The average company stays out of trouble, and the regulatory authorities seem to be fairly effective in supervising moderate-sized bodies. Clearly, however, in view of their slowness in addressing major cases such as those described above, it is questionable just how effectively the regulators use the information and intelligence available to them.

As indicated above, there is far too little exchange of information between regulatory agencies. They collaborate only when they are aware of a crisis already in process—and not always, even then. Unless something suspicious is discovered in the course of a review of a specific company, the authorities do not share information with the company's outside directors and auditors. By so failing to improve the exchange and free flow of available information and intelligence between all parties linked to corporate governance, they guarantee collapses that could otherwise be forestalled. One might think that the BCCI scandal in 1991 was so embarrassing and so traumatic that regulators and auditors alike learned their lessons—and that controls would be tightened and other debacles avoided or, at least, discovered sooner. But, as Barings rogue trader Nick Leeson showed in Singapore early in 1995, as the crisis at the New York branch of the Daiwa financial group indicated sometime earlier, and as the shenanigans of Yasuo Hamanaka of Sumitomo Corporation[22] demonstrated, the bucket is still leaking—and will probably continue to do so.

The roguery that led to the collapse of Barings Bank continued for a relatively short period (less than three years), commencing soon after the arrival in Singapore of Nick Leeson in March 1992.[23] By contrast, the deceptions at BCCI, Daiwa, and probably at Sumitomo all lasted for over a decade without the regulators or auditors learning about them. Yasuo Hamanaka single-handedly managed to cause ten years of losses in excess of $2.6 billion at Sumitomo. A $58 million loss from unauthorized trading in 1985 was compounded in the following decade by secret deals in which he attempted to erase the shortfall.[24]

Sadly, there is little reason to believe that lessons have been learned and that adequate safeguards are now in place to prevent fraud or similar acts of mismanagement. The success of Toshihide Iguchi, who, operating out of New York, hid $1.1 billion in losses from his Daiwa Bank superiors over an eleven-year period, or of Nick Leeson at Barings, is a savage affront to the credibility not only of these institutions and their internal auditors but also the outside auditors, the banks, and regulators. Such escapades could not have happened without the continued weaknesses of trading controls at the different companies, as well as the absence of tough and well-informed staff willing and able to challenge the information they collect from their traders.[25]

The regulators (not least the New York Federal Reserve examiners, considered by many to be among the finest supervisory institutions in the world) should have been concerned when, in November 1992, they discovered irregularities in Daiwa Bank.[26] Calling for improvement in the internal audit procedures, they expressed anxiety about the quality of the asset portfolio but they did not investigate Daiwa's shift of securities trading from the downtown location to the midtown office. (This change in location was effected to prevent the Fed from reporting to the Japanese Ministry of Finance that trading was being conducted at the former office without the Ministry's authorization.) These clues notwithstanding, it took another three years for the eventual unmasking of Toshihide Iguchi's illicit dealing (see note 18).

Consider the observation made by New York State Banking Department officials that bank examinations are "not designed to detect fraud. Detection of fraud is primarily the responsibility of the bank's auditors, both internal and external.''[27] This peculiar position statement points to a serious gap both in public expectations and in actual responsibility, for external auditors have repeatedly stated that fraud detection is not an inherent part of their assignment. In his tell-all book, published in Japan in January 1997, a former Daiwa bond trader (later jailed) stated that although the bank had tried to cover up the losses, both the American and Japanese regulators had been negligent in not detecting his wrongdoings.[28] Continuing his efforts to describe the laxity, the author shares with the reader his impression that the external auditor appeared to have been emasculated and was little better than an expensive rubber stamp. He quotes Daiwa's auditors, Ernst & Young, as explaining that they were not obliged to audit the (major) New York branch, and he adds the opinion that, while banks clamor for the imprimatur of a Big Six auditing seal of approval, its value is questionable.

While officials at the Daiwa Bank were forced to resign, those at Barings were fired, and those at BCCI all but dispersed, the regulators all stayed in office (with the exception of one minor casualty at the Bank of England in the aftermath of the Barings debacle) (see note 26). In an article in *Banker*, Stephen Timewell noted that bureaucratic camouflage represents a knotty problem, but he made no suggestions for solving it. In any case, it is clear to those who study these affairs that the regulators were careless in their tasks.

The clearing houses with which Barings was trading should have taken a more aggressive attitude toward it. They should have asked for more details about the bank's position and should not have allowed it to increase the riskiness of its position. The Bank of England ignored the reports from Barings acknowledging large margins deposited with the Far East exchanges in excess of the 25 percent of capital base exposure limit imposed on all British banks. Lulled by Barings' conservative reputation, they kept quiet (see note 14). Similarly, Singapore-based SIMEX sent letters to Barings querying discrepancies in the activities of Barings' Future Singapore. These queries remained unanswered, but the regulators did not follow up until it was too late.[29]

That the auditors of both BCCI and Barings were sued was to be expected; they were ''perceived to have deep pockets.'' Coopers & Lybrand, the accountants of the latter, decided to fight back, not only defending itself but also suing nine former directors of the bank on the grounds that, in reality, Barings' management was liable.[30] It should be noted that in this litigation merry-go-round, no one considered (or, apparently, dared to) suing the regulators. Among the explanations offered is that one does not take up proceedings against government staff. Another is the relatively modest salary of the supervisory regulators and the fact that they are not covered by insurance, thus reducing the chances of their being rewarded.

The reaction of the Commodity Futures Trading Commission (CFTC) agency regulator, an organization less known to the public and less involved in litigation, to its shortcomings was first to confer and then to introduce new rules to strengthen its controls and increase surveillance. Accordingly, regulators from eighteen nations met in Britain late in November 1996 to formulate a safeguard against another scandal in the murky world of trade in key raw materials like the Sumitomo affair. (An earlier meeting had been held in Windsor, England, in 1995 to deal with the collapse of Barings.)[31] Although Sumitomo confirmed that Hamanaka had actually confessed to hiding a web of unauthorized deals, early in 1997 the CFTC still had not completed its investigation and would not predict when it would do so (see note 18). Apparently, regulators still enjoy the luxury of being free, if they so wish, to learn their share of the lesson from recent debacles without being accountable and running the risk of suffering legal and other penalties.

Are regulators, indeed, incapable of doing a better job? Has the complexity of today's business world—especially financial services—made truly effective controls next to impossible? Are there a variety of factors (not all spelled out in this book) preventing efficient supervision? There are different opinions on this issue. One former U.S. regulator is quoted as saying, "No one individual is held responsible, no individual's job is on the line." So far—maybe because they have never been seriously challenged—regulators explain the system's shortcomings in terms of the prevailing bureaucracy, and they continue to make errors in judgment and performance with immunity. They have not been considered accountable and are rarely charged with negligence.

THE SAGA OF CLARK CLIFFORD

In the arena of corporate governance and accountability, in between and including both boards of directors and regulatory authorities, there is a throng of lobbyists, old boys, and other operators who know how to cut red tape—and charge you for it. Their numbers are constantly replenished by officials who, at the end of the term of office of the outgoing president, retire from government and join the ranks of the consultants. They operate out of Washington, D.C., and in every state capital, as well as in London, Paris, and Tokyo. In the course of their activities, most stay genuinely within the law. Henry Kissinger, who acts as consultant and serves on several boards, is a good example; and there other lobbyists just as respectable. Sooner or later, however, certain individuals are discovered either to have been used or, worse, to have abused the trust they built up over the years, embarrassing their friends and government contacts and muddying their own name. One might say that they are contaminated by the "Clifford syndrome."[32]

As a practicing lawyer from 1945 through the end of the 1980s, Clark Clifford was a dominant force in the world of American decision making. Confidante to all presidents in office, from Harry S Truman through Jimmy Carter, and secretary of defense in the Johnson administration, he had access to every federal office in the capital. Clifford thrived because his clients knew he could pick up the phone and call anyone in high places. But there was more than that: Clifford had become a stamp of approval. Anyone who retained him was guaranteed respectability and prestige. His word alone had become a prize commodity. The BCCI bankers, eager to gain recognition and obtain permission to operate in the United States, hired President Carter's budget director Bert Lance and used the former president himself, former Atlanta mayor Andrew Young, former CIA head Richard Helms, and other well-known people to front for them in their U.S. operations.[33]

They also engaged Clark Clifford. For over a decade, from the end of the 1970s, he seemed to serve BCCI well. When, for instance, BCCI began trying to acquire Financial General Bankshares of Washington, Clifford used his clout to persuade the Federal Reserve Board to approve the purchase. At an April 1981 hearing with staffers, he tried to convince them that allowing this group to invest in an American bank would be good for the country, and he put his personal integrity on the line by assuring the Board that BCCI would have no role in the management of the bank.

At this point, he had put himself in a situation where there was an obvious conflict of interest. He was supposed to protect Financial General from the influence of BCCI, while, at the same time, receiving legal fees from Agha Hasan Abedi, the president of BCCI. Soon afterwards, the Arab investors in BCCI suggested that Clifford become chairman of the new bank. They agreed that he continue his law practice and act on behalf of both the bank and BCCI. Around that time Financial General Bankshares was renamed First American Bankshares. The relationship continued throughout the 1980s. Clifford and his key partner, Robert Altman, filled multiple roles. They were lawyers for both BCCI and First American's holding company. As chairman and president, re-spectively, of First American, they made decisions on the purchase, including the final price; and they personally borrowed a substantial amount of money from BCCI. By means of a complex structuring, they invested in the group's shares for less than half the price paid by another investor a few days earlier.

Eighteen months later, they sold 60 percent of the shares at triple the price, the highest amount ever commanded by shares in the holding company. From the proceeds, they paid off their entire BCCI loan, shared a profit of close to $10 million, and retained, debt-free, the remaining 40 percent of the original block of stock. Not very long after, the sinful saga of the BCCI group began to unravel and Clark Clifford's halo vanished. Now an old man, he could only struggle to avoid spending days and months in court trying to disprove allega-tions of conspiracy against the U.S. government—a sad end to an extraordinary career.

Although there were any number of tidbits of information concerning possible criminal acts by BCCI and members of the group, there was no serious, con-certed effort by the regulators to put them under the magnifying glass until the end of the decade. Clark Clifford and some of his peers colluded in this negli-gence, as did the authorities who at least suspected that something was wrong. There is no evidence that the latter tried to warn Clifford. After all, they all belonged to the "old boys' club," the least likely institution to deal with corporate governance. Although BCCI is no more, the club has not closed down; it just has different members. It is part of the establishment, and there seems no way to make it disappear.

A MATTER OF PROPER GOVERNANCE

Long gone is the age of innocence, when a chief executive officer was trusted and had no reason to expect his directors to question his activities. Hardly anyone doubted that the facts presented in the (far more simply designed) financial statements, unencumbered by pages of notes and supported by the auditors' opinion, represented a "true and fair" picture of recent events. Was that trust justified, or were unethical transactions simply hidden under the carpet and negative publicity avoided? Was integrity really esteemed and honesty respected? Did such integrity ever exist? If so, who is responsible for changes in business ethics and morals? New rules and regulations are continuously introduced and adopted in attempts to prevent shenanigans and give some measure of comfort and assurance to those who rely on corporate representation of facts, published or otherwise. Are these new rules needed because of deterioration in the level of trustworthiness today, or should they already have been in place in the previous era? Government authorities, regulators, business professionals, analysts, and the public in general continue to wonder—sometimes with some skepticism—whether the progress made in corporate legislation is sufficient. There are those who doubt that the additional edicts for further disclosure contribute to better governance.

In any case, such rules, regulations, and professional instructions have been introduced. Among the recommendations introduced in the early 1990s were:

- separating the office of CEO from that of chairman of the board;
- a board composed predominantly of independent, nonexecutive directors;
- a far more active board, composed of nonexecutive directors and involved in the management of the company through the audit, compensation, and other subcommittees; and
- reporting of the internal audit division (or department, or staff) and independent auditors directly to the chairperson of the audit committee or the chairman of the board, rather than to the CEO.

There is, in fact, a seemingly continuous output of proposals intended to strengthen controls, implying some distrust of the ethics of the primary actors in governance. In sum, it can be stated with some assurance that the call for further regulation indicates lack of confidence in the system.

Most of those concerned with corporate governance—not least the gurus of the distinguished business schools—spend many hours considering how to strengthen regulations and the practice of governance. Few, if any, consider how much of the resources spent on bureaucratic mechanism could be saved if the instruments of corporate governance and those who administer it were more creditable, dependable, and honest. If corporate governance were more trustworthy and if the public were better schooled in applying accountability, far less regulation would be needed. But hardly anyone believes that such an upstanding business climate can be achieved today. Without investment in more education, fresh scandals of all sizes are brewing and will boil over, sooner or later—to be met with more moral indignation and new, more stringent regulations.

Hardly any resources, government or private, are being devoted to strengthening the moral fiber, honesty, and ethical conduct of society as a whole or the business world in particular. Perhaps the best starting point for those concerned with corporate governance would be to devote more time and money to improving and expanding the study of ethics into a continuous educational program, commencing in kindergarten and continuing throughout school into college.

TOWARD HONEST GOVERNANCE

The number of corporate governance ordinances, regulations, and edicts has been continuously increasing since the early 1930s. What influence have they had? They have certainly helped make corporate accounting and reporting functions far more powerful. Also, the volume of paperwork has mushroomed and will continue to increase, as companies grow and diversify and move overseas.

We cannot precisely quantify losses incurred through business mismanagement and substandard levels of corporate governance. One can only add up the losses from dishonest conduct that have been recorded; those undetected—and therefore unquantified—can only be guessed at. The consequences are far-reaching. Taxes are not collected on income generated in the subterranean economy, increasing the burden on honest taxpayers. The national economy is deprived of income which, but for the folly of substandard economic performance, could have been produced.

Also, it would not be practical even to attempt to determine whether the level of white-collar crime has decreased as a result of more thorough reporting. Most white-collar crime of the past generation or two was a result of the greed of people responsible for ensuring that corporate governance be properly implemented. That does not mean that they were always the beneficiaries of the stolen money. Preferring not to know all the facts, however, they were often greedy recipients of funds that had not been honestly earned. Greed was certainly at work when Clark Clifford aided and abetted the owners and managers of the BCCI financial group in their financial crimes, and it was what motivated many of those who controlled the savings and loan associations in the 1980s.

It was also clearly the motivation for the executives of Barings Bank who permitted Nick Leeson's rogue trading in Singapore. In his autobiography, Leeson wrote that duping the company was sometimes as easy as falsifying a fax. The senior executives were perfectly content to let him do whatever he pleased as long as he generated those fantastic earnings. Management knew that Leeson was providing "profits" in total contravention of proper control procedures, both executing trades on the Singapore Exchange and overseeing the bookkeeping of those trades, but they preferred not to be too inquisitive. This contravention of proper internal control was noted in an internal report prepared in the summer of 1994, warning that he could do real damage to the firm.[34]

Leeson's achievement, thought to be unique of its kind, was that he caused the largest financial loss ever suffered up to that time by a single institution— about $1.4 billion. (A year later the losses to Sumitomo Trading were revealed— some $2.6 billion.) It was not until a few days after he disappeared into the jungles of Malaysia that his superiors in the bank began showing some curiosity about his machinations. Indeed, Peter Baring, the bank's chairman, had told the head of banking supervision at the Bank of England in late 1993 that "The recovery in profitability has been amazing, leaving Barings to conclude that it is not actually terribly difficult to make money in the securities business."[35]

Like the Clark Clifford case, the Barings experience provides yet another instance of the effect of greed on trust. Both instances indicate how difficult it is to attain quality corporate governance. As long as managers regard profit-based bonuses as their right, some will be only too happy to turn a blind eye to suspiciously oversized profits. Until there is a general agreement to do everything to eradicate its influence, greed will be a stumbling block to good corporate governance. Simply put, it must be acknowledged that proper governance means asking tough questions continuously and relentlessly; that curiosity and the desire to understand are essential characteristics of management; and that those in charge—officers, directors, and auditors—should never believe that any transaction is too complex for them to understand, or requires too much time for close scrutiny. Until that day comes, some people will exploit weaknesses for their personal gain.

NOTES

1. "Review and Outlook": BCCI Opening, editorial in *Wall Street Journal* (September 5, 1995): A14.

2. Richard Kerr, "CIA admits it failed to tell the Fed about BCCI," *New York Times* (October 26, 1991): 34.

3. E.O. 12333 is the most recent in a series of executive orders governing U.S. intelligence activities. Previous orders had been issued by President Carter in 1978 (E.O. 12036) and by President Ford in 1975 (E.O.) 11905. Page NT018, February 23, 1996: http://www/access.gpo.gov/int/int018.html/.

4. *New York Times* (August 27, 1992).

5. "Business brief—Bank of Credit and Commerce: Bank of England cleared of 'corrupt links' to BCCI," *Wall Street Journal* (October 21, 1992): A13.

6. Eugene Robinson, "Report says British regulators bungled supervision of BCCI," *Washington Post* (October 23, 1992): A25.

7. *Defining the Roles of Accountants, Bankers and Regulators in the United States*: A Study Group Report, by the Group of Thirty (1994): 13–14.

8. Karen Wells, "Bank of England partly blamed for BCCI," *Wall Street Journal* (October 23, 1992): A9.

9. "Britain on BCCI," editorial in *Wall Street Journal* (October 26, 1992): A16.

10. *1988 Current Biography Yearbook*, 365.

11. Roy Greenslade, "Question time for Maxwell's friends," *Guardian Weekly* (November 10, 1996): 27.

12. "Coming a cropper in copper," *The Economist* (June 22, 1996): 85–86.

13. Paul Murphy and Lina Saigol, "The $3 billion copper caper," *Guardian Weekly* (February 23, 1997).

14. Hans R. Stoll, "Lost Barings: A tale in three parts concluding with a lesson," *Journal of Derivatives* (Fall 1995): 109–115.

15. Jeremy Mark, "International Singapore blasts management; Ministry of Finance Report says Leeson supervisors share blame in collapse," *Wall Street Journal* (October 18, 1995): A16.

16. Nicholas Bray, "With Barings collapse study imminent, the fallout begins at Bank of England," *Wall Street Journal* (July 17, 1995): A7.

17. Alex Brummer, "Gamble of a lifetime," reviews of two books on the Barings collapse in *The Guardian* (March 10, 1996): 8.

18. "Banking's bad jokes," *The Economist* (April 12, 1997): 71–77.

19. Dan Atkinson and Sarah Whitebloom, "Barings bosses set to face charges," *The Guardian* (March 24, 1996): 16.

20. "Blind Faith," and "Discord in Switzerland," *The Economist* (January 31, 1998): 16.

21. "Investment banking—NatWest holed," *The Economist* (March 22, 1997): 106.

22. "Japan prosecutors arrest copper trader," Reuters (October 22, 1996): 106.

23. S. Rajagopal, "Barings and Daiwa: Lessons in bank management," *State of India Monthly Review* (August 1996): 407–417.

24. "Sumitomo's Hamanaka faces more legal trouble," Reuters (November 12, 1996).

25. "Sumitomo probes grind on in U.S., Britain," Reuters (February 14, 1997).

26. Stephen Timewell, "Too hard to hold," *Banker* (November, 1995): 22.

27. Timothy L. O'Brien and Norihiko Shirouzu, "Fed's scrutiny helped reveal Daiwa Losses," *Wall Street Journal* (September 29, 1995): C1.

28. "Japan's Asahi Bank cleans up U.S. branch," Reuters (February 14, 1997).

29. Paul Stonham, "Whatever happened at Barings: Unauthorized trading and the failure of controls," *European Management Journal* (June 1967): 269–278.

30. Jim Kelly and John Gapper, "Ex-Barings chiefs to be sued by bank's auditors," *Financial Times* (November 30, 1996).

31. "Regulators meet on commodity scandals," Reuters (November 25, 1996).

32. Douglas Franz and David McKean, "Friends in high places," *Common Cause Magazine* (Fall 1995): 12.

33. Scott Shepard, "BCCI used Carter, Young and Lance to commit fraud, Senate panel says," *Atlanta Constitution* (October 2, 1992): A6.

34. Stanley W. Angrist, "The corporate world's super-egos," *Leisure & Arts: Business Bookshelf, Wall Street Journal* (n.d.)

35. Michael Lewis, "Snobs and yobs," *New Yorker* (June 17, 1996): 97.

Chapter 4

How Governance and Accountability Affect Corporate Growth

To survive as vigorous entities, democracies must adjust to change. To preserve, societies must renew themselves, which they do in different ways—not least through economic development and through legislation. The United States of today, for example, is not only very different from what it was in the days of George Washington; it has also developed dramatically from where it stood early this century. Its progress from white-male-minority rule to general suffrage was the result of growth, social demand, and constitutional decisions made over time.

Similarly, it is generally accepted that a government based on the dominant long-term presence of one party will with time become stale. A two-party or multiparty system provides a better chance for both good governance and the renewal of political ideas. A political pendulum that throws one party out of office from time to time and replaces it with its opposition enables reinvigoration. By spending time out of power, the defeated are not only reminded of their human frailty but also provided with an opportunity to rejuvenate themselves, to reexamine old policies, and to initiate new programs more in line with the needs of the future. In the last two centuries the bi-party system has had considerable success in the United States and Great Britain, and no less impressive results in some of the smaller democracies. Businesses, however, do not operate democratically; therefore, other means must be found to keep them vital, competitive, and responsive to current conditions.

ON THE DYNAMICS OF CORPORATE EVOLUTION

A compelling theory holds that when the market is allowed to act with total freedom, the best will come out on top. But there are numerous sectors of society that do not form an integral part of the market or have any inbuilt renewal mechanism. Also, in the civil service, education, medicine, science, or business, the systems that help encourage renewal are not always parallel or similar. Therefore, except for the Libertarians, most economists believe that the free market economy requires certain governmental regulation and supervision. In practice, however, they do not usually expect that the instruments of government will be reassessed periodically and that those in charge of their implementation will be held to account.

Federal Reserve chairman Alan Greenspan observed, "Regulation, by its very nature, becomes increasingly obsolete; regulation imposed in an earlier period would be wholly or partly inappropriate for something that evolves at a later date."[1] Understandably, some rules guiding regulators have become antiquated over the years. He added that, to ensure that they remain focused on today's issues, both Congress and the regulators should periodically review the existing laws and regulations that guide the regulators. A policy providing for the reassessment of laws and regulations—say, every seven years—would not be a minor undertaking, demanding, as it would, additional bureaucracy. The results, however, if the proceedings were conducted with determination, could be of benefit to all concerned. Ways of making the different functionaries in these areas accountable will be discussed in the following pages.

Corporate Governance and Accountability

On entering a profession or business, people born in the second half of the twentieth century discover an economic world that to them seems to have existed for ages. Few are aware that, although the concepts of capitalism and free enterprise have been identified with America since the Declaration of Independence, most economic and social laws relating to how the country functions and to its instruments of government—ranging from the regulatory authorities to the tax system and to who is responsible for managing transfer funds—have been in effect only since the early 1930s. That is to say, they were enacted in response to the Great Depression at the earliest. Some came even later, after World War II.

It is hard to imagine today how relatively small government was then, how little of business life was taken up with accounting and paperwork. Compared with the one-third of the gross national product spent by the government each year in the 1990s, the administration's share in the GNP was only 8.6 percent in 1937 and as little as 1.8 percent in 1913.[2] Only with the evolution of economic and social legislation did government bureaucracy and the larger corporate establishment begin to grow to their present elephantine proportions, and only then, to keep a semblance of order and control, did the service industry mushroom, manned by people—both staff and independent—whose task is to ensure the accurate recording of events and their proper disclosure and to help link every business to the appropriate government authorities and other business organizations.

As they do with the corporate world, a large flock of political scientists address such topics as the quality and size of government, the need for taxes, or the advantages of privatizing various government services. Publications are written by or derived from the work of theorists, often business school professors or interested parties such as outside directors or auditors. Some emphasize the need to strengthen a certain area of governance, while others explain—sometimes defensively—the history of a particular corporate event. In response, politicians sometimes raise questions (usually technical), but the curiosity and capacity to question, to reassess, and sometimes to change national priorities, laws, and practices hardly ever exists in either government or the corporate world. In addition, quite a few CEOs have written at some length about their personal contribution to a company's success, but few have asked whether the present corporate structure is the most suitable for conducting the business. Nor have they dwelt on their experience in corporate governance or discussed the need for accountability of the role played by the company's directors and auditors.

No matter what its source, however, no study of modern corporate governance and accountability is complete without taking into account the overwhelming impact of the federal securities legislation administered by the Securities and Exchange Commission (SEC). The SEC was established in 1933, in the wake of the 1929 crash. The commission and its modus operandi have been studied at great length, and many volumes have been written about how this truly great regulatory authority guides corporate America. Its outstanding characteristic is its unobtrusive size and its commitment to maintain as low a profile as reasonably possible, so that the business of the nation can continue with minimal intrusion or interference.[3] Although the traditional framework of discussion of corporate governance does not include the regulators, the very real role of these participants in governance must be examined and they, too, ought to be held accountable.

Corporations as Living Organisms

Although intangible and structured by law, corporations—somewhat like plants, animals, and people—have a finite lifespan. That has been true ever since the legal structure of companies took shape. The contemporary concept of the limited liability company has grown rapidly in a climate of optimistic ideology and economic growth following the establishment of the SEC and other national undertakings ranging from Medicare to Social Security.

Over time, however, even successful companies, once established with much entrepreneurial enthusiasm, tend to grow fat and weary. They become producer- rather than consumer-oriented. Their "arteries" harden, their layers of management increase, and gradually they grow old and disappear. At least in part, the aging of companies can be explained by the fact that, with time, management grows overly conservative, captive to governance instructions introduced in the past. It fails to recognize social change or to perceive shifts in public needs. The executives lose their sense of mission and purpose. Many companies close after only a few years of existence, but even those that are successful and perform for decades may well in time go into a gradual decline. According to *The Economist*, the life expectancy of a typical multinational is between 40 and 50 years, and about one-third of the firms on the *Fortune* 500 list in 1996 will have merged, broken up, or gone out of business by 2010.[4]

Companies operating in a free economy will only survive when there is a satisfactory, commonly accepted level of governance. But society is not static, nor is the business environment. They are both dynamic environments, colored by changing circumstances and priorities. Accordingly, the term "proper governance" should periodically be redefined. The appropriate questions must be asked: To whom, actually, do companies belong? Whom should they serve? The shareholders? Their own workforce? How about their effect, good or bad, on the environment? What about suppliers and other creditors? Do they allocate their resources sensibly? Do they distribute their proceeds fairly?

The point is that the answers to these and other questions are different today from what they were a generation ago. For example, today it is fashionable to count job security, health insurance, and vocational and other forms of training among the ingredients of good corporate governance, whereas in the past they were not usually considered among the basic rights of the employee. When such concepts of governance change, those responsible for reporting should be clearly told how to adapt their supervisory function accordingly.

Unlike a democracy, where the system of political parties ensures sensitivity to the voters and encourages renewal, a business is subject to governance far more authoritarian than democratic. Annual corporate reports rarely provide insight or self-criticism, and neither regulators nor corporations have established a discipline of self-assessment or reevaluation of modes of operation in the light of prevailing economic rules. In the mid-1990s, few in the world of corporate governance were aware that, under the American Law Institute's 1994 "Principles of Corporate Governance," the failure of corporate officers and directors to institute and periodically assess compliance systems in corporate organizations can form the basis for a personal liability claim.[5]

Ultimately, the business success of the United States and other democracies will depend, to a large degree, on the quality of their corporate management and governance and their ability to address successfully both the market and the regulators' demands. And yet, what appears to be lacking is a mechanism that would periodically trigger a reassessment of business practices of various accounting systems, and that would examine whether corporate governance answers current needs. Perhaps the system suffers from an ostrich-like inability to face unpleasant facts, or maybe management lacks the confidence or interest to seek an honest evaluation of its performance. Whatever the case, management leaves judgment to the market, the final arbiter.

Judgment, Governance, Power, and Accountability

Despite the many calamities such as those described above over the years, determined intellectuals and business leaders have undertaken to design instruments for guiding corporate governance to improved performance. Some believe that they have produced the rules necessary to regulate the normative use of power and the proper application of authority, thereby ensuring that all those who hold office are held to account.[6] How effective these instruments are and what should be done to make them even better is a subject that requires continued attention.

Proper corporate governance must be based on sound judgment and on an understanding of the respective power and accountability of the different elements involved. This end cannot be achieved unless all relevant information is available, hence the need for full disclosure.[7] This concept is a means to achieving sound business judgment which, in turn, is a tool of judicial review used in analyzing executive conduct.[8] If the regulator and the chief executive officer, the outside director, the full board, and/or the independent auditor use their independent judgment, proper governance will prevail.

On the subject of corporate governance, it is difficult to exaggerate the importance of good judgment. Courts rarely interfere with the judgment of a board of directors unless gross and palpable overreaching is shown. That is to say, a board is normally presumed to have sound business judgment, and its decisions will not be overturned by the courts.[9] Accordingly, the 1978 ABA *Guidebook* observes:

Recognizing that business decisions may seem unrealistically simple when viewed in hindsight, and expressing reluctance to substitute their judgment for that of the directors, courts have generally refrained from questioning the wisdom of board decisions. For the Business Judgment Rule to apply, a director must have acted in good faith and with a reasonable basis for believing that the action authorized was in the lawful and legitimate furtherance of the corporation's purposes, and must have exercised his honest business judgment after due consideration of what he reasonably believed to be relevant factors.[10]

This position was reiterated in Rule 4.01(c) of the American Law Institute's 1994 "Principles of Corporate Governance," which explains that if directors or officers have undertaken reasonable fact-gathering and evaluation prior to making a decision about the scope and adequacy of a compliance system, and unless their decision is irrational, it will not be a basis for personal liability (see note 5).

In the 1970s and early 1980s, much of the discussion concerning the Business Judgment Rule revolved around company mergers. Since then, however, there has been a shift in focus from particular board conduct on a specific transaction to more general board procedures involving corporate performance.[11] Accordingly, where the use of good judgment is lacking or questionable, the chances are that corporate governance will be flawed or unsatisfactory and that questions of accountability will arise. The exercise of good judgment is essential to provide confidence in the relations between management, agents and shareholders, and principals (see note 8). It is just as applicable to auditors as it is to outside directors.

In the corporate structure, there is a complementary relationship between the use of judgment and the application of power. It is not always easy to discern how power is applied. Bertrand Russell said in 1938 that he thought that the fundamental concept in social science is power, in the same sense in which energy is the fundamental concept in physics, and that power is generated, maintained, and lost in the context of relationships with others.[12] When the performance of the regulator, the outside nonexecutive directors, the CEO, or the independent firm of CPAs is being assessed, the question is how each uses the power vested in him. Much depends on there being a clear understanding of and respect for the sources of power of each functionary, and this, in turn, depends on the prevailing level of communication. But, in fact, the performance of a director or, for that matter, an auditor can only be tested in crisis situations. Although theoretical examinations are of some help and past performance is an indication, there is no assurance that an individual will apply good judgment and rise to the expected level of accountability in an emergency.

Although in theory it is the shareholders and/or principals who appoint directors, in fact the CEO quite often has great influence over their selection. This may be a flawed practice, but it is common. The directors perceive that they are far more dependent on the CEO than on the shareholder, and this consideration more often than not will influence their thinking and decision making, at times impairing their independence.

Compared with the regulator or senior corporate officer, the nonexecutive director has considerably fewer opportunities to apply those minimal instruments of power he is allowed to have. As will be shown in the following pages, the outside director's expression of power often may be negative—for example, voting against the majority or, at best, swinging the vote. Exerting a positive influence requires far more knowledge of the company than most outside directors have gathered or, alternatively, a much stronger power base than most have built.

THE ETHICS FACTOR IN GOVERNANCE

Ensuring that ethical standards are maintained in a company often calls for a nonstop, uphill campaign. The quest for quick financial rewards as expressed, not least, in the demand for ever-better quarterly results, tends to undermine the basic mores expected of the business community. In our mercenary world, in which consumerism prevails and more capital goods are to be had than ever before, and where production keeps increasing, some members of society may pontificate about the importance of being ethical. Others, however, respond to the call for good ethics with mere lip service, asserting that few individuals in our everyday life actually regard ethical behavior as a priority in their business considerations.

Business ethics is a well-publicized topic sometimes discussed at tedious length in the economic world. Different codes of professional conduct (sometimes Talmudic in their complexity) have been adopted by various organizations to describe how one is expected to behave when ethical questions arise, but they are not necessarily helpful. There is, in fact, an endless variety of questions that require ethical judgment in the business world: When to "blow the whistle?" When to oppose executive decisions? When to break off trading with a client? The decisions often require a certain amount of boldness—even bravery; on the other hand, playing it safe might expose one to accusations of carelessness and, possibly, violation of business rules.

Ethics, of course, embraces a whole range of issues, from the abstract and philosophical to the mundane. One would expect any professional, employee, or independent practitioner to recognize an ethical question when it arises. When addressing this subject, one soon discovers that like politics, ethics is a lot easier to study as a theory than to apply in practice. Endless nonsense and much hype is uttered daily on the subject, with little opposition, and sermons on business ethics are common but apparently of little help in improving the moral standards of those at whom they are directed.

Questions of business ethics generally fall into one of two categories: Some are abstract, involve little risk, and are usually impersonal; in other cases, an individual must make an ethical decision that could be costly and of significant impact to him. An example of the former is the nationwide consensus reached in the late 1970s to boycott apartheid South Africa. Gradually, the subject became an issue not only for investors but also for traders who heretofore had business links with this country. At annual meetings of corporate America, CEOs were expected to state, in no uncertain terms, not only that their company did not conduct any business with South Africa but also that it had sold any and all shares in other companies that did. Any company that continued to have ties with South Africa—for example, through branches or agencies—ran the risk of being ostracized. Similarly, universities, hospitals, and museums were expected to declare that they owned no shares and had no other involvement, direct or indirect, with South Africa. This very effective boycott helped bring down the white government. Enforcing it was basically an ethical decision requiring no significant amount of personal courage and, with few exceptions, causing no business loss.

An example of the second category of ethical question, also with international ramifications, is the manufacturing of goods in low-wage countries: The use of cheap child labor in India, Indonesia, and other Far East countries, as well as in some Latin American nations, became a matter of public interest. There was, for example, publicity about several successful U.S. apparel and shoe companies that had some of their products manufactured in countries where children were employed at what appeared to be, by U.S. standards, strikingly low wages.

Among these corporations was Seattle-based Starbuck's, a boutique coffee retailer that sourced Guatemalan workers who were paid about $2.50 a day, as well as Nike, KMart, JC Penney, and Reebok—all of which rushed to pass sourcing codes, publicizing their decision to avoid exploitation of labor in the developing world. Some contended these measures were not far-reaching enough. The question: Were they exploiting overseas child labor in a way that would have been totally unacceptable within the United States? Some, like Levi Strauss and The Gap, have exerted direct pressure to establish minimum wages and working conditions. Levi Strauss has a written code of conduct stating that it will "seek to identify and utilize business partners who aspire as individuals and in the conduct of all their business to a set of ethical standards not incompatible with our own."[13] The company can show that it severed relations with suppliers which did not meet its standards.[14] Still, such decisions are often complex.

The counterargument, expressed mainly by companies that, when accused of such abuse, have reacted with general noncommittal declarations rather than come up with remedies, has been that this situation is preferable to the alternative—that is, without these seemingly meager wages, the children's families would starve. Few such firms make a serious effort to examine the intricacy of the issues, and the accusation remains an unresolved matter of concern.

It is especially noteworthy that the current administration is troubled about these modern sweatshops. In April 1997, President Clinton announced the recommendations of a task force appointed by him and including U.S. clothing manufacturers, labor unions, and human rights groups. They called for a code of conduct on wages and working conditions and for a mechanism to inspect apparel factories worldwide.[15] There were specific proposals to limit the working week to a maximum of 60 hours and to demand that factories not use workers under the age of fifteen. The recommendations, the product of compromise, were criticized by bodies such as the San Francisco Global Exchange Group, which stated that the agreement watered down important issues, sanctioned excessive overtime, was not specific about the wage requirement, and did not include any provision for monitoring labor practices by human rights groups.

There are other ethical issues: Whereas directors did not usually find it difficult to conform with the anti-apartheid measures, they are hesitant and slower when ethical matters affecting them directly in the boardroom are first raised— for example, affirmative action policies inviting women or African Americans to join the board. But in this instance also, even though boards are still composed of a majority of middle-aged white males, there is evidence of a slow but steady increase in minority representation.

The position of an individual confronted by an ethical problem deriving from corporate greed is different. When employees take a firm stand, such as "blowing the whistle," they find that some colleagues might admire them but few, if any, will actually support them. Even more unpleasant, they may be regarded as troublemakers, a label that could affect their careers and chances of promotion. Worse, their chosen course of action could mean losing their jobs or other forms of material damage. It can be a case of ''No good deed goes unpunished,'' and choosing the ethical path is not often rewarded.

Company board directors do not always feel comfortable in dealing with ethical questions. There are various explanations for such reticence. Perhaps they do not regard the matter as significant or material, or they may consider the question to be a management affair and none of their business. Many simply prefer not to stick their necks out, and it is not often that directors deal with ethical matters. When ethical questions do appear on the board's agenda, they are usually the result of pressure from senior corporate staff or the outside community.

In the business world, as in society at large, the decision to take a stand on an ethical matter is not always made on purely moral grounds. It may also be influenced by consideration of who is likely to know that one was faced with the dilemma and what the cost will be. There maybe a trade-off and/or a compromise—for example, an accounting firm hates to lose a client; a director would be sorry to leave the board; a CFO (Corporate Financial Officer) doubts whether he or she could easily find another position with equal pay.

Sometimes ethical questions evolve gradually and are at first hardly noticeable. When the presence of a conflict is realized, the individual involved may feel that he or she can either keep it in the background or ignore it entirely—believing or rationalizing that the larger project at hand is far more important for the community or the company. When individuals finally wake up to the implications of the situation, they find it difficult—and, often, unrealistic—to voice their concerns, and thus they are drawn into collaboration in the unethical act.

There is really only one good decision for those confronted by such a dilemma: Choose the ethical course. In the long run, one is more damaged by any other (see note 13). Sadly, too few people in the business world follow this dictum.

AUTHORITY TO THE MARKET

In our increasingly complex bureaucratic environment, it is not always simple to determine just where, exactly, the buck stops. For instance, it is not clear that regulators and internal and external auditors are all accountable together, nor is the critical share of each in financial control systems clearly perceived. One fact, however, is fairly certain: Absolute reliance on the individual functionary, to the extent that it ever existed, is no longer practical.[16] The question to be answered is whether controls can be made more effective than they have been so far—that is, are there other ways of ensuring proper governance?

One suggestion has been that the market itself, rather than regulators, should develop an appropriate supervisory responsibility. According to Bert Ely, a U.S. consultant, regulators delegated to address economic matters should no longer be government staff but, instead, agents of the banks. Under a system of cross-guarantees (reminiscent of the way an insurance system functions), banks, through independent agents, would monitor each others' financial condition and guarantee that each can meet its obligations. Inherent in this view is the idea that markets regulate the banks and that failure prevention must lie with direct guarantors. Markets composed of a multitude of involved individuals would give their view on the risks and would pay the price if their judgment turned out to have been faulty. This proposed alternative to the present system has certain difficulties, especially for companies in their start-up period. Before a bank could commence operations, it would have to establish a syndicate of financial institutions prepared to honor its obligations in the event of failure. The guaranteeing banks would provide their service for a risk premium and the cross-guarantees would provide a market price for the risks involved.

Early in the 1990s the governor of the New Zealand Reserve Bank came up with a similar proposal. Rather than having them report to the regulatory supervisors, he would have banks report directly to the market. To permit the market to make the judgment, banks would be forced to disclose far more information than has so far been required.

According to both proposals, regulatory responsibility would be transferred from the central bank to the (hopefully) less bureaucratic, more readily accountable market. They want to see a clearer system of accountability, confirming the suspicion of some that the outside auditor has become a low-quality, low-responsibility supplier and a reluctant risk taker.

Other approaches to enhancing common controls are embodied in ideas expressed by a European Union committee and, more recently, by a committee of the Bank for International Settlements in Basle, the leading monetary cooperation forum of the advanced democracies of the West. In presenting the committee's set of 25 core principles, chairman Tommaso Padoa-Schioppa, a senior Bank of Italy official, hoped that "a mixture of market forces, peer pressure, the need for respectability and credibility on the part of national authorities and banking systems would help enforce this agreement."[17]

It is probably too early to commence planning for public bodies that would take over responsibility from, say, the SEC or the FDIC, but studying the pros and cons could be a valuable exercise. Such a pursuit would address, at least in theory, whether a market regulator would be more effective than the present government-operated system.

The above proposals might be regarded as utopian and unrealistic by many who are involved in ensuring proper controls and accountability, but the fact that suggestions have been made for a radical change indicates that there is an increasingly vocal lobby of different people contending that the present system of controls is unsatisfactory and cannot be fully relied upon when times become turbulent.

The Cost of Regulation

A characteristic of all modern governments, small as well as large, is to be involved in the economic and social activities of the nation. Some believed they could execute a wide range of social welfare and medical services better than the private sector could. When they discovered that the cost was too heavy, they began considering privatization. They acquired the habit of being involved, if not in the outright execution of budgetary resources then, at least, in regulation. Some countries, such as Japan, Switzerland, and the United States, with relatively smaller budgets at their disposal than socialized democracies such as Sweden, Germany, and Holland, knew that through regulation they wielded as much and, at times, more power than through direct budgetary expenditure. Understandably, then, the regulatory agency has gained in stature and become a popular instrument of government. Regulation applies not only to economic activities such as banking, insurance, and trading in securities and commodities but to a whole world of activities—from medicine to aviation. Through regulation, it is presumed, the authorities can achieve more and better quality and safety standards.

It is not quite clear, however, whether there is an optimum level of regulation. Some of the former supporters of direct government ownership, who now believe in the expediency of regulatory devices as an alternative, are nevertheless concerned by the implicit threat of overinterference. One school of thought advises caution, taking care not to overregulate. These advocates point out that extensive government interference in business can be costly not only in money but also in the use of resources, and it can lead to reduced corporate productivity and profits. It is impractical to calculate the price exactly, if indeed there is redundant regulation. Some attempts are being made in Congress to measure the cost of regulation, but these are still in their preliminary stages.[18]

Many of the regulatory agencies have made much progress toward a better-organized, more equitable and open business system. But, like other bureaucrats, some regulators have grown fat, self-satisfied, and lethargic over the years. They find it difficult to define their mandate precisely or to evaluate whether their original terms of reference and instruments of office are still applicable in today's environment. They fail to set new or revised objectives in keeping with the current climate.

Possibly because some regulators have not structured instruments of periodic assessment, they do not cover all the ground for which they are responsible. Their lack of focus is one reason for the growth of multiple layers of regulation at both federal and state levels. In the case of banks, for instance, the Federal Reserve Board, the FDIC, the State Banking Commissioner, and other regulating bodies assigned to financial institutions produce endless reels of red tape, and their rules sometimes overlap, duplicate, or contradict one another.

Regulation, especially in relation to the banking community and financial institutions, is a popular topic for debate in U.S. politics. The call to regulate banking was probably first heard during the tenure of President Andrew Jackson early in the nineteenth century. In recent years, following the establishment of modern accounting and disclosure systems, efforts have begun to streamline and simplify the different regulating agencies not only because of the increasing costs of management, but also in part as a result of the shortcomings of the regulators such as those related to the collapse of the savings and loan institutions. Although they recognize the general need for regulatory agencies, some regulated companies assert that the agencies are today overly demanding and time-consuming—indeed, that they are overregulated.[19] In a more general statement, they point to some forms of regulation as unnecessary, even contrary to the needs of society, and prohibitively expensive. There is some evidence that the current U.S. administration is gradually becoming aware of the need to become more efficient in its regulatory demands. Calls to implement reform in the regulation of financial institutions have been gathering momentum since the early 1990s.[20] It is of interest to note that, although the term "accountability" has been increasingly prominent in calls for modernization, there has been no clear attempt to hold staff regulators accountable like people outside government. Nor is there evidence that those who call for regulatory reform are in agreement as to what changes should be made in the system and how to make it both more efficient and more effective. As an example of some soul-searching, consider a speech made by SEC commissioner M. H. Wallman, in which he stated that in 1995, Americans "invested nearly $3 trillion in 5,600 investment companies—an amount nearly half a trillion dollars more than is on deposit with banks."[21] Yet, he added, "the regulatory burdens on these two industries are quite dissimilar. By some counts, there are over 14,000 banking regulators, while there are only about 500 SEC personnel working in the mutual fund area." It is generally accepted that some regulatory consolidation would prove to be advantageous to all concerned, but those who support this idea realize that working toward a consensus on what should be done and how will require considerable time and resources.

The cost of government remains a heavy burden on the economy in general, and the cost of being regulated by any of the different agencies is an additional inconvenience for business. Many agree that the United States is overregulated. With some 60 federal agencies issuing more than 1,800 rules a year, the Code of Federal Regulation is now more than 130,000 pages long.[22]

For over a decade there has been an apparent recognition in Washington of the need to simplify the way financial institutions are regulated. Banks have many regulators, often with rules and responsibilities that overlap, duplicate one another, and sometimes are in downright conflict, yet little progress has been made toward streamlining. Just to name a few, there is the Federal Reserve System, the Office of the Comptroller of the Currency, the Federal Deposit Insurance Corporation (FDIC) and the Federal Home Loan Banking Board (FHLB) on the national level, to which one can add the various agencies regulating financial institutions on the state level.[23]

Late in 1996, the General Accounting Office (GAO) recommended that the Office of Thrift Supervision (OTS), which oversees savings and loans; the Office of the Comptroller of the Currency (OCC), which supervises national banks; and the FDIC, which regulates federally insured, state-chartered banks that are not Federal Reserve members, be combined.[24] According to the GAO report, "this new independent agency, together with the Federal Reserve, could be assigned the responsibility for consolidated, comprehensive supervision of these banking organizations under its purview." It said the U.S. central bank should have direct access to supervisory information as well as influence over supervisory decision making in the banking industry. It is still unclear whether, and if so, when, Congress will adopt and rule on these recommendations, but they are an important step in the right direction. Understanding how regulation might best be put into practice at the most reasonable cost is among the more important challenges facing Congress and the consultants.

The Legislative Aspect

A multitude of new bills are tabled by Congress each season. Most are complicated products created in large committees and they are the results of compromises reached between representatives of different interests. Government operations are just too extensive for any individual to be familiar with them all. Indeed, on most issues, senators and members of Congress have neither the time nor the expertise to go into full detail as to how, specifically, proposed laws will further the general policies they are expected to support (or oppose). This lack of knowledge is particularly true for financial appropriations: Congressmen do not really know whether the budgets they allot to the various government agencies are appropriate, whether there is waste or whether expenditure is redundant, nor do they have yardsticks to monitor the degree of accountability of these offices.

Because regulators are perceived to address many different issues and because they are expected to operate smoothly, with no glitches or scandals, federal and state politicians usually devote minimal attention to the mode of operations and the efficacy of regulatory authorities. In this age of privatization, one would expect that members of Congress—Republicans and Democrats alike, committed as they are to market economics—would be keen supporters of the regulatory agencies, especially those that supervise and oversee the working of the market. Most, no doubt, are supporters, but, especially in the years that federal departments were running up huge deficits and Congress began seeking ways to reduce the overruns, pressures increased for cuts in the budgets of the Federal Reserve Board, the SEC, and other agencies. Obviously, some cuts could be beneficial, but other reductions could lower the quality or range of services provided by regulators. How does Congress address such a threat?

There is a built-in element of inefficiency in the operations of any government regulating agency, because it functions in an uncompetitive climate. No satisfactory system has ever been developed to make such an agency supremely efficient or to work out the optimal cost at which it should be operated. When cuts were called for, the SEC provided one example of the pressures on the regulators' budget. In 1995, its division of corporation finance employed 343 people. The Office of the Chief Accountant had 24 people. When Congress cut the budget for the 1996 fiscal year by 10 percent, it was clear that this was going to affect both regulators. Arthur Levitt, Jr., chairman of the SEC, cautioned all 100 senators in a letter: "The capital formation process could be hindered significantly by delays in responses to requests from attorneys, accountants, and the public for interpretive advice concerning such matters as new financing methods and novel securities, corporate restructuring and beneficial reporting requirements."[25] But what seems to be missing is a team of competent, independent and knowledgeable peers who periodically—say, once in five to seven years—assess the work of the regulators and report to Congress on their findings, recommending regulation budget cuts or increases, and explaining why.

Although there are no precise—let alone audited—figures on the aggregate costs of regulation, a study by regulators found that in 1991 American banks forked out between $7.5 billion and $17 billion to comply with financial regulation. Was this expenditure worthwhile? Nobel prize-winner in economics Merton Miller, of the University of Chicago, thought that "it is an act of faith, that the benefits of regulating markets exceed the cost." Citing the FDIC, which in giving insurance possibly provides an incentive for banks to be less prudent, he suggested that some regulations may increase rather than decrease systematic risk. Without the theoretical comfort of the regulatory safety net, firms quite possibly would be more cautious in carrying out their activities.[26]

Today, there still is a general consensus that regulation, in principle, contributes to the well-being of society. Professor Miller was raising a question rather than expressing a doubt. What we might expect to hear more often are calls for periodic reassessment of the usefulness of the services provided by the regulator. Also, without instruments to set market prices for the services provided, it is impractical to assess precisely what the regulators' cost should be. Although experience shows that ultimately these matters are resolved amicably in compromise, it is less clear whether they are dealt with efficiently.

NOTES

1. "President says that he's working 'like a bulldog'," quoting historian Robert Dallek, author of *Hail to the Chief: The Making and Unmaking of American Presidents*, in *USA Today* (April 25, 1997): 1A, 2A.

2. "The world economy survey," *The Economist* (September 20, 1997): 11.

3. Possibly the most comprehensive popular study of the SEC is that written by Harvard professor Louis Loss, whose *Fundamentals of Securities Regulation*, published by Little, Brown and Company (1983), remains topical today.

4. "How to live long and prosper," *The Economist* (May 10, 1997): 69.

5. This liability would be in the amount of corporate losses (including fines and punitive damages) suffered in a situation where an effective program would likely have prevented the losses. Richard S. Gruner, "Corporate governance: Officer and director liability for inadequate legal compliance systems," Wittier College School of Law, Los Angeles: http://www/pacificrim.net/~ncpl/ODArt.html.

6. Ken Starkey, "Opening up corporate governance," *Human Relations* (August 1995): 837.

7. John Pound, "The promise of the governed corporation," *Harvard Business Review* (March–April 1995): 89.

8. James M. Tobin, "The squeeze on directors—Inside is out," *Business Lawyer* (August 1994): 1712.

9. Ibid. James Tobin quotes the Delaware Supreme Court in *Sinclair Oil Corp. v. Levien*, 280 A.2d 717, 720 (Del. 1971).

10. Ibid. James Tobin quotes the 1978 ABA *Guidebook*, supra note 5, at 1604, then adds, "the 1994 ABA *Guidebook* restates this analysis and incorporates the type of explanation of the relationship between the business judgment rule and directors' fiduciary duties appearing herein. See supra notes 36 through 42 and accompanying text. The references to reasonableness as opposed to rationality evidence a further evolution of the treatment of the business judgment rule."

11. John W. Pratt and Richard J. Zeckhauser, eds., *Principals and Agents: The Structure of Business* (Cambridge, Mass.: Harvard Business School Press, 1991).

12. Andrew Pettigrew and Terry McNulty, "Power and influence in and around the boardroom," *Human Relations* (August 1995): 845.

13. Jon Entine, "Corporate ethics and accountability": http://www/corpgov.net/entine1.html/.

14. Thomas Donaldson, "Values in tension: Ethics away from home," *Harvard Business Review* (September–October 1996): 18–62.

15. "Clinton to announce deal on sweatshops," Reuters (April 13, 1997).

16. Stephen Timewell, "Too hard to hold," *Banker* (November 1995): 22.

17. Alan Friedman, "Banking rules for all: Accord sets global guidelines," *International Herald Tribune* (April 9, 1997): 11.

18. "The hidden cost of red tape," *The Economist* (July 27, 1996): 13.

19. "Overregulating America: Tomorrow's economic argument," *The Economist* (July 27, 1996): 19.

20. Bernard Shull, "How should bank regulatory agencies be organized," *Contemporary Policy Issues* (January 1993): 99–106.

21. Steven H. H. Wallman, remarks before the Investment Company Institute's 1995 investment company directors conference and new directors workshop (Washington, D.C., September 22, 1995): http://www/sec.gov/news/speeches/spcho54.txt.

22. "In love with regulation," *The Economist* (August 2, 1997): 35.

23. Banking Brief, "A tangle of bank regulators," *The Economist* (August 25, 199): 65.

24. "GAO: Bank regulators should be consolidated," Reuters (November 21, 1996).

25. Stephen Barlas, "SEC budget cuts could stymie exam of financial statements," *Management Accounting* (November 1995): 12.

26. "Hooked on financial red-tape," *The Economist* (July 22, 1995): 73–79.

Chapter 5

Disclosure as an Instrument of Regulation

THE NEED FOR DISCLOSURE

Most of those concerned with economic regulation are in agreement that full disclosure remains their most potent tool of implementation. They would concur with Justice Louis Brandeis, who noted in 1913 that "publicity is justly commended as a remedy for social and industrial diseases. Sunlight is said to be the best of disinfectants." Close to total secrecy was being practiced by most of corporate America and nearly 20 years were to pass before the SEC was established, with its basic tenets of full disclosure and accounting standards. The concept was that with such rules the investor would be informed, aware, and protected.

The Role of Government

Between 1897 and 1905, Westinghouse Electric and Manufacturing did not hold any open annual meetings or publish any financial statements, and that was not untypical of corporate behavior.[1] This cavalier attitude toward shareholders continued until the stock market crash of 1929. Only then did what should have been clear far earlier become apparent: Owners had lost control of powerful public companies and management had gained the upper hand over the disparate small owners whom they ostensibly represented.[2] When disclosure was selected as the priority of the SEC, the question of how to ensure its proper execution was crucial. The decision to delegate supervision to the private sector proved to be critical to what is regarded up to the present day as a basically successful system. Although granted the authority to formulate accounting disclosure rules, the SEC preferred, from its beginning, to delegate this task to nongovernment professionals. At first, committees forming part of the AICPA drafted the necessary rules and opinions. For over two decades, the FASB has carried most of this burden.

The record speaks for itself. The vibrant growth of America's economy, led by its publicly traded companies, is the best justification for the existence of the SEC and the way its regulations are enforced. It is reasonable to presume that without the SEC, investor confidence could not have reached and maintained the levels of trust witnessed in recent generations. So why are an increasing number of people questioning whether the system is adequate for present-day operations? No matter how extensive disclosure is, its effectiveness depends on the presence of enough expertise and knowledge to analyze the existing data properly. An increasingly vocal school of specialists contend that, in recent years, with the call for more specific and more frequent reporting, the sheer volume of detail sometimes precludes intelligent, sharply focused review. And in any case, they add, clever technicians always eventually find ways to circumvent many of the disclosure rules. In theory, as long as the regulator, the executive, the director, and the independent CPA stick to their brief, keep their eyes open, and focus clearly on their assignments, proper governance is ensured. But if their intellectual commitment flags and their dedication to perfection slackens of if they cease to regard accountability as supremely important, no amount of additional disclosure will compensate for their lack of vigilance.

The business world is far more complex than it was at mid-century, as can be seen when questions of accounting treatment and disclosure arise. The preferred approach to stock options, accruals for pension and severance, and, most recently, derivatives are all exclusively modern-day issues. Different lobbies advocate different treatments, and the SEC has been criticized in public (for the first time ever) for the way it suggests pursuing some issues. On the subject of derivatives, chairman Arthur Levitt, Jr., has come under fire from a congressional panel asking why his commission supports accounting rules which other regulators warn might harm U.S. investors.[3] Rather than maintain its "umpire" position, the SEC was being sucked into an argument where it was not in full control.

There have been other instances in which SEC decisions were questioned. Despite its policy of full disclosure, for instance, it has permitted 55 of the 1,800 institutions required to file quarterly holdings reports to withhold information concerning their holdings. In providing such exemptions, the agency uses subjective criteria that are not made public.[4]

One SEC Remedy: Plain English

In the mid-1990s the SEC realized that disclosure could be compromised by the verbose language in which financial facts were being presented. As early as the mid-1970s, accounting pundits had begun to grow disenchanted with such adjectives as "objective," "credible," and "timely" being used in professional literature to describe the desirable qualities of disclosure instead of giving a clear description of their meaning and implication. Professor P. W. Wolnizer notes the "habit of using words to conceal rather than to make clear, of using words with the intention of an audience understanding one thing, when detailed analysis of the words shows a different meaning." Calling this practice a form of "intellectual dishonesty," he concludes that accounting will continue to fail in its mission until remedies are found for the particular defects and anomalies in reporting.[5]

On January 13, 1997, after a two-year study, the commission announced that it proposed to make disclosure documents easier to read by requiring the use of plain English in prospectuses. This rule, prepared by the Division of Corporate Finance, would provide standards on the meaning of the existing requirement for clear and concise prospectus information. In the summer of 1997, the Office of Investor Education and Assistance released *A Plain English Handbook: How to Create Clear SEC Disclosure Documents* to assist lawyers and others responsible for filing prospectuses.[6] Chairman Arthur Levitt, Jr., expressed concern that investors were not getting adequate disclosure of the risks involved in stock and bond investing, with the following observations:

Disclosure has two aspects: the information that is made available to investors, and the information that actually gets across to investors. We have excelled at the first part; now we need to focus on the second. We need to acknowledge that disclosure is not disclosure if it doesn't communicate. The proposed rule requires prospectuses to . . . [be] . . . in plain English. It asks issuers to use the hallmarks of plain English . . . active voice, short sentences, everyday language, tables, and no legal or business jargon. Our eventual goal is to purge the entire document of words that, in the famous phrase of George Orwell, *fall upon the facts like soft snow, blurring the outlines and covering up all the details.*[7]

To encourage investors to read prospectuses, Levitt suggested relegating less relevant information to a separate document and ensuring that they were written in "plain English." He also proposed a rule that would allow management companies to describe their funds in a four-page profile that summarized the key points of the prospectus (see note 7).

At the time of the publication of the *Plain English Handbook*, Levitt asked "What is the point of disclosure if the people who need it most don't understand it?" and answered his own question by saying that "communicating in plain English is the best way to serve investors. Gobbledygook must go." Many investors considered the SEC action courageous and forward-looking. Others, more testy, questioned its appropriateness, asking where responsibility actually lay if, as a result of unsatisfactory English in past disclosures, some investors misunderstood the thrust of a prospectus and were misled by it. Was it the fault of their lawyer, their broker, the issuer, or, possibly, a regulator at the SEC? And if someone was found accountable, how could the damage be measured?

In January 1998, the SEC approved a rule banning arcane jargon in specific sections of investment documents. Effective October 1, 1998, it would require companies and mutual funds to write the cover page, summary, and risk factor sections of prospectuses in short sentences, using definite, concrete, everyday words in the active voice. SEC chairman Arthur Levitt, Jr., said, at a commission meeting on January 22, 1998, that the demand is for "clarity, it's being able to convey complex ideas in a way where individual investors will be to able to understand."[8]

TIMELINESS OF STATEMENTS

A basic point of potential friction and misunderstanding between the public, the regulators, and those responsible for the conduct of corporate governance is that the public seeks clear knowledge about what will happen in the future, while the only seemingly precise information that can be given relates to the past. However impressive corporate performance is perceived to be, it is based on reports of events that have already taken place.

As in other parts of life, predicting the future in business is hazardous, and those who attempt to do so need both experience and a measure of luck. Management can make fairly accurate short-term predictions, but longer-range forecasts require venturing on far riskier terrain. Forecasting is especially difficult in the case of larger companies, where thick layers of bureaucracy reduce sensitivity to warning signals. Only alert, intelligent officers can discern which alarms require attention and which can be ignored, and, even then, they need some luck. It is difficult to decode threatening signals correctly, but pressures of time and limitations inherent in the ways in which information is gathered reduce the chances that potentially unmanageable crisis situations will be detected before it is too late.

In the expectation that they will prevent crisis affecting the well-being of the market, regulatory authorities enact their laws, regulations, and guidelines. This approach can, however, create problems. For example, the demand from within the SEC and from such outside parties as analysts for ever-greater disclosure encourages regulatory authorities to call for increasingly elaborate reporting, instead of using their good judgment to draw up new regulations in the interest of achieving the optimum amount of disclosure for the public. In 1994, Ray Groves, then chairman of Ernst & Young, strongly urged that steps be taken to simplify disclosure requirements and make them more concise. He was not the first to raise the issue, yet it took several years for the SEC to realize and recognize the need and to take steps to make disclosure documents more readable. "Prospectuses have become so thick and language so technical that it's difficult for the average American to go through them and pick out key points they need to know," Joni Hamilton, spokeswoman for the Investment Company Institute, said early in August 1995; and SEC chairman Arthur Levitt, Jr., conceded that "clearly, the SEC is partly responsible for the current state of the prospectus, and . . . we want to make it better."[9] Accordingly, in mid-1995, the SEC began experimenting with a simplified prospectus in the form of an eleven-point questionnaire that mutual fund providers printed on a single folded sheet of paper. So far, there are few signs that they have considered introducing yardsticks to measure the impact and effectiveness of the information produced, seemingly ignoring the need to assess the benefits of their policies or to confirm that all the data they call for are essential.

One of the more radical developments in business America in the past generation was the introduction of quarterly statements of operating results, first demanded by the New York Stock Exchange. The SEC suggested how to proceed with them and provided guidelines as to how they should be prepared. It did not take long for corporate CEOs to become entrapped by this manifestation of the culture of instant results and to adjust their management policies to these new rules. Most executives today are eager to have their success measured by such short-term results. Aware that their period of office is relatively short, they are not overly concerned with the longer perspective; many quickly reach the conclusion that they should give priority to quick gains over long-term growth. In other words, they have learned to live with the system and to exploit it for their personal benefit. The stock exchanges have encouraged this approach.

The corporate structure, of course, is hardly ever democratic. Until close to retirement, the chief executive is often an authoritarian officer, very much aware of the power and prerogatives of his office. It is not long before he claims the "rights" bestowed on those responsible for improving corporate results, including higher bonuses, more stock options, and salary increases. As long as quarterly results continue to improve, the corporate heads may expect to receive greater financial recognition. There is no doubt that this reward system, a modern version of Russian roulette, is a temptation few CEOs have the courage or strength of character to refuse.

But what is the real value of quarterly statements? Or do they have negative effects? Do they, for example, hinder strategies that might yield better long-term rewards? Are they worth the cost, quantifiable and otherwise, to the shareholders, the company, and the nation? What is their long-term contribution/cost to the economy at large and the investment policies of the specific corporation? To what extent do they affect the infrastructure of corporate fixed assets or the company's investment strategies?

These questions have ethical implications. The pressures of having an ongoing quarterly growth reporting system sometimes lead to questionable manipulations, such as shifting income or expense items between quarters or seemingly innocent window dressing of entries, all contrived to show growth stability. Even though moved about, the facts are essentially correct but, in retrospect, the timing may appear to be controversial. Is not the decision of the knowledgeable insider to tell a white lie preferable to the overreaction of a nervous public on learning of a drop in the quarterly operating results? There is another question: Just how much information should the CEO share with his independent directors and outside auditors? Does the CEO share this "minor" piece of deviousness with his directors? If so, what is the danger that such collusion among corporate officers will become habit-forming? It is rare for outside directors to voice public queries about such policies or to caution against the preference for such hasty decisions versus carefully thought-out, longer-term, wealth-creating strategies.

John J. Cullinane, an extraordinarily successful entrepreneur of the 1980s who was CEO of a fast-growing software company, wrote a study of reporting. In both the introduction and body of his work, he made the following point:

CEOs grow to hate the treadmill of quarterly reporting. I certainly did, and I was CEO of a company that boasted 29 consecutive quarters of sales and profit growth in excess of 50% and four stock splits. We were the first software company to reach $1 billion in valuation. However, the more successful my company became, as quarter after quarter it met projections and the price earnings climbed, the greater the pressure to continue to perform. Even a slight slowing in growth rates could cause a dramatic fall in the price of the stock and threaten to trigger a class-action lawsuit against management. Conse-quently, management diverted inordinate amount of time and energy to the quarterly reporting process, particularly as each quarter drew to a close.[10]

A close study might well reveal that a heavy price is often paid for the ongoing supply of fresh information provided by quarterly statements—that is, diversion from strategic thinking and long-term growth investment. And, it is worth noting that nowhere else among the English- or non-English-speaking post-industrialized nations is there such emphasis on providing shareholders with quarterly reporting.

THE SEC AND THE DISCLOSURE OVERLOAD

The SEC is the main regulator on all matters concerning corporate gover-nance. In its seventh decade, it is perceived as embodying authority, solid judg-ment, conservatism, and gravitas. It is scandal-free. Probably not all its commissioners have been inspiring personalities, but some were true leaders. Without extensive executive authority, they used their office—or, as they some-times proudly call it, their "bully pulpit"—to guide and moderate methods of governance, with considerable success. The concept of full disclosure remains the main instrument through which they attempt to ensure that the companies registered with them provide the public with all pertinent information.

Much of their work is maintenance, often quite mundane in nature; rarely do they take part in "fireworks." Some idea of their activities can be gathered from their annual reports to Congress.[11] In 1994 these reports devoted a moderate amount of space to the fact that the SEC worked with the FASB in the areas of derivatives, loan impairments, and stock-based compensation; with the Emerging Issues Task Force on reconstruction charges; with the Accounting Standards Board on risk alerts; and with the Accounting Standards Executive

Committee on advertising costs, risk and uncertainties, and environmental liabilities—subjects that do not usually generate much interest in the business
world.

Most sophisticated readers of financial reporting suspect that the amount of
data demanded by the reporting system has passed the saturation point, and some
believe that disclosure as practiced today is overextended in detail and therefore
of little help, possibly even confusing shareholders, stakeholders, and other interested parties. Not only are the recipients of the information in something of
a quandary; some of the providers are as well. Financial officers and managers
feel that too much is expected of them, and auditors, too, are dissatisfied and,
at times, perplexed by the extent of reporting. A few of the latter have the
courage to actually go on record. Ray J. Groves, former chairman of Ernst &
Young, put it this way: "In our ever more complex business environment, the
sheer quantity of financial disclosure has become so excessive that we've diminished the overall value of these disclosures."[12]

According to Groves, if disclosure demands keep increasing the way they
have recently, annual reports will soon be too heavy to lift. But that won't be
the only burden; they will be so packed with technical data that most readers
will be unable to understand them anyway. He gives the following warning:

Excessive financial disclosure requirements by the FASB, SEC, AICPA, and others are
causing the number of required financial disclosures to grow at significant rates. As a
result, end-users of various financial statements already find it increasingly difficult—in
some cases, impossible—to distinguish between what is important, decision-critical information and what is not. And disclosure will only get worse if steps are not taken to
change the incremental approach for setting disclosure requirements.[13]

Groves suggests a two-tier disclosure. Annual reports would be simplified,
but the full disclosure in SEC Form 10-K would remain. Among those who
have joined in the campaign to push forward such changes is P. Norman Roy.[14]
His argument is that transferring lengthy and complex footnotes out of the annual report would actually make it easier to understand, yet provide at least as
"true and fair" a view as before. The SEC, headed by Chairman Arthur Levitt,
Jr., liked the recommendation in principle. Similarly, Commissioner Stephen
M. H. Wallman acknowledged that there was concern "that at some point you
give people so much information, they do not read any of it."

The SEC came to realize that the demand for ever-greater disclosure, which
had always been a dominant feature in their policies, could, if continued, become
counterproductive. The commission recognized that the time had come to reduce
the burden of reporting by some of the smaller traded companies. Accordingly,
in 1994 the SEC issued draft proposals to permit the use of abbreviated financial
statements, annual reports, and other disclosure documents, including prospectuses delivered directly to investors. These statements, however, would require

a special full audit report and full set of audited financial statements to be filed with the SEC and provided to investors upon request.

These draft proposals met with noisy opposition from security analysts who believed they understood the makeup of the companies they scrutinized and knew what was missing. They kept pressing for ever more financial detail— more disclosures, new FASB and other regulatory instructions. The SEC soon got cold feet and withdrew its initiative. The commission retreated as a result of the offensive by the analysts, who mobilized as a lobby and sent in a substantial number of letters opposing the simplification; they succeeded in putting it on hold.

The simplification would, actually, have been quite modest and would have given companies the option of transferring most of the annual report Footnotes to Form 10-K. What aggravated veterans like Ray Groves was both the self-interest of those who opposed the amendment and the lack of enthusiasm on the part of those who should have been its natural supporters. He and others believe that their call for improvements, although on hold, will soon be heard.

The above incident could be interpreted as just one more example of slow, ever-cautious pondering (which some would wrongly name indecisiveness) by the regulator. But if we delve more deeply into the matter, it becomes apparent that the subject of accountability is lurking in the background: Companies and executives might be sued for withholding information that the amendments would have made redundant; and, of course, as of now, the regulatory staff would not be taken to account for any of the ensuing difficulties.

HAS THE FASB LOST TOUCH?

Bureaucracies that are not held accountable tend to lose touch with society. True for administrations in general, this maxim is applicable also to those responsible for regulating corporate governance, be they government staff or employees of public organizations. The increasing discontent of the business community with the FASB is related not only to how the board issues its pronouncements but, more important, to whether its proposals still serve to fulfill its mission, and to establish and improve standards of financial accounting and reporting for the guidance and education of the public, including issuers, auditors, and users of financial information.

The FASB was established in 1973, with the warm approval of the SEC, to be a private sector organization for establishing standards of financial accounting and reporting. SEC chairman Arthur Levitt, Jr., explained the commission's ties with the FASB as follows:

In Accounting Series Release (ASR) No. 150, the Commission stated that the standards and interpretations issued by the FASB would be considered by the Commission has having "substantial authoritative support." ASR 150 emphasized that the Commission was not abdicating its authority to set accounting standards and that Commission staff would continue to take appropriate action to resolve registrants' specific problems of accounting and reporting as they arose on a day-to-day basis.[15]

And he added that the SEC monitors all FASB standard-setting projects. Over the years, the FASB has issued over 120 statements, all with the purpose of establishing and improving standards of financial accounting and reporting for the guidance and education of the public. The financial information provided about the operations and financial position of individual entities for the public is based on these statements.[16] During this period, the board has gained the trust of the business community, especially investors and analysts.

Financial statements drawn up under the guidance of the FASB are subjected to oversight by the SEC and a number of nongovernment regulators, ranging from the AICPA to the NYSE, and they are perceived to present an honest and consistent description of a reported company. Recently, however, it has become apparent that although they are presented in accordance with Generally Accepted Accounting Principles (GAAP), they do not necessarily always provide a clear and therefore reliable basis for determining the real value of the reported company.[17]

Point 5 of the FASB Mission Statement states that it should "improve the common understanding of the nature and purposes of information contained in financial reports" (see note 16). A large portion of the newer pronouncements, many corporate executives contend, increases administrative burdens and costs, with little contribution to the general public's understanding or benefit. In the early 1990s, an increasing number of those involved in the financial disclosure arena began sensing that the FASB rules were becoming excessive and were not always useful to those wishing to understand the companies. From the 1992 FASB Rules 106 and 107, to its proposals on stock option treatment announced in the summer of 1993, to those more recent ones on derivatives, it has become evident that queries concerning the FASB's objectivity would be increasing. Financial executives have begun to ask whether all the newer FASB statements and demands are essential to comprehending the financial conditions of the reported corporation. In other words, is the additional information a significant aid to grasping the true state of a company?

Some FASB pronouncements have a significant impact on the way financial statements are presented. In 1992, the Board began requiring companies to record retirement and health benefits as liabilities. This raises the question of whether financial statements issued for earlier years, with no such provisions, gave full disclosure or fairly represented equity. If they were misleading, were the FASB or, for that matter, the SEC tardy in requiring the inclusion of these benefits as liabilities; were they responsible for the liability included in the earlier statements being underprovided?

Members of the accounting profession have become immersed in the overwhelming flood of regulations poured out by the various standards and opinion organizations led by the FASB. Before he retired, Ray Groves (until 1994 chairman and managing partner of Ernst & Young) urged all those with influence over the profession to build some discipline and self-control into the disclosure system. He urged that standard-setting bodies such as the FASB, SEC, and AICPA make the disclosure issue a top priority in order to make financial information more meaningful to users.[18]

On the basis of a "nonscientific" survey of the 1972, 1982, and 1992 annual reports of 25 large, well-known companies, including AT&T, Bank of America, Coca-Cola, GE, GM, IBM, and Xerox, Groves found that during those 20 years the size of the companies' annual reports increased by an average of 83 percent, from 35 to 64 pages; that the average number of pages of footnotes increased by 325 percent, from 4 to 17; and that the average number of pages of management discussion and analysis trebled from 4 to 12 pages. But he noted that there are no signs that the FASB and the SEC, bent on requiring additional disclosures in areas ranging from derivatives to stock options, are sensitive to these drifts, adding, "Users often cannot find, or recognize in a reasonable time, those disclosures that affect their investment decisions" (see note 18).

As noted in the previous section, the SEC, after considering the subject for a number of years, began taking cautious steps in 1997 toward simplifying disclosure requirements, but it is still too soon to assess how far it will move to simplify disclosure requirements. Criticism has been directed at both the extent and the content of the requirements. Probably the most controversial of its recent proposals was the FASB plan that would require companies providing their employees with stock options to calculate their value and charge it against earnings. In a way it was a populist move, a reaction to the monumental eye-popping bonuses being given to senior officers around the country. That stock options have become popular among CEOs is evident; in 1987 some 17 percent of their remuneration was given in the form of options. This portion rose to 29 percent by 1993, and it continues to climb.[19]

A hot debate followed, with people arguing that such a practice would cause havoc to many companies' earnings. Others asked whether the concept was fair or economically sound. Among the latter were those who pointed out that in issuing stock options to CEOs and senior officers, the company kept all its assets in full, and that what actually happened was a reorganization or redistribution of equity rather than a distribution of income. Finally, the controversy reached Congress. In a letter to Arthur Levitt, Jr., Congressman Ed Markey quoted Susan Eichen, a principal in William Mercer, Inc., to the effect that "the proposal may give us good accounting rules that end up encouraging questionable business practices. The hardest-hit victims are likely to be high-tech and new public companies that use options extensively. . . . They may have little choice but to reduce drastically the number of employees who participate or the size of the grants" (see note 15).

In 1994 another controversy, this time between SEC commissioner J. Carter Beese, Jr., and Dennis R. Beresford, chairman of the FASB, concerned "the truth (that) will set investors free."[20] On that issue and others that have followed, the FASB, committed to truth and integrity, took a position that other sound economic thinkers with records just as honest as the Board members' disagreed with. So far, no acceptable candidate for umpire is in sight.

Since 1995 some members of the 14,000-member Financial Executives Institute (FEI) have begun putting pressure on the Financial Accounting Foundation (FAF), which provides the funding for the FASB and has the authority to change the way it is structured. They wanted to reform the Board, make it smaller and more compact. The aim was not only to make the FASB better focused on business needs but also to enable the business community to block new accounting standards that it believes unnecessary.[21] In letters to the *Wall Street Journal*, first on February 13, 1996, and then on April 24 of that year, FEI member Kenneth Johnson, controller of Motorola, explained why the FEI believed that the FASB should be changed and why the FEI had attempted to force wholesale changes on the SEC and the FASB. "They are so enamored with theoretical accounting purity," he said, "that they are unable to look at the practical effects of what they are trying to do." He pointed out that many FASB procedures had been established 25 years ago and could probably be improved. He reminded readers that, currently, standards take up to 14 years to be formulated and approved, and he asserted that there is a responsibility toward the users of financial statements to "attempt to improve this obviously inefficient process."

Other FEI committee members urged that FASB operations need restructuring because some of the Board's standards are difficult and costly to implement and do not provide a proportionate benefit to investors or other financial statement users. They also suggested that a new, small, outside organization should be established to control and oversee the FASB's agenda and make it accountable.[22] Not surprisingly, both the FASB and the SEC opposed these proposals. Neither the general public nor the average investor, however, seem very curious about the controversy. Most would probably agree that professional demands have become burdensome and exaggerated and that not all are necessary, but they do not show much concern with the subject. Maybe they feel that the accountancy profession resembles a priesthood, with its own rites, mysteries, and ideology. To some laymen, the debate over accounting principles resembles an arcane dispute between medieval scholars over the sex life of angels.[23]

Sensing that the current work of the FASB is sufficiently controversial to cause its public interests to be at risk, SEC chairman Arthur Levitt, Jr., has demanded a larger role in deciding who selects the people who write the rules. Aware that the Motorola controller was not alone in his criticism of his own role as regulator and umpire, Levitt is determined to ensure that investors not be losers and thus lose faith in the market. Protective of the FASB's responsibilities, he has emphasized that the FASB "has filled the role of impartial standard-setter admirably for a quarter century . . . [it] has consistently sought to ensure the accuracy of financial information, protecting the basic rights of the investor and strengthening public confidence in our markets."[24] He is determined to protect what he believes to be the integrity of the FASB, especially in view of the increasing professional opposition to the FASB call for greater disclosure concerning business involvement in derivatives which, in fair weather conditions, are sometimes difficult to explain to the public. As Levitt sees it, "the FASB sets standards for preparers, in order to protect the interests of users and the public ... [and] the FEI ... issued a series of recommendations that would put FASB in the corporate equivalent of leg irons." He added that "the FASB is charged to create the most hallowed rules of accounting," and he believes that these rules should be practiced by corporate America. Although the accounting world and all involved in public share ownership and trading would like to reach absolute disclosure, that may not be possible (see note 16).

Every few weeks the FASB produces its financial accounting series status report. The report of February 26, 1996, a typical issue, is devoted to a series of logistical decisions that have little bearing on governance or accounting; it signifies how inward-looking and remote from the business world the Board has become. There is little evidence that it recognizes any obligation to make its requirements understood by the nonprofessional.

Relative to the widening schism between the public's expectations and what the FASB deems pertinent, Chairman Levitt recently observed, "Farsighted business leaders over six decades have supported the independence of the process and accepted even those standards that may have worked against their short-term interests. The positive economic consequences of a visibly independent and well-protected FASB far outweigh any potential dislocations and temporary discomforts it may cause."[25] He was acknowledging (inadvertently perhaps) that the FASB is not only detached from reality but on the defensive as well. The delicate equilibrium between business growth and reasonable governance seems threatened. The accounting guardians of full disclosure seem to have stopped focusing on their mission, and the independent auditors find it difficult to explain what the present-day contribution of the FASB to disclosure actually is.[26] Despite its reluctance to intervene, the SEC may have no recourse but to propose ways to bring the voluntary organizations down from their ivory towers.

NOTES

1. "A useful analogy—The origin of the SEC," *Harvard Business Review* (March–April 1996): 100.

2. Roger Lowenstein, "Corporate governance's sorry history," *Wall Street Journal* (April 18, 1996).

3. Joanne Morrison, "SEC's Levitt comes under fire in Congress," Reuters (October 2, 1997).

4. Joanne Morrison, "Wall Street's big players can hide their moves," Reuters (August 23, 1997).

5. P. W. Wolnizer, "Are audit committees red herrings," *Abacus* (March 1995): 56.

6. "SEC to consider plain English proposal, handbook draft," bulletin released in Washington, D.C. (January 13, 1997): http://www.sec.gov/news/plaineng.htm.

7. "SEC to help investors understand mutual funds," Reuters (February 25, 1997).

8. "SEC adopts plain English rule for prospectuses," Reuters (January 23, 1998): http://www/yahoo.com/headlin . . . /business/stories/sec_1.html.

9. Daniel S. Levine, "An end to mutual confusion: BofA says prospectuses could be one page if funds killed the mumbo jumbo," *San Francisco Business Times* (August 4, 1995), Section 1: 3.

10. John J. Cullinane, "Widows and orphans," Center for Business and Government, Weil Hall, John F. Kennedy School of Government, Harvard (undated).

11. William J. Coffey, Gary Illiano, and Lewis Schier, "The SEC's annual report to Congress," *The CPA Journal* (December 1996): 42.

12. "Financial disclosure: When more is not better," *Financial Executive* (May/June 1994).

13. "The disclosure overload issue," in a speech given to the Financial Executives Institute on current financial reporting issues (November 13, 1995).

14. P. Norman Roy, "Three cheers for two tiers," *Financial Executive* (May/June 1995): 1.

15. "An exchange between the honorable Edward J. Markey, Chairman, U.S. House of Representatives Subcommittee on Telecommunications and Finance, Committee on Energy and Commerce, and the Honorable Arthur Levitt, Jr., Chairman, Securities and Exchange Commission," *Accounting Horizons* (March 1995): 71–78. (Quoting Susan Eichen from "Taking account of stock options," *Harvard Business Review* (January–February 1994): 29.

16. Facts about the FASB: The mission of the Financial Accounting Standards Board: http:/www.rutgers.edu/Accounting/raw/fasb/facts/fasfact1.htm.

17. See also "The American corporation at the end of the twentieth century: An outline of ownership-based governance," speech given by A. G. Monks at Cambridge University (July 1996).

18. Ray J. Groves, "Here's the annual report. Got a few hours?" *Wall Street Journal* (August 4, 1994): A12.

19. "High anxiety: Accounting proposal stirs unusual uproar in executive suits: FASB's stock option plan threatens pay packages; lobbying gets intense: a risk to high-tech firms?" *Wall Street Journal* (March 7, 1994): A1.

20. Dennis R. Beresford, "Letters to the editor: In accounting truth above all," *Wall Street Journal* (March 21, 1994): A13.

21. Floyd Norris, "The SEC chief wades into the battle over accounting rules," *New York Times* (April 25, 1996): 75.

22. Lee Berton, "Business group wants smaller FASB, more influence on rule-setting process," *Wall Street Journal* (February 2, 1996).

23. David Waller, "Priesthood accounts for mystery," *Financial Times* (April 11, 1991), quoting Anthony Sampson, who first commented on the similarity with the priesthood in his *Anatomy of Britain* (Hodder & Stoughton, 1962).

24. Remarks by Arthur Levitt, Jr., chairman, Securities and Exchange Commission, speaking before the Conference Board (New York, October 8, 1997): http.//www/sec.gov/news/speeches/spch178.txt.

25. Remarks by Chairman Arthur Levitt, Jr., Securities and Exchange Commission, made at the Financial Reporting Institute, University of Southern California (Pasadena, Calif., June 6, 1995): http.//www/sec.gov/news/speeches/spch106.txt.

26. Itzhak Sharav, "Viewpoint: No accounting for this plan," *New York Times* (March 24, 1996): 13.

Chapter 6

What to Expect
from the Director

THE ROLE OF THE DIRECTOR

Rarely does an outside director or, for that matter, an independent auditor contribute to the growth of a company. Of course, many will argue that it is not the duty of the board member or the CPA to do so and that it is enough if, by establishing adequate early warnings, they help prevent a crisis that could damage the company. But, here too, their record is unsatisfactory, for they are commonly among the last to know about difficulties, which often come to their attention when it is far too late for remedial action.

Although there are few subjects in the realm of business on which more has been written, in practice the role of the director is more indistinct today than ever. The definition of the responsibilities of directors depends, at least in part, on whom one asks. In the eyes of the National Association of Corporate Directors, the terms "professional director" and "director professionalism" have altogether different meanings.[1] Even among the one group that should have a clear, experienced view of what to expect from directors—CEOs—there is no consensus. CEOs interviewed for this study were asked two questions: Do you receive constructive advice or ideas from your outside directors, and, assuming the absence of regulatory or corporate governance requirements for a board to be composed predominantly of outside directors, would you still recommend their retention?

The answers were far from unanimous. In larger, older companies, with a greater equity spread and a strong finance and audit department, there was less use and respect for outside directors. The perception was that outside directors rarely contributed original or helpful ideas to the company or to the proceedings of the board. A relatively higher regard and greater use for the director was shown in companies where the founding entrepreneur still held a major stake and had structured a small board of trusted acquaintances, all specialists complementing his talents and creativity. Although these entrepreneurs generally recognized the fiduciary responsibility of their directors for proper governance, they gave it less weight, regarding advice as their primary contribution.

Myles Mace, one of the most important first-generation theoreticians of corporate governance, wrote: "The Board provides advice and counsel; the Board serves as some sort of discipline; the Board acts in crisis situations; it often does not have primary influence, nor does it establish the basic objectives, corporate strategies or broad policies of the company, ask discerning questions, or even select the president."[2] Ten years later Peter F. Drucker added, "In every major business catastrophe . . . [since the Great Depression] . . . down to recent debacles . . . the Board members were apparently the last people to be told that anything was awry . . . and it is futile to blame men. It is the institution that malfunctions."[3]

Many self-satisfied directors—from university business schools and elsewhere—believe that the relationship has changed since the mid-1980s. It is, however, difficult to prove that the power of the board as compared with that of the CEO has become stronger; one may just as safely argue that little has changed on the board. One subject of greater emphasis in recent years, however, is the requirement that directors be "financially literate." It is now generally agreed that directors cannot be ignorant of such matters as the difference between return on equity and return on assets. They are expected to be able to read financial statements, to understand how to use financial ratios, and to evaluate company performance.

Time Spent on Directorships

Until recently, hardly anyone asked how much time the director really devotes to the company. Now it has become clear that the days when a director could carry out his responsibilities with little investment of time are past. Rising expectations for directors mean that fulfilling this function requires far more commitment than was customary in the past. Yet, board members still apportion only a relatively small part of their time to their directorships, usually spending less than fourteen days a year on the company's affairs—and that includes preparatory reading, travel, and committee meetings in addition to the board meetings themselves.

This situation has been a subject of some concern to SEC chairman Arthur Levitt, Jr.[4] "You can't be a good watchdog if you're only on patrol three times a year," he told directors in 1995. "The commitment of adequate time is an essential requirement for directors," he added, stating that he believed that "outside directors serving on committees and attending both special and regular meetings should contemplate approximately two days per month to understand and respond to the dynamic needs of today's major businesses." In practice, even the most committed board members rarely spend more than half that time on their company's affairs.

In line with the SEC chairman, governance experts are calling on directors to budget a full day's preparation for every board or committee meeting; and if they are chairing a committee, they should spend two to three days preparing for the session (see note 1). But most directors, unless fully retired, have what they consider to be more important concerns. In the moderate amount of time they are willing to allocate, they can hardly become proficient and knowledgeable about the company's affairs. Most directors fear being overwhelmed by material and provided with too much rather than too little information.[5] Indeed, the way information is obtained by most corporate boards, observes Clifton Wharton, is one of their greatest weaknesses.[6] The few who try to gather more data usually discover that their only communication link with the company is the CEO and, sometimes, the CFO.

Directors usually do not initiate contacts with other corporate officers. On the rare occasions when they try, they are almost always discouraged from involvement by the CEO. Whether recently appointed or veteran, directors are often not sufficiently alert to their fiduciary responsibilities, are too cozy in their relations with the CEO, and have little concern for accountability.

The Duties of the Director

Although it would be reasonable to expect directors to address matters such as long-term strategic programs, where their contribution can be beneficial, it is far more common today for them to be required merely to approve current quarterly statements. These reports are usually unexciting, and the input of the directors is marginal. Accordingly, directors are rarely tempted to delve into the details of such statements, and many are content to be a rubber stamp.

Today, directors are expected to be cognizant of an ever-increasing galaxy of rules. Regulators seldom consider how their new rules will affect the performance of directors or how long it will take directors to understand their new assignments. As mentioned previously, regulators attempt to draw lessons from business collapses and to introduce new preventive measures, rather than recognizing that they themselves may have fallen short of an acceptable level of performance. This tendency increases the burden on management, for if directors would fulfill their responsibilities instead of merely reiterating the need for caution, diligence, and responsibility after the fact, many a corporate crisis might be foreseen and prevented.

Most directors are not kept informed about production, labor, or marketing problems and lack independent information and analysis regarding the company's performance (see note 6). All too often they receive relevant information slowly, and they are hand-fed according to the whim of the CEO. Consequently, in most companies, they lack the curiosity or motivation to seek out analysts or institutional directors to obtain their observations on their firm's operations. In these circumstances, directors have little influence over their contribution to the company, although some senior corporate officers exploit their specific talents and qualifications as they see fit for the welfare of the shareholders and the stakeholders. All in all, it is not surprising that the one subject to which most are sensitive is the market price of the company's shares.

The original concept of a board of directors was a team of persons of repute and quality to oversee the operations of the company and its CEO on behalf of the shareholders. Although there is a general consensus that boards are essential for shareholders' protection, far too many appear to be mere ornaments.[7] Directors' connections with the CEO are usually far stronger than with the shareholders. Except for the obligatory material the company publishes—that is, annual and quarterly reports and other data as required by the various regulatory authorities—no way has been established to generate a dialogue between director and shareholder, and there is little evidence of any constructive thinking about how to strengthen links. In fact, in medium-sized and large corporations, in which the number of shareholders is considerable and no single individual holds a significant number of shares, there is no effective communication between shareholders and directors. Accordingly, the latter, over time, may well get the sense that they are agents only of the CEO.

CEOs in large, publicly held companies have a considerable influence in the choice of directors. A CEO may look for the retired politician or ex-government officer who can lobby for the company, as well as for a talented lawyer, banker, or other professional consultant. In many cases, the CEO is swayed more by the expertise of the prospective board member than by his capacity to fulfill his fiduciary responsibilities to the shareholders. The ideal director would combine consulting expertise with integrity; but possibly such a mix would result in an insurmountable contradiction in tasks. "Serve as a director or be a consultant," advised John Nash, president of the National Association of Corporate Directors. "If I'm accepting a consultancy, can I truly maintain my independence as a director?"[8] Although conflicts between the two functions are infrequent, they can, indeed, occur, and there is pressure to separate the two roles. One way to accomplish this would be to set up advisory boards that consultants would be asked to join and thereby ensure that the directors perform solely in their fiduciary capacities.[9]

In conclusion, currently expected performance of directors can place them in a rather awkward position—possibly untenable. Indeed, perhaps too much is now expected from this function in corporate governance. If one extrapolates from recent writings and legislation, it may be deduced that the increasing demands would overburden any director. An alternative way to enable the director to do what both the public and corporate management expect is to reduce the load of his or her responsibilities, not least by separating the advisory role from that relating to fiduciary responsibility, accountability, and corporate governance. It is possible, however, that the patching up cannot continue and that the whole system has to change.

Independence and Time Constraints

With the time that directors apportion to the company limited to some 20 days a year, can they, in this world of giant, diversified multinationals often involved in state-of-the-art innovation, really be independent? Can they be sufficiently knowledgeable about corporate activities to carry out their fiduciary responsibilities, look after individual shareholders' concerns, and be accountable to the diverse groups of stakeholders? Or is independence impossible, given the constraints of time?

What other options are there? Possibly the importance attributed to independence is exaggerated. Could it be that the corporate world is ready for a new profession, that of the full-time, salaried director, retained and paid by the shareholders? This is a question that needs to be considered in a separate study. Another suggestion is to establish a public intermediary to contract and retain directors who would be expected to spend a significant amount of time on corporate matters. They would sit on a smaller board and receive a reasonable salary.

CHANGES FACING THE DIRECTOR

In November 1996, *Business Week* made a startling statement: "Slowly but surely, . . . a quiet revolution is going on in America's boardrooms. The directors around the conference table are waking up. They're taking the job more seriously."[10] If that is true, what had the directors been doing up to then? How badly were they performing in the 1970s or 1980s? Were they dormant, careless, or just uninterested? And if their performance was so unsatisfactory, where were the business pundits? Had they been exaggerating when, in their publications, they repeatedly declared that those changes described in *Business Week* in 1996 had in fact already occurred much earlier?

Business Week has been watching the boardroom for many decades. As early as 1971 it observed:

The problem of the modern director is to define his role so that he does not meddle with day-to-day management but nevertheless knows what is going on and makes his influence felt in the determination of board policy. . . . If corporate management is to survive in anything like its present form, directors will have to take on new responsibilities. They must make sure that corporate goals are consistent with the larger goals of U.S. society. And they must monitor management to see that it pursues these goals effectively.[11]

Some four years later, Myles Mace observed, "There have been some cosmetic approaches by many companies to create the impression that directors have a lot more to do on the board. . . . But there has been no real improvement in what directors do or don't do."[12] These observations are just as topical today as when they were written. Despite the many publications over the past 20 years concerning corporate governance and the need to upgrade systems, there is no quantifiable evidence that directors' performance has, in fact, improved.

To be fair, shareholders have no way of clearly assessing how well the board of the company in which they have an interest actually performs, nor do the directors themselves. Various research studies show that most directors are confident that they operate properly and are knowledgeable on all important issues. But rarely are directors concerned about future crises; they are simply not trained or equipped to predict or prepare for threatening situations. They will concede that "there is room for correction, modification, and improvement in the board's activities," but they will deny vehemently that they are part of an old boys club, that they need to spend more time on company matters, or that they are lazy. On the contrary, they believe that they fulfill their responsibilities and that they care for the shareholders' interests. Because there are so many different facts and issues involved, it is often difficult either to agree and support or to take issue with them. One area, however, in which their decisions could be vital to the company can be measured: mergers. Unfortunately, there is little evidence that directors exert any influence for the good in merger decisions.

According to the FTC, there were close to 3,600 major corporate mergers in the United States in the year ending September 30, 1997, compared with 3,087 in the previous year and with the 1989 record of 2,883.[13] The paper value of these mergers is impressive. In 1996 it totaled $659 billion, compared with $519 billion in 1995. It is rare for the FTC to oppose mergers, and roughly 98 percent of them go through without question. The burden and responsibility of such transactions is clearly on the officers and directors of the companies involved. When Mercer Management Consulting of New York studied 300 big mergers that took place starting in the mid-1980s, they found that three years after merger, 57 percent of the companies lagged behind their industries in total return to shareholders. The long-run failure rate appears to be even higher.

When dealing with company business, the CEO has an inbuilt advantage over his directors in terms of knowledge and training. The difference in their relative experience in assessing the market or the current corporate operations should not, however, be as great when it comes to corporate mergers. Often, a diligent director could collect data that would enable him independently to know as much about a proposed merger as the CEO, yet one hardly ever hears of a board blackballing a merger proposal. Why are so many directors party to bad bets, just to support their CEOs?

In recent years, various topics have been discussed in efforts to modernize the operations of the board of directors. They include the following:

1. Separating the role of board chairperson from that of chief executive officer. This distinction would certainly make it easier to hold the CEO accountable to the board and thus facilitate more orderly governance. Some people, however, believe that the accompanying cost in paperwork and bureaucracy would offset the advantages.

2. Providing a fair and proper procedure for selecting new board members, especially

when the shareholders are widely dispersed and have little say in the election, and taking steps to ensure the directors' independence from the CEO.

3. Limiting the terms of directors, to avoid members becoming entrenched in office and losing their objectivity. The counterargument is that a limitless term of office affords directors time to get to know the company, especially when it is complex technologically or in other ways. Directors can learn to work with their colleagues as a constructive team, but their objectivity and alertness is often affected by the intimacy these relationships nurture.

4. Finding different ways of rewarding directors to induce them to give their best. Among other attractive incentives are cash or pension plans and stock options.[14]

The accusation that capitalism permits exorbitant amounts of cash and equity to be given to CEOs and, at times, to members of the management team is a related issue and one of the main reasons for pressure to introduce a tighter system of corporate governance. Corporate directors, stung by the fuss over what is perceived to be excessive executive compensation, have indicated that they are beginning to take the demands of the more powerful and vocal shareholder groups at least somewhat more seriously.[15] But recent published figures of rewards to senior corporate officers show that, in practice, the influence of the critics has not yet resulted in action.

THE SCARCITY OF GOOD DIRECTORS

Unlike a generation ago, when company officers formed the majority of the board, in the 1990s well over 90 percent of boards of directors are composed mainly of outsiders. Close to 30 percent have only one insider (usually the CEO) and another third have two. Because of the increased weight of their fiduciary responsibilities, however, outside directors are becoming a scarce resource. Jack Lohnes of Spences Stuart Board Services declares that "the turndown rate is the highest it's ever been. Eight out of ten people we approach say no."[16] This is true despite the fact that few honors are more sought after than being invited to join a board of directors. Despite the threat of litigation and the burden of fiduciary responsibilities, board membership still radiates a certain aura of mystique and power.

Little has changed since Harvard professor William A. Sahlman stated in 1990 that "the corporate governance system makes being the director of a public company an unattractive, if not outright dangerous proposition."[17] He explained that people should not make economically stupid decisions and, as the economics of being a director are fundamentally off balance, he has a simple rule: Never join the board of directors of a publicly traded company.

The Legal Exposure

The statistical data support Sahlman's point. While many regard the S&L debacle as an exception, at the end of 1994 a total of 233 professional liability lawsuits had been filed by the Resolution Trust Corporation against financial institutions and their directors or officers, and 542 settlements or judgments, totaling more than $1.3 billion, had been executed.[18] Clearly, the cost of fending off lawsuits against corporate directors and officers is growing significantly from year to year.[19] Small companies—especially those involved in technology—have seen a sharper increase in lawsuits against directors than larger ones. The theory is that less stable stock prices make smaller companies more vulnerable to suits alleging failure to disclose information. The only relatively safe way to avoid such litigation is to ensure that the company's stock price keeps increasing—something that cannot continue forever.

These dire warnings notwithstanding, a directorship is still widely perceived as a soft, comfortable post in which one's experience and ideas are admired and appreciated. In short, prospective directors often expect a cushy job in a modern version of the exclusive club of a century ago. They do not even imagine being faced with a company crisis or having a confrontation with management, fellow board members, or shareholders, and they certainly do not anticipate being charged in class-action suits. In the case of companies where growth is moderate but steady, where the CEO is conservative and not overly ambitious, and the wishes of the shareholders are reasonable, these expectations may be realistic. But experience shows that few companies exhibit all these characteristics and that the demands made on directors cover a wider, often more complex terrain. The many guidebooks and precedents aside, the definition of directors' duties often remains blurred, and even those who are keen to learn find that following the rules is anything but easy. Many directors discover that they simply do not know what they let themselves in for, including a substantial commitment of time.

In any case, directors are right to worry. There has been an annual average increase of 10 to 15 percent in legal claims since the early 1980s. The likelihood is that three out of four companies involved in a merger, acquisition, or divestiture may, in the aftermath, expect to face a suit brought by some unsatisfied party. Quite naturally, directors do not want to be involved in litigation. According to the results of a 1993 survey, approximately half of all directors on the boards of the top 1,000 companies had been sued at least once in their careers in connection with their board service. Of these, 93 percent said that the probability of being sued again in the following three years was higher than it used to be. Robert Leitman of Louis Harris and Associates, who conducted the survey, concluded, "It's clear that outside directors live in an environment where being sued is almost part of the process of doing business" (see note 16).

The high exposure to litigation is a fairly recent development. Not long ago, directors believed that they were protected by their business judgment. They thought that only fraud, insider trading, or self-dealing could expose them to litigation. This assumption changed in 1985 in *Smith v. Van Gorkom*. In that case the Delaware Supreme Court found the directors of Trans Union Corp.

guilty of gross negligence for nothing more than accepting too low a price for the sale of the company, although it was substantially above the market price and there were no other bids. The directors were found to be personally liable for the losses sustained by the shareholders!

Although in the Delaware case the concept of business judgment was not modified, the expectation that directors be better informed when being party to board decisions became significantly higher than ever before. Later the Delaware legislature passed a statute permitting corporations to protect their directors from such situations, but lawyers and their director clients remain wary. Although such charges are often dismissed or settled out of court, preparing for litigation—even if it does not reach the courts—is expensive in terms of both time and legal fees. Many concerned about the current reluctance of qualified people to join boards pray that the tide of litigation will turn, but they are pessimistic about its' doing so.

Many directors are considering ways to improve their position on the board and reduce their exposure to legal charges. They see themselves analogously as sitting on a little island in the middle of a roaring river. They can't return to the riverbank they left, and it is dangerous to go on to the other side. The riverbank they left was one of trust in management based on the record of many years of sound judgment and ethical performance. It was a safe spot until there were overreactions that led to the building of the small boat in which the directors set out to seek better governance. The climate on the other side is hostile, reminding one of a stern authoritarian police state, rigid with rules that deter growth. Although the directors found refuge on this tiny island, they will soon have to decide which course to take. Allegories aside, there are those who question whether outside directors have become an endangered species. It is probably too soon to write their obituary, yet clearly the institution of directorship is in a state of turmoil.

Incentives for Improvement

To enhance the attractions of joining the board, many companies have been increasing the financial rewards, either in cash or in stock. According to Korn/Ferry International, these emoluments grew at close to double the pace of the consumer price index in the 20 years leading up to 1993—that is, 387 percent, compared with 216 percent. As previously noted, there has been little research on whether the quality of directors has improved correspondingly, remained unchanged, or deteriorated. Also, greater attention is being given to the specific qualities required in the director. Unless directors are chosen for their specialized knowledge and are regarded as a resource and rewarded as such, the quality of directors might decline, leading to an even lower level of corporate governance—a worrying prospect (see note 16).

The fact remains that no one has yet come up with a comprehensive blueprint for the role of board members, nor has anyone worked out how the shareholder and the public can be reasonably sure of not being let down by the board. Many are seeking ways to improve board performance, and some of the ideas that have been put forward require courageous changes. There is, however, no evidence of plans to assess the ability of potential directors to discern and address tough company situations, to know when painful decisions are called for, to nurture their own independent opinions, and to decipher the conceptual errors of corporate officers.

Among the measures that have been proposed (as mentioned previously) are separation of the position of CEO from that of chairman of the board, emphasis on board members being independent outsiders, and delegation of some board functions to subcommittees, thereby saving time that can be better spent on the company's business. Some boards have even called for an annual self-evaluation by the board and its various committees. There are still, of course, many almost narcissistically self-satisfied and complacent directors who will take no steps to establish instruments of self-assessment, unless required to do so by an outside regulatory or other body of authority.[20] It is too soon to judge whether this commendable step will yield constructive criticism or serve only to massage the egos of board members.

Director Education

Board members are not born to the position, whatever they might think. Ideally, they get a seat on the board by virtue of a combination of general knowledge and specific expertise, ranging from legal training to schooling in economics, to technical knowledge. No matter how important these talents and experiences are, however, the director should, within a reasonable time after joining the board, become knowledgeable about the company's affairs. Sadly, this does not always happen. Directors often do not take the time to master the information essential for them to fulfill their roles. Neither regulators nor any voluntary organization have formally set up a system to ensure that directors have the basic information required to provide the services expected. But institutional investors such as the California Public Employees' Retirement System (CalPERS), who regard themselves as shareholders' agents, recognize the need for high-quality directors, and they are also seeking ways to jettison ineffective ones. As W. T. Hawkins, managing director of Russel Reynolds' board practice, stated, "Investors are really looking for a better sense of the value of each director. . . . They want more personal information, more about their business track records and contributions."[21] And addressing the same subject, Wirthlin Worldwide, an opinion-research group, found that investors' unhappiness with directors overall was clearly evident when "88 percent of those questioned agreed that boards need to be more aggressive in weeding out underperforming members" (see note 21).

Some companies have taken well-defined steps toward instructing the director. One conducts an annual weekend retreat to discuss strategy and study long-term projections, with presentations by senior management.[22] Such a program has a number of purposes, among them education of board members on the special risks of the business. It is also an opportunity for the board to assess its collective effectiveness and that of its individual members. In the relaxed environment of the retreat, members can speak freely with senior managers and get to know their talents and shortcomings. It also gives them an opportunity to grasp the strategic direction of the company, an essential understanding for the serious director who is trying to get a better understanding of how the company operates.

There are, of course, other ways to ensure and to improve the education of the director. The essential point is to provide directors with as many tools of the trade as possible. As we move into the next century, it is probable that more attention will be given to structuring various continuing education programs for directors.

DIRECTORS UNDER PRESSURE

Proper governance requires that directors fulfill their assignments, not only in normal times but particularly when extraordinary events occur, such as restructuring, merger, or unexpected trouble. It is then that they must fulfill their fiduciary-agent responsibilities for their principals, the shareholders, and the general public. This, as directors who have experienced tough times well know, is easier said than done.

The Need to Spend More Time

With an ever-greater number of business and corporate transactions being carried out daily and with the global range, diversity, and complexity of today's marketplace, it is increasingly difficult for the director to master all the essentials necessary to enable fulfillment of his or her fiduciary responsibilities. Some observers doubt whether even the most dedicated director—one who attends meetings, reads material, seeks information, and gives generously of his or her time—can meet modern demands, especially in times of stress, when decision is urgent.

Directors often find themselves in a maze of facts that obscure the best decisions. Their main responsibility is to see that full information is provided, in the interest of ensuring the financial security of the stockholders. But even if they perform cautiously and sensibly, seldom can they prevent company losses or suggest a course that would increase returns. When an emergency occurs and the company is faced with hard times, directors—however careful they have been—often find themselves exposed to angry principals who may bring a legal suit against them or accuse them of negligence or, at least, carelessness. Is there any way directors can reduce these risks of office?

Participating in policymaking should be an important task for directors. In practice, however, they often lack the basic knowledge required to share in such decisions, so they depend on management, which, as previously noted, often fails to present them with the facts. Board members are expected to be fully informed. As individuals willing to allot only a limited amount of their time, however, they seldom acquire all the tools needed to handle pressure. What, for example, will they know about the pros and cons of a proposed merger being put before the board by the CEO? How can we ensure that they have enough knowledge to satisfy the investigator or regulator inquiring about the sequence of decisions taken prior to a crisis or to initiate action crucial to the well-being of the company?[23]

Quite clearly, directors should spend the time necessary to assess all risks, including such types of market risk as competition, new technology, and product innovation. They also need to be aware of inflation risk and fluctuating interest rates, as well as operational risks. Directors should know enough about the company's operations to ask the right questions and, not less important, to evaluate answers received. And, in addition to their fiduciary responsibilities, directors may be expected to provide guidance to the company's officers and senior staff in such matters as approving strategies, testing the logic of possible management assumptions, and evaluating performance. The question is, how can they be conversant with the full gamut of the company's activities when they devote only a limited portion of their time to it? Finally, for directors there is no such thing as too much curiosity; it is not enough to ask all the right questions or to speak one's mind at the risk of upsetting other members of the board or alienating the regulators, the shareholders, or the public.

Any person willing to become a director should take all these considerations into account. While they may fairly safely assume that most of the time they spend in the boardroom will be uneventful, they should always be prepared for their performance to be examined in terms of the role they played when a sudden crisis occurred. Above all, directors should understand that there are no formal preparations for dealing with such contingencies.

Judgment as a Prerequisite

As in all other facets of life, the future is largely unknown in business. The ability to look ahead, however, is vital. There is usually more than one option, but once chosen, it may well be irreversible. Accordingly, sound judgment is an important quality in a director. To prevent needless mistakes and to ensure the best chance for success, the decisions of board members should be based on the facts, on sound projections, and on knowledge of the market in the context of a philosophy of active stewardship. In such a setting, it will be easier for the directors to fulfill their mission and see that corporate resources are used efficiently.

To prepare themselves for their role, beyond selecting the CEO, approving the appointment of senior company officers, and being attuned to the question of succession, the board members should:

1. determine the broad policies and general direction the efforts of the company should take;
2. establish performance standards, both ethical and commercial, by which the management will be judged and communicate them clearly to management in unambiguous terms; and
3. review top management's performance in following the overall strategy and meeting the standards set by the board.[24]

Complex business matters and organizational problems cannot be overseen by directors who have little or no specific experience and who devote only a limited amount of time to the subjects brought before the board. Such a board will be unable to guide the CEO and management through turbulent times or to prevent the exposure of employees, owners, customers, and suppliers from incompetent leadership. Indeed, the chief executive would rightly be hesitant to present a risk-laden proposition to a board whose members do not really understand the fine points of the business at hand and are unwilling to actively support tough courses chosen by management.

As we have seen, most directors are outsiders. Unless they make themselves knowledgeable in the company's business, a CEO with a powerful personality may intimidate and subdue them. If that happens, the board members may find it difficult to evaluate management performance, and they may also be unable to interpret indications that the company is headed straight for the rocks. Such a danger can be averted only by the application of stern discipline and judgment. In other words, the majority of the board should be self-confident, worldly, informed individuals well-versed in both current affairs and company business.

There are, of course, other basic requirements. It is not enough for directors to act as advocates of the company on whose board they serve; rather, they should be deeply involved in their roles and committed to the overall objectives of the organization. They must be able to obtain the information they need from the same company officers and staff as the managers do, and they must be shown, should the need arise, the same data and reports.

NOTES

1. John A. Byrne, "Listen up—The National Association of Corporate Directors' new guidelines won't tolerate inattentive, passive, uninformed board members," *Business Week*, cover story (November 25, 1996).
2. "Directors: Myth and reality," Division of Research, Graduate School of Business Administration, Harvard University (1971).

3. "The bored board," in *Towards the Next Economics and Other Essays* (Heinemann, 1981): 108, 110; first published in *Wharton Magazine* (Autumn 1986).

4. Arthur Levitt, Jr., "Shareholder interests as the director's touchstone," remarks at Directors' College, Stanford, California (March 23, 1995): http://www.sec.gov/news/speeches/sch032.txt.

5. "Bored directors," *The Economist* (January 27, 1990): 74.

6. Clifton R. Wharton, Jr., "Advice and dissent: Rating the corporate governance compact," *Harvard Business Review* (November–December 1991): 138.

7. Arch Patton and John C. Baker, "Why won't directors rock the boat?" *Harvard Business Review* (November–December 1987): 10.

8. Richard Gibson, "Double duty: Board outsider, paid consultant," *Wall Street Journal* (March 17, 1995): B1.

9. G. Bruce Knecht and Joann S. Lublin, "American Express board using directors as paid consultants; company takes lead on issue that irks many investors. Kissinger is an exception," *Wall Street Journal* (April 12, 1995): A3.

10. John A. Byrne with Richard A. Melcher, "The best and worst boards, our new report card on corporate governance," *Business Week* cover story (November 25, 1996).

11. "What are directors for?" *Business Week*, (May 22, 1971): 90.

12. Myles L. Mace, *Fortune* (April 29, 1985): 209–210.

13. "U.S. corporate mergers seen at record levels," Reuters (April 11, 1997).

14. Colin Boyd, "Ethics and corporate governance: The issues raised by the Cadbury Report in the United Kingdom," *Journal of Business Ethics* (February 1996): 167–182.

15. William H. Bonner and Alan E. Ellstrand, "CEO successor choice, its antecedents and influence on subsequent firm performance," *Group and Organization Management* (March 1996): 105–123.

16. Dan Cordz and Jennifer Reingold, "The vanishing director," *Financial World* (October 1993): 22.

17. William A. Sahlman, "Why sane people shouldn't serve on public boards," *Harvard Business Review* (May–June 1990): 28.

18. Diane Mastrull, "Lawyer's advice: Don't yearn to be a bank director," *Philadelphia Business Journal* (February 10, 1995): 3.

19. Wade Lambert, "The business of law—legal beat: Corporate settlement costs hit a record," *Wall Street Journal* (March 10, 1995): B3. "Accordingly, the cost of settlement in suits against directors and officers rose 39 percent, to an average of $4.6 million for the nine-year period ended in 1994, from an average of $3.3 million for the nine years ended in 1993, according to Wyatt Co., a Washington consulting firm." The article provides additional staggering data.

20. Ronald Berenbaim, "Corporate boards come of age," speech on corporate governance before the Conference Board, *Vital Speeches of the Day* (September 1, 1995): 680.

21. Judith Dobrzynski, "Boardrooms under scrutiny," New York Times Service, *International Herald Tribune* (March 8–9, 1997).

22. David H. Atkins, "Corporate governance lessons from abroad," *Canadian Business Review* (Autumn 1995): 24.

23. Dawn Marie Driscoll, "The ethical responsibility of directors and trustees," *Montana Business Quarterly* (Autumn 1995): 10.

24. Irving S. Shapiro, "Corporate governance," *Power and Accountability* (The 1979 Benjamin F. Fairless Memorial Lectures): 45–51.

Chapter 7

What to Expect
from the Board

DIRECTORS FOR MODERN TIMES

Profit versus Governance

When Harold Williams headed the SEC in the late 1970s, he warned the public
not to expect the performance of boards to improve through legislation. He
believed that proper governance cannot be imposed from above and that those
involved must cooperate and comply with the system. He explained that legis-
lated measures, by definition, impose one solution on all corporations and de-
stroy the flexibility needed to tailor the board to the needs of the particular
corporation. He pointed out that a law seeking to establish independent boards
and independent directors would, of necessity, focus on structure, form, and
other objective criteria rather than on the unmeasurables that determine how
well a board discharges its responsibilities. It would, he said, divert attention
from the efforts of individual companies and boards to mechanical compliance
with the law.

The success of American business will depend, in the future as it has so far,
on the ability and effectiveness of its corporate governance. But it should be
recognized that not all well-governed companies automatically do well in the
marketplace, nor is there necessarily a correlation between company performance and the adherence of the board to governance guidelines. In short, the
mission of management is economic, and long-term profitability is the measure
of its success. There are, however, hurdles to clear in negotiating the profit track.
Sometimes, for instance, there are directors who face a conflict between duty
and self-interest; they may stand on both sides of a transaction or they may be
able to realize some personal benefit from a certain action.[1] Or, management
may unwittingly create a climate that tempts subordinates into compromising

their ethics—for example, taking inappropriate action in order to enable the company to show an ostensibly better record.

If an ambitious individual is in a business setting in which every action is judged purely on economic grounds and in which rewards are based on short-term economic performance, ignoring all social and moral issues of fairness, then, quite naturally, he or she will strive to maximize the economic returns of the entity, even at the expense of social or ethical values and even though such a materialistic course might result eventually in the business destroying itself. The same principle applies to the corporation. Society will not permanently tolerate a major institution that justifies itself solely in economic terms.[2] It is with this in mind that the board of directors should undertake its mission of governance and accountability: There are responsibilities beyond profits.[3]

The board is not a weapon that can be used effectively in adversarial situations in the corporate world; it is easier to call board members to account if they are not performing in a hostile environment. In the same vein, a chronically hostile relationship between board and management prevents the efficient performance of either, just as does a relationship characterized by board passivity. Boards and management are best viewed as two supportive links in the chain, with management expected to respect its board and carry out the policies set by it, while not being overly dependent on it. Because of real or perceived outside pressures on business executives, however, there is always a danger that management will not risk being second-guessed or failing and that it will tend to play it safe at the expense of the primary economic mission.[4] But such caution is not necessarily a negative trait; indeed, there are many companies with cautious, uninspired boards that ensure solid, if somewhat dull, continuity.

Good management, in the context of concern for the future of the company, will achieve a harmony of profit, the interests of the stakeholders, and other ethical goals. Conversely, when management fails to think in terms of the broader social dynamics in which it operates, it will be unlikely to anticipate changing client needs and its performance will, over time, decline. No government regulations, no board of directors, no federal agency can offset the consequences of inadequate management. It is vital to guard against usurping management's role or crippling able management. It is the quality of managerial leadership—its willingness to venture, to take risks and seek rewards—that will determine the future of both individual business and the economy as a whole. In this relationship, the board should act as guide and mentor to management.

The Classic Perception of the Board

An army can look impressive parading on a national holiday. Although it may be used as an exhibition of the power of the military forces, the ceremony provides no clue as to how the troops will perform under fire. Because the eventuality of war has, hopefully, been reduced to a minimum today, the behavior and judgment of most military officers can be observed only in training or in war games.

There have been some attempts in the business world to stage parallel war games as tests for directors and candidates, but the experiments have not been successful. It simply is unrealistic to regard the results as convincing indicators of how individuals would operate in real time in the business world. Harvard and other business schools have developed teaching programs that include case studies, but they have not discovered the criteria for assessing how directors will perform under duress, nor are these criteria applied to candidates by boards or CEOs in choosing new directors. At this time, it is not practical to guess whether boards that faced an emergency would have performed more impressively had their directors been so evaluated before being invited to join.

Unlike medical and law schools, where faculty usually include experienced doctors and judges or lawyers, respectively, business schools and management institutes do not engage senior corporate executive officers to give students in their core program the benefit of their decades of practical wisdom and experience. When they do teach the role of the director, the faculty—a number of whom are also board members—usually groom students to participate in the classic board under fairly good weather conditions, as if they could always be assured of continued business growth.

While it is rare to have a full-time practicing CEO teach at a graduate business school, quite a few enjoy giving public lectures to advocate their concepts of management. One of them, Lawrence Perlman, recommends three basic principles that should guide the board.

1. To effectively select and monitor senior management, directors must be independent of management.
2. The board must actively participate in developing long-term strategy and financial goals, but it should not become too involved in detail.
3. The CEO and his corporate executives should work under the authority of the board.[5]

Perlman adds that it is the authority in item 3 that legitimizes the actions of executives—a humbling and healthy reminder to certain CEOs.

Although many people assert that the quality of board members and their level of performance have improved, others will admit that little has changed since 1983, when Dr. R. Holzach, chairman of the board of the Union Bank of Switzerland, quoted an unnamed American bank counsel: "Ten years ago, directors were selected for three reasons which were interrelated: their position in the community, the business they could bring in, and the advice they could give on the creditworthiness for borrowers in the community." "A good board," he went on, "should have its nose in and its hands out. Understand thoroughly the time commitment. If you do not have time . . . do not go on the board. And, above all, if you can't bring something to the party, don't come."[6]

Corporate officers and board directors should identify role models. Doing so can be good publicity and possibly bestow educational benefits as well. An example is the 1995 first "board of the year" award presented jointly by the Wharton School of the University of Pennsylvania and Spencer Stuart, an international executive search firm. The recipients were the directors of Mallinckrodt Group, Inc., a St. Louis–based company with sales of $2.2 billion that supplies human and animal health care products and special chemicals worldwide.[7] The jury chose the directors of Mallinckrodt, a successful growth company, because the directors were dedicated and committed to their responsibility. They attended six regular, two-day meetings per year and visited the corporation's operating facilities. Included in the commendation was a quotation from the group's chief executive officer, C. Ray Holman, who observed that "their interest in and understanding of our business facilitate synergistic board-management dialog which helps us achieve our goals and objectives ... The attribute we appreciate ... is the viability of the board members to consult with management at any time." Also, because the board members believed that shareholders should have confidence in the board's ability to understand and do its job, they developed, adopted, refined, and published their formal principles of governance.

The announcement of the award and the reasons it was given to the Mallinckrodt board included a description of the impressive, highly qualified jury. They had six standards of outstanding board performance:

1. acts productively, in a timely fashion, to add value;

2. understands and acts on its responsibilities to the shareholders;

3. understands and can articulate its role and relationship to management;

4. understands and acts on its responsibilities to employees and to society;

5. encourages discussion and exhibits courage in the handling of difficult issues; and

6. supports strong ethical and moral standards of business.

In normal times, most boards can prove that they act in accordance with the first four standards, which should be expected from any board. It is not, however, common for boards to be tested as to whether they meet the last two criteria. That is to say, most boards do not usually find an occasion to instruct management in choosing the moral course or to exhibit courage in threatening or otherwise difficult circumstances. If there were instances in 1994 or 1995 in which the Mallinckrodt board could be measured by the last two standards, there was no reference to them in this document of commendation. Certainly, there was no description of difficult moral decisions the directors of Mallinckrodt had faced with courage, nor was there any indication of what the deliberations of the jury were or on what basis they rated the behavior of the Mallinckrodt board and ranked them in comparison with other companies. The question therefore needs to be asked: Did the performance of the Mallinckrodt directors really meet all the criteria spelled out by those who initiated the prize? Although the Mallinckrodt directors were surely a splendid group of people and dedicated to their assignment, they have not been tested in crisis situations.

But even when a company makes national news, its board is rarely mentioned. In the summer of 1997, Mallinckrodt was trying to assure investors it would work quickly to reduce the massive debt that accompanied its planned $1.9 billion acquisition of Nellcor Puritan Bennet Inc., and Mallinckrodt's CEO acknowledged that the high debt load could be risky. There was, however, no indication of the extent to which the company's directors had been consulted or whether they supported the move. Although the company was often in the media, the board's role in the decision making was not mentioned.[8]

In the autumn of 1996, in the magazine's first corporate governance ranking, *Business Week* chose Campbell Soup Company as having the best board of directors. Explaining the choice, the magazine pointed out the valuable and probing questions the board members had posed to the company's CEO, David W. Johnson. On a series of strategic matters, to quote director Philip E. Lippincott, "there was vigorous and challenging discussion in the boardroom over all these issues." And John Byrne, who wrote the article, concluded that the board would be tested if Campbell's turnaround faded or its new strategy failed, but that at the end of 1996 it strongly desired to stay the best-governed (if untested) company in the nation.[9]

In summary, it is important that boards be inquisitive but also supportive of management. It is, however, more important that the board be capable of pulling its weight in damage control and other crisis situations. There is no evidence that those who grade boards today look at these capabilities.

The Desired Attributes

The term "leadership" has become inflated and ambiguous. According to Webster's dictionary, a leader is "a person who leads, a directing, commanding, or guiding head, as of a group or activity." Many describe the ideal choice for board member as a "strong leader," but that obviously is not what they really have in mind. Rather, they are looking for a person who will be *part* of a board that speaks with *one voice*, preferably through one spokesperson.[10] In other words, the director is expected to have several commendable qualities, but in the ordinary course of events, leadership is not one of them.

The reason, of course, is that it is difficult, if not impossible, to expect a group of leaders to speak with one voice, for they are far too individualistic. A board composed of true leaders would find it difficult to keep quiet for long or to allow the CEO to act as its perennial representative. Perhaps, then, the basic quality to be sought is not leadership but sterling character—the ability to differentiate between right and wrong and the courage to stick to one's principles. A good director will not even think of fearing confrontation with the CEO or outside pressures. And, in fact, no one—whether shareholders, stakeholders, or the company itself—will benefit from having weak-spined directors.[11]

But good character is not the only attribute directors should have; realistic modesty as to what they can achieve is also called for. As Bevis Longstreth advocates, ''More modesty about the claimed contributions to corporate performance that any particular form of corporate governance will provide is highly recommended.''[12] He goes on to call for a diversity of approach to corporate governance, for the right of corporations and their leaders, management, and directors to experiment with the widest possible range of different approaches where legal and other options exist. These are two open-ended recommendations, very different from those of the ''one voice'' school.

A director should not have either blind trust in management or total distrust of the CEO and skepticism about his actions. Extremes in either case ensure that his or her tenure will be ineffective; it is the middle road that board members should strive to travel. Good judgment by directors is essential to their accountability and corporate governance. A typical, simple example would be a request to approve a significant expenditure, investment, or commitment: How would the director act if the decision were to be made for his or her own company?

Choosing Board Members

When companies are small and controlled by the founders or when the main shareholder is also the CEO, there is little doubt about how a board director is chosen. This situation gradually changes as the company grows, as other shareholders come in, and when the company goes public. At this point, shareholders other than the original ones become interested parties and have a say in the choice of directors. Later, when the equity begins splitting into very small portions and the number of small shareholders rises to many thousands, individuals lose their power to influence the annual general meeting or to choose the directors. The choice, then, almost by default, returns to the CEO. Alone, or with the support of an influential board member, he or she fills the vacancies that have occurred.

In response to the call for tighter corporate governance and public criticism, some companies have (formally or informally) changed this system. More frequently, new directors are being invited to join not by the CEO or one dominating member but by the entire board.[13] This trend has been strengthened by the lobbying and real power of investment groups such as the California Public Employees' Retirement System (CalPERS) that have prevailed on small shareholders to organize in order to have a greater say. As a larger body, they should, so the case goes, be able to influence governance, not least by choosing some of the directors on the board. Has this development changed the structure of the board significantly? It is probably too soon to say.

THE CHANGING ROLE OF THE BOARD

Some people call for more decisive corporate governance because they want a higher standard of business ethics and credibility. The motive of others is more calculating and mercenary. CalPERS, for instance, wants more decisive corporate governance to improve its members' income. CalPERS and similar institutions are unwilling to remain passive when the companies in which they have invested fail to provide positive and improving results. They become especially irritated in the face of disappointing corporate performance and that insupportable but common concomitant, excessive executive compensation.[14]

In theory, advocates of proper governance do not regard instant gratification as a high priority. They view with approval policies that balance the maximization of the wealth of today's shareholders and the company's future growth potential. They weigh new marketing strategies against the business dictum that the best companies are those that retain the best people.[15] These are not necessarily the views of institutional investors, who do not always have the patience to wait for longer-term results.

Duality or Separation of Roles?

Various proposals have been made to raise the level of corporate governance. As mentioned previously, one is to separate the position of CEO from that of chairman of the board. It has been suggested that separating the two roles would enable the board to better supervise the executive actions of management. At first, the potential cost of this governance solution and whether it is appropriate at all or only in some circumstances was barely discussed. Later, some serious reasons surfaced for questioning whether splitting is such a good idea, not least of which is that the governance advantages might be offset by greater administrative costs and other disadvantages.[16]

The proposal has two important weaknesses. The first is the handicap of directors who spend only a moderate amount of time on the company's affairs and therefore do not usually become conversant with its complex corporate machinations. It is difficult enough for full-time executives to achieve an adequate understanding of the details of the business of which they are in charge; for a nonexecutive chairman, it is close to impossible. Hence, if this post is separate from that of the CEO, it is likely that the chairman will lack the extensive knowledge and sensitive understanding necessary to lead the company.

The second weakness relates to the fact that the CEO who is also the chairman draws strength from the clarity and decisiveness of his or her dual position. Separation would require extra management time and lead to delays in the corporate decision-making process. Further, it would not be easy for the other directors, very much dependent on the information they receive, to choose between divergent positions taken by the chairman and the CEO.

But care should be taken not to generalize on these matters. There may be situations where duality is preferable, mainly in companies where business is stable and policies focused and conservative, as in public utilities. In contrast, independent chairmen can contribute and be valuable in growth companies, when the CEO is pursuing bold, somewhat risky strategies or when the company is facing turbulent times.

The Art of Asking Questions

"Corporate governance is something more than sitting around a boardroom table debating grave matters in measured tones," says William Dimma, chairman of the board of Monsanto Canada.[17] He points out that the board cannot run the company, but that doesn't mean that the role of the directors should be belittled. Their major challenge is how they perform when the company, or a segment of it, is about to go sour or is already in difficulty. Even in normal conditions the director has an important role to play.

When there is a crisis, the most effective director is the one who has the curiosity and confidence to ask tough, possibly embarrassing questions. He rejects glib replies and insists on full, well-argued answers. Such a director can avoid mistakes and become a well-informed, responsible observer and a constructive critic of corporate policies, strategies, procedures, and governance plans.[18]

Tough queries are helpful when posed in a positive vein. It is also possible to question corporate officers firmly without antagonizing them if it is done courteously and respectfully. Care should be taken, however, to avoid pitfalls such as becoming:

1. the adversarial director, contentious and negative;
2. the contrarian director, suspicious and pessimistic;
3. the nit-picking director; or
4. the "do nothing" director who rarely contributes to the proceedings but meticulously collects his fees.

When directors show empathy for the company's senior officers and maintain a keen curiosity about corporate affairs, the odds are that their contribution to governance will be effective and appreciated.

Are Boards Becoming More Cautious?

Board members like to believe that their level of performance is gradually improving, and most would say that they respect their role and mean business. In an effort to become more effective, most boards are becoming smaller. In 1982, the typical board was composed of sixteen members, of which about half were corporate officers. A decade later their average size had dropped to twelve, with only three of them company executives.[19] Since then, the average number of members is believed to have dropped further to between nine and eleven. The composition of the board is changing in other ways, as well: There are more directors with academic and scientific training and more women and minority group members. The smaller size still allows for a reasonable spread of director expertise, besides reducing the time spent on speeches and making the proceedings more efficient.

There is also a general trend toward delegating many of the board's assignments to subcommittees. Most prominent in this regard is the audit committee; whereas in 1973 only half the larger U.S. corporations had one, by 1995 virtually all did (see note 19). In addition to the decades-old institution of audit and executive committees, it is increasingly common to have committees for reviewing business conduct, as well as committees on finance and/or investment, on human resources, and on corporate governance. It is encouraging that the usefulness of these subcommittees seems to be periodically evaluated by the board. The executive committee, which in the era of larger boards was essential to sensible management, has all but disappeared, while the strategic planning committee, theoretically of major importance, exists only in a small number of boards.

Another significant step toward more effective governance is the near disappearance of salaried officer-directors (often limited to two or even to the CEO alone), coupled with a policy that the key subcommittees be comprised solely of outside directors. There are, however, different schools of thought as to who qualifies as a fully independent outside director. The author accepts the criteria formulated by James R. Booth and Daniel N. Deli: A fully independent outside director is one whose only affiliation with the company is as a director. Employees, former employees, relatives, block-holders, people who derive personal benefits such as consulting fees or personal loans or members of organizations with contractual relations with the firm such as banks, commercial firms, or investment institutions, or lawyers should not be classified as outside directors.[20]

These measures are important steps toward better governance, and they should provide an opportunity for the board to be a more prominent factor influencing the company's operations. But this theoretically increased role should not be overstated; a board can influence but never manage the company. One reason for recommending that the board maintain a low profile is that its contribution to the company's results in normal times is generally passive and limited at best. It is management that develops the strategic plan.

Previously, it was noted that many boards spend far too large a portion of their time reviewing quarterly and other financial results. Even where, in theory, they might contribute more, as in long-term strategy, they depend to a large extent on management for information. Management usually presents its program to the board or its strategic committee in the course of a morning or, possibly, a full-day meeting, most of which is devoted to formal presentations by the company's officers. The time reserved for questions and full, frank, and constructive discussion, before the board is asked to endorse the plan, is minimal. Realistic board members, who know how modest their input is, recognize the limitations of such meetings. Most seem unaware of the full implications of their fiduciary responsibilities, and seem unfazed by being asked to play such a minor, passive role.

INCREASING EXPECTATIONS

What makes boards of directors such peculiar social structures, with seemingly inbuilt contradictions? It is commonly accepted that boards were formed to provide essential protection for shareholders, but it is suspected that many functions are no more than window dressing for the CEO and the company's management. Formally, a corporation's board of directors is charged with ultimate responsibility for managing the company's affairs; accordingly, they are required to act in good faith, and in an informed manner, with the goal of furthering the best interests of the company and its shareholders.[21] Unfortunately, boards do not always conduct themselves in such an ideal fashion, for various reasons. For example, some are so large that even those directors willing to spend adequate time are not able to achieve an independent, informed, and helpful perspective on corporate affairs.[22]

The modern company is required to provide quarterly statements and other ongoing reports, mainly financial, that offer a fairly detailed description of its economic conditions. Reviewing and approving these facts and figures takes up much of the allotted time of the board meeting. How, in these circumstances, can directors work toward long-term financial success? Will they devote the time required to learn the facts and then support or influence management policies? How can they support the CEO's risk-taking without detailed knowledge of the plans? Will they put in the time necessary to monitor management throughout their term of office, not just when trouble is brewing or has already boiled over?[23]

Obviously, the respective characteristics and personalities of the CEO, the chairman of the board, and other directors influence their mutual relationships. It is the CEO who proposes the agenda for the proceedings to the board's chairman, while the directors play a fairly passive role. The latter come to the meetings as listeners; they may make comments and advise on certain matters but, as mentioned elsewhere in this study, they spend only a relatively small part of their time on the company's matters.

Even when directors have a modest equity involvement, the company's affairs are not their main concern. Recognizing the primary position of the CEO and his or her need for independence, they usually refrain from forcing changes in the higher levels of performance. In other words, they are not inclined to be back-seat drivers. More friendly onlookers than central actors, few of them volunteer ideas or initiate policies that might lead to bigger profits for the firm.[24]

Traditionally, the most important task of the board was to determine when it was time for the CEO to retire and to choose his or her replacement. Over the years, however, as the task of corporate governance has grown, the public has come to expect far more from the board. But it is noteworthy that those who want more corporate governance do not necessarily have a clear idea of what all the extra director chores should be or which activities are more important than others. There is, in fact, no guarantee against a repeat of the embarrassments of the early 1990s, when losses were discovered at IBM, GM, American Express, and Westinghouse, and it was the companies' CEOs who inadvertently sparked the process that toppled them from office. In hindsight it is clear that the directors were too late to learn and to take action, and we cannot be sure that the scenario in which the directors sit idly by while crisis mounts will not be repeated in similar circumstances in the future.

The case of IBM, as briefly described by professor Amar Bhide, dramatizes the inadequacies of many boards in the 1980s and early 1990s.[25] IBM's stock lost more than 60 percent of its value between the summers of 1987 and 1993, while the overall market rose by about the same percentage. Although the size of the paper (and real) loss to the shareholders was significantly larger than the GNP of several countries, the company's officers felt secure in their posts and the board did not appear concerned by what was apparently occurring in front of their eyes. Business magazines actually carried glowing cover and other stories in 1991 and 1992 about how successfully CEO John Akers was carrying out his assignments. A year later he was out, but what did the directors—who sat by as the state of IBM deteriorated—have to say for themselves? Some retired in the aftermath, but in hindsight it appears as if most took a detached ivory-tower view of a crisis they should have done more to prevent.

Similar questions could have been addressed to the directors of General Motors Corp. Beginning in the spring of 1990 and in the following two and a half years of the tenure of CEO Robert C. Stempel, they had sufficient indications that the company was in the red. By the end of 1990 it had become clear that, whatever his other merits, the new CEO was not a crisis manager and was incapable of operating aggressively. During this time, the behavior of this board was hardly more impressive than that of IBM. The members lay dormant for some two years, even after they learned in 1991 that GM had lost $7 billion in its core North American auto operations. When the board finally did reach the conclusion that Stempel had to go, rather than outright firing, their preferred weapon was press leakages.[26] Most of the credit for the nerve to proceed at all should go to New York lawyer Ira Millstein, who orchestrated the board coup. It is impossible even to guess how long GM would have remained in the doldrums without his initiative.

The shock of these crises was surpassed only by the wonder that the dramas had taken so long to unfold. Where *were* the directors? The answer could be found in the composition of the board, whose members—as a result of their many past and present ties with the company—were not independent in the full sense of the word. The upheavals showed that boardroom culture and politics were still very much dependent on the CEO. As a result, it took the board far too long to acknowledge that the company was in trouble and even longer to conclude that the CEO had to be removed.[27]

In addition to reviewing the company's quarterly and annual financial reports, receiving the CEO's current and policy reports, and delegating tasks to audit, financial, remuneration, asset investment, and strategic planning subcommittees (whose meetings some of them attend), members are also expected to be involved in the company's full board meetings and ask questions for which there are, at times, no immediate answers. These expectations are patently unrealistic in view of the short time most directors can allot to the board when they must also be active in their main careers.

It has been suggested that diversity of experience results in a better functioning board. In practice, however, companies—especially those in trouble—benefit more from board members with direct business knowledge. The latter should not, of course, be the CEO's cronies but outsiders who nominate additional board members and operate with a fully independent mind (see note 27).

Board members should have the time to set performance goals and deadlines; they should be free to reassess the executive's skill frequently; and they should feel comfortable in asking the wide range of questions that directors should ask both in the interest of sound governance and for their own protection. The following basic questions are essential for the director who often wears two hats: that of the specialist consultant to the CEO and management and that of the accountable shareholder's agent. The thinking director should be aware that getting satisfactory answers requires a considerable investment in homework.

1. To what extent have the company's strategic planners considered the strength of its competition, the threat of market turbulence, and changing consumer habits?

2. Are the company's financial resources adequate to meet its goals?

3. Have the budgetary policies taken into account the cash flow projections?

These are not theoretical questions, nor are they one-time issues. They should be asked periodically, and detailed information should be provided by management to support their answers.

Here is an afterthought: In the second half of 1997, with the beginning of the biggest financial crisis ever in East Asia, several international financial institutions including such U.S. banks as Chase Manhattan, J. P. Morgan, Bank America, and Bankers Trust discovered that they had a considerable stake in the troubled area. Although they were determined to get all their money back, billions of dollars were set aside for potential losses. Asked whether the risks taken in financing the region were reasonable, they gave the familiar-sounding answer that "there was a huge euphoria about Southeast Asia." Whatever the process of decision making, there was no evidence that any of the bank directors had stood up before the crisis to warn of the business shakiness of the region.[28]

THE FATIGUE FACTOR

From time to time, there are stories about the length of time it took a board of directors to realize that management was incompetent, that corporate performance was deteriorating, and that the senior officers should be turned out. The time lag is usually attributed to the timidity of the directors, who feel compelled to compromise and tread lightly rather than advocate their own views forthrightly. They are, in short, not truly independent when their personalities, their friendships, or their pocketbooks stand in the way of sound judgment. Some boards leave one with the impression that little has changed since Professor Peter Drucker, more than 20 years ago, characterized the board as an "impotent ceremonial and legal fiction."[29]

In an interview published in *Newsweek* in October 1986, Carl Icahn, the renowned corporate raider of that decade, described what he believed was wrong with many U.S. boards. He described one, of which he was member, where "meetings were held at eight in the morning out in Cleveland . . . Literally half the board is dozing off. The other half is reading the *Wall Street Journal*. And then they put slides up and nobody can understand the slides and when it gets dark they all doze off. The CEO at that time was a very intimidating sort of a guy. A big, tall guy, strong personality, and he was in control of that board. I mean nobody could say anything."[30]

The Economist noted in 1986 that although, theoretically, management is accountable to the board and the board is accountable to the shareholders, in fact, when the shareholders ask no questions, boards are too often answerable to nobody. The magazine also observed that boards, like other groups of people, will often act to quash deviant views and even agree that black is white to avoid jarring the harmony of the group. In such circumstances, groups become less than the sum of their parts (see note 30).

A full decade later, a money manager for a corporate pension fund observed that "in most cases, boards are a joke. They spend little time understanding the business or knowing much about management performance other than reported results."[31] He might have added that their main concern, to which they give considerable thought, is how to avoid being sued.

Corroborating the above is the observation of a cautious and experienced director, Professor Walter Salmon, who said that "critics of the boardroom have plenty of substantive ammunition, and we can no longer avoid the glaring evidence that too many corporate boards fail to do their jobs."[32]

Boards do, indeed, have structural problems that are exacerbated when management's primary criterion in choosing board members is to find people compatible with, and sometimes indebted to, the CEO. When they convene, such directors tend to work together in a tension-free, harmonious atmosphere. In their consultant capacity, they may render invaluable service to the company, but management is not as accountable to them as it would be to truly independent directors (see note 2).

Any overly close, comfortable relationship poses a threat to accountability and discipline, and boards of directors are not immune to such a danger. Indeed, a long-standing board with veteran members tends to become clubby, overly trusting, and insufficiently sensitive to warning signals. A possible antidote would be a corporate strategy establishing sufficient tension to keep their performance and compatibility in equilibrium. Unfortunately, little has evolved in the 1990s to enhance the boardroom as a group or to encourage individual members to express themselves independently. So far, no one has come up with a satisfactory proposal that provides for both a friendly climate in which board assignments can be executed efficiently and board members who can carry out their fiduciary responsibilities.

As alluded to earlier, it has not been long since U.S. corporations accepted the concept of reducing to one or two the number of salaried executive officers acting also as directors. If this change was a slow, gradual process in the United States, it took the British some 20 years more. Only in the aftermath of the Cadbury report did they adopt the principle that the majority of the directors should be outsiders.[33] Not everyone is happy with this new policy. Some involved in corporate management assert that operating a business is a professional activity and that a board should be run by people who know how to conduct the business. "You don't need a lot of independent directors to spy on managers," David Kimbell in the United Kingdom is quoted to have replied to a query.[34] He cautioned that if nonexecutive directors were to police the executives, the unity of the board would be disrupted. U.S. boards have found this threat to be exaggerated, but it has also become clear that even a board predominantly composed of independent directors will not always avoid coziness with management and laxity in fulfilling fiduciary responsibilities.

In 1979, Harold Williams, then head of the SEC, expressed optimism that a board could institutionalize accountability without having government intervene by introducing more regulations. Yet, the introduction of additional government regulations has not stopped but is constantly increasing. As shown in this study, the number of FASBs and other accounting measures continues to increase, with many professionals, analysts, and others pressing for more. The possibility that a regulator will make substantial new demands is less likely today, although additional demands for technical quality are another matter. As a result, laws and regulations constitute a considerable burden for corporations and contribute to significantly higher administrative, management, and accounting costs.

REWARDING DIRECTORS

The financial arrangements some companies—encouraged by their CEOs—make with their directors are, to say the least, cozy. There is a sense that boards often fail to monitor management adequately because their members reap such generous pay and perks. With this in mind, the National Association of Corporate Directors' blue ribbon report of June 1995 stated that director pay programs "often have little or no relationship to corporate profits or shareholder gains."[35] And they might have added that one could question the value they add to the company's well-being.

The way many directors are rewarded tends to make them beholden to the CEO. "The norms of behavior in most boardrooms inhibit independent directors from asserting leadership among their peers," Wall Street lawyer Martin Lipton is quoted in a *Forbes* article. The perks, ranging from pensions and life insurance policies to stock options and medical care, often deter them from taking an objective, unbiased approach to corporate governance matters.[36]

There is considerable diversity in the way directors are rewarded. According to Dana Wechsler Linden, nearly 70 percent of the largest American industrial corporations grant pensions to retired outside directors (see note 36). Now, however, there is a trend toward rewarding directors with stock options. In either case, the question is: How can a board get tough with a chief executive officer who showers it with benefits? And as Wechsler Linden points out, "companies pamper their outside directors with so many goodies that the board's objectivity could be compromised." According to compensation consultants Pearl Meyer & Partners, the average annual pay of directors of the 200 largest industrial companies in 1994 was some $68,300. In the following year, according to Towers Perrin, the New York–based management consulting firm, pay plus retirement benefits reached $71,000.

In the quest to improve directors' performance, there has been some rethinking of directors' remuneration. As mentioned above, corporations are using stock rather than retirement benefits to compensate outside directors. On December 1, 1995, Campbell Soup—a company recognized for its advanced corporate governance philosophy—introduced a policy that would reward each outside director with a $43,000 annual retainer entirely in stock. The company also requires outside directors to own 1,000 Campbell shares within a year of joining the board (see note 35). Richard Osborne, chairman of Asarco Inc., replaced his board directors' pension program with a stock plan that annually sets aside shares equal in value to 75 percent of the director's annual retainer. "Tying directors much more directly to the fortunes of outside shareholders has real merit," he said. Confirming that there has been decline in retirement plans for directors, Towers Perrin found that in 1995 only 44 percent of 250 large corporations surveyed used defined retirement plans for their outside directors, down sharply from 69 percent in the previous years. They expected this trend to continue.[37]

Do companies get a fair return for these retainers? In periods of good weather, it is probably impossible to judge. If, however, the aim of good governance is to have as talented and independent a board as possible, do not exaggerated rewards to directors serve as a bribe, keeping them quiet and impairing their objectivity? As long as the sun was shining at Morrison Knudsen, W. R. Grace, Digital Equipment, IBM, General Motors, and American Express, among others, nobody imagined that their directors would be unable or unwilling to deal with their companies' management problems. When the management inadequacies were finally discovered, managers were removed from office, but no estimate has been made of the cost of the directors' tardiness. To what extent were the directors at fault or negligent in not discovering their CEO's shortfalls sooner? Were the distinguished individuals who adorned these boards doing no more than renting out their names?

In the aftermath of the above, it should be asked whether directors take proper precautions to protect the shareholders. Is it possible to prevent them from developing an unhealthy affinity for CEOs with whom they may meet once a month or even more often? Conversely, directors have no such direct contacts with the shareholders; thus, they are far better attuned to arguments made by the CEO than to any distant call for attention by the shareholders.[38] Clearly, this problem is another facet of the difficulty in ensuring high quality in board members.

In a society that encourages an open market economy, it is almost as difficult to limit the rewards to board members as it would be to curtail the pay of the CEO. Certainly, the regulator would be ill-advised to interfere, but public pressures seem to be achieving a turnabout. Although it is too soon to assess how much change there will be, "more and more companies want to ensure that directors remain closely focused on shareholder issues," according to Paula Todd of Towers Perrin. She added that "to achieve this objective, companies need to set a substantial stock ownership target for directors and tie a significant portion of the director's pay package to the value of the company's stock." Indeed, most of the companies she studied had restructured their directors' pay packages to provide a larger proportion in stock (see note 37).

LIMITING BOARD MEMBERSHIPS

Increasing emoluments are an important incentive for those keen to collect directorships, and to some it has proved a rewarding occupation. The study of "America's least valuable directors" issued by the International Brotherhood of Teamsters early in 1996 was an eye opener, not least because, in normal conditions, it is almost impossible to judge how effective any one board member is. It is difficult to argue with one assertion made in the article: Participation on more than five boards of directors is probably too much. A director who sits on too many boards cannot do justice to any of them.[39]

Limiting the number of directorships any one person could undertake might be accomplished by regulation, but there would be resistance to such a move. The clubby, incestuous board relationships continue despite the Teamsters' observations and the recommendations of the National Association of Corporate Directors published in November 1996 (see note 31). At AT&T, six of the nine outside board directors serve on four to eight boards each. Five of Coca-Cola's directors serve on five or more boards each—and CEO Roberto G. Goizueta sits on seven. The chairman of the board of NationsBank Corp., Hugh L. McColl, Jr., is a director on five outside boards.

In the spring of 1995, Vernon Jordan was a member of twelve boards and his wife, Ann, of seven! Frank Carlucci, onetime secretary of defense, was a member of fourteen. Retired CEO of the Jewel Cos. supermarket chain Donald S. Perkins, a member of ten different boards who, in 1995, was honored by the NACD as the director who had done the most to advance and strengthen the principles of good corporate governance, claimed a year later that in the first ten months of 1996 he had missed just two of the 150 board and committee meetings he was invited to attend. He defended his proliferated activities by saying that "there is no substitute for having experience doing this."[40]

All this notwithstanding, there is a gradual realization that nobody can attend so many meetings and provide wise insight or be knowledgeable about the details of the company's structure and problems. The companies that invited these people to become directors were looking for their support in the form of consulting and lobbying, not to carry out any fiduciary responsibilities. It would obviously not be realistic to expect such directors to be overseers of corporate governance.

In its recommendations of November 1996, the National Association of Corporate Directors (NACD) strongly urged that boards limit the number of seats any individual may hold, so that a director would be able to devote enough time to the boards he or she serves.[41] In the case of chief or senior executives, the association urged that companies select individuals holding no more than two public company directorships in addition to the individual's own board; it recommended that other directors hold no more than six. Among other proposals that would help make the board more independent and more effective, the NACD recommended limiting the tenure of directors, so as to obtain fresh ideas and critical thinking from new board members. Not a binding organization, the association nevertheless has considerable influence on corporate governance in the United States. Its experience gives its president, John Nash, hope that NACD recommendations will be commonplace in the boardroom in the next three to five years.

When reviewing the various recommendations for improving the role of the director that were made by regulators, by prestigious commissions, or by specialists, one is impressed by the emphasis on technical detail—for example, the duality of the role of the CEO-chairman of the board; the length of tenure, and the reasonable number of directorships. What does not seem to exist is any emphasis on the intrinsic characteristics of the individual board member. That is to say, all the recommendations relate more to form than to substance. Presumably, all concerned—from the regulator to the graduate business school teacher—are convinced of the need to improve quality of performance. The difficulty is finding a way to ensure the rigorous self-discipline required in a good director.

NOTES

1. "Review of board actions: Greater scrutiny for greater conflicts of interest," *Harvard Law Review* (May 1990): 1698.

2. Harold M. Williams, "Power and accountability—The changing role of the corporate board of directors," *Corporate Accountability and Corporate Power* (1979): 25.

3. Ibid., 21, 22.

4. Ibid., 23.

5. Lawrence Perlman, "Corporate governance: A postmodernist view," speech given to the National Investor Relations Institute silver anniversary conference in Scottsdale, Arizona (June 5, 1995): http://www.ceridian.com/speech_06.05.95.html.

6. R. Holzach, "Changing responsibilities for corporate boards," *UBS Business Facts and Figures* (May 1983): 3.

7. "Directors of Mallinckrodt Group are named 'Board of the Year,' " *Directors and Boards* (Winter 1996): 52–43.

8. Robin Sidel, "Mallinckrodt says it can handle debtload," Reuters (July 24, 1997).

9. John A. Byrne, "Why Campbell's copped the top spot?" *Business Week* cover story (November 25, 1996).

10. Craig M. Wassernan, "Growing pressures in the boardroom," *US Banker* (September 1995): 93.

11. Hoffer Kaback, "Principles to govern by," *Directors and Boards* (Summer 1995): 6.

12. Bevis Longstreth, "Corporate governance: There's danger in new orthodoxies," *Journal of Portfolio Management* (Spring 1995): 47.

13. "Getting underway in board formation," *Directors and Boards* (Fall 1995): 23.

14. William A. Dimma, "The changing role of the board of directors," *Vital Speeches of the Day* (January 15, 1996): 217.

15. David Allen, "Judged by the company you keep," *Management Accounting* (London: February 1995): 107.

16. Andrew Campbell, "The cost of the independent chairman," *Long Range Planning* (December 1995): 107.

17. William A. Dimma, "Some thoughts on corporate governance: The board of directors and the CEO," speech delivered to the Canadian Bar Association in Toronto, Canada (May 13, 1994).

18. Robert Lear, "The hair-shirt director," *Chief Executive* (December 1995): 12.

19. Claire M. Hinsberg, "The corporate board's changing role," *Corporate Detroit Magazine* (August 1995), Section 2: 44, quoting statistics based on a 1994 article by Murray Weldenbaum, director of the Center of American Business in St. Louis, entitled "Corporate governance, today and tomorrow."

20. James R. Booth and Daniel N. Deli, "Factors affecting the number of outside directorships held by CEOs," *Journal of Financial Economics* (January 1996): 81.

21. "Review of the board actions: Greater scrutiny for greater conflicts of interest," *Harvard Law Review* (May 1990): 1697.

22. Arch Patton and John C. Baker, "Why won't directors rock the boat?" *Harvard Business Review* (November–December 1991): 10.

23. Judith H. Dobrzynsky, "Activist boards, yes. Panicky boards, no," *Business Week* (December 28, 1992): 40.

24. Some of these ideas are noted in a different context and direction in Regina E. Herzlinger, "Can public trust in nonprofits and governments be restored?" *Harvard Business Review* (March–April 1996): 87–107.

25. Amar Bhide, "Efficient markets, deficient governance: U.S. Securities regulations protect investors and enhance market liquidity. But do they alienate managers and shareholders?" *Harvard Business Review* (November–December 1994): 128–139.

26. Paul Ingrassia, "Board reform replaces the LBO," *Wall Street Journal* (October 30, 1992): A14.

27. "Lessons from boardroom dramas" (about poor management by boards of directors), editorial in *Business Week* (February 8, 1993): 134; and Judith H. Dobrzynsky, "Those board revolts prove the system works, right? Wrong," *Business Week* (February 15, 1993): 35.

28. Timothy L. O'Brien, "Banks were slow to see warning signs in Asia," *The New York Times on the Web*, Business Section (January 28, 1998).

29. "The bored board," *Wharton Magazine* (1976): 19.

30. "Wanted: A cure for board stiffness," *The Economist* (December 20, 1986): 13–126.

31. John A. Byrne with Richard A. Melcher, "The best and worst boards—our new report card on corporate governance," *Business Week* cover story (November 25, 1996).

32. Walter J. Salmon, "Crisis prevention: How to gear up your board," *Harvard Business Review* (January–February 1993): 68.

33. The report was published in 1992 and named for Sir Adrian Cadbury, who headed the Committee on Aspects of Corporate Governance.

34. "The quest for the best in governance practice," interview with David Kimbell, chairman of Spencer Stuart, in *Directors and Boards* (Fall 1995): 40.

35. Joanne S. Lublin, "Management: Give the board fewer perks, a panel urges," *Wall Street Journal* (June 19, 1995): B1.

36. Dana Wechsler Linden, "The cosseted director" (about generous salaries and benefits paid to corporate boards of directors), *Forbes* (May 22, 1995): 168.

37. "Survey: Stock replacing retirement plans," Reuters (October 3, 1996).

38. James W. Michaels, "Watchdogs rarely bark," *Forbes* (May 22, 1995): 16.

39. Suzanne Barlys, "Management tips from the teamsters," *Fortune* (April 15, 1996): 15.

40. John A. Byrne, "Listen up—The National Association of Corporate Directors' new guidelines won't tolerate inattentive, passive, uninformed board members," *Business Week* cover story (November 25, 1996).

41. "Group proposes changes for U.S. boardrooms," Reuters (November 12, 1996).

Chapter 8

A Realignment of Interests

LEGISLATION AND GOVERNANCE

The proper conduct of business requires a level of social order and rule enforcement that only the state can provide. Government has to ensure that the public believes in the integrity and legitimacy of business—in other words, it should guide the accountability process. It should do so with care, recognizing that too much corporate regulation can be self-defeating and that corporations exist to generate wealth. For the purposes of this study, the term "corporate governance" applies to quoted companies as well as to utilities and financial institutions, but not to the corner drugstore or the Mom and Pop haberdashery.[1]

It sometimes seems as though there is a never-ending stream of questions concerning corporate governance. Some have been repeated for years, while others are of more recent vintage. Among the more persistent are the following two: Does the quoted company belong to all its shareholders and only to them? Should the corporation be focused exclusively on maximizing shareholder returns? These questions address present-day questions about the complex, changing relations between the company and its environment.

Among the parties interested in the corporation are the short-term speculators who are interested only in immediate results and, if dissatisfied, sell their stock. By contrast, institutional investors and many others are vitally interested in the well-being and accountability of the corporation because they regard their equity as a long-term investment. And there are the stakeholders and the general public who care about what is going on and are interested in the company, even if they have no direct ownership in it. Scattered among these interested parties are those who recognize that corporations are subject to social demands. They know that today's business enterprises are expected not only to produce, serve, and make profits, but also—especially if the business is of significant size—to assume certain social obligations that, in the past, either did not exist or were met by individuals or communities. This school of thought maintains that corporations have a duty to help bring about a better society which, the argument runs, should ultimately also benefit the company by increasing its long-term profits.

These social demands have not been fully defined, however, and as a result companies may exaggerate their responsibilities, even though doing so impairs their primary effort—that is, to produce the best product they can, as efficiently as possible, and at the most advantageous price. Accordingly, expectations of corporate responsibility are tricky terrain, one in which both the general public and the government have more than a passing interest. One must remember that additional duties (or expectations) on the part of the corporate governance process may serve to diffuse accountability.[2]

In this complex society, government, through its laws and regulations, is a de facto partner in business decisions taken by the corporation. Hence, it must have a sound understanding of the impact of social legislation on business. Government should consider the price paid in terms of productivity, innovation, and capital formation when its regulatory demands reduce the rewards that otherwise would accrue to the corporation, its investors, and the nation.

In trying to find the optimal governance balance, government has toyed with a variety of policies over the years. One was to have federal rather than state government dispense corporate charters, in order to tighten the grip on corporate action. Another was making room on the board for constituent groups (employees, consumers, and minorities), as practiced in Germany and Sweden. There was also a proposal that boards be equipped with private staff that would report directly to the directors and would not be controlled by management. Legislators and regulators alike should be commended for having so far avoided the pitfalls that these ideas entailed.[3] Even without such interference, the flow of regulation has spread so wide that it is impeding economic creativity.

REDISTRIBUTING CORPORATE POWER

Today, there is no clear consensus on whose interests corporate governance serves. Is it the shareholders or, possibly, the stakeholders, who were not really recognized as factors in the past? If the latter, who are they? Who actually are the owners, individuals or the composite? Some consider the term "governance" a "discreet, academically correct way of referring to the struggle for corporate power and the uses to which it is put."[4] It surely is a process that was not planned but, rather, evolved to become what it is today. This process of evolution has produced a covenant that ensures that the public corporation will function within the social framework accepted by the nation, as it fulfills its obligation to create real wealth. More than ever, "the notion that corporations have responsibilities, just like real people, touches a deep chord," says Jonathan Rowe.[5]

Scholars debate whether corporations should serve the interests of their shareholders or their stakeholders. Contrarians argue that firms should maximize
shareholders' value, while communitarians maintain that there should be a balance of interests between shareholders and stakeholders.[6] Brookings Institute
economist Margaret Blair joins the latter to remind us that shareholders today
benefit from their limited liability, and they can sell their shares in the highly
liquid market if they are dissatisfied with the company's performance. It is
common knowledge that many modern shareholders lack sufficient information
about the firm in which they invest, have little incentive to monitor management
performance, are scattered and passive observers, and, she adds, are "in a poor
position to exercise all the responsibilities of ownership in large corporations"
(see note 6).

In contrast to the passive average shareholder, she says, the employees are a
human capital investment who generate wealth for the firm, who become specialized in the course of serving the company, and who thus are at risk in exactly
the same way as the (financial) stake held by the shareholders. These employees
possess inside knowledge of the business, may be more capable than those
distant shareholders of monitoring management, and probably contribute far
more to the company on an ongoing basis. They therefore, according to Blair,
have as much claim to being owners of the corporation as do shareholders.

To amplify her message: It is accepted that people become shareowners in
both tightly and widely held companies by contributing capital, financial or
other. In exchange, they receive a security that gives them the right to certain
distributions made by the firm and, usually, the right to elect directors.[7] In fact,
in long-existing companies, most are usually not the initial investors who created
real wealth but purchasers of stock that has already been traded many times on
the market.

On average, according to Morgan Stanley Capital International, turnover as
compared with market capitalization was 48 percent in 1996, a drop of 2 percent
from the 50 percent of 1995 and an average of 54 percent in the preceding
decade. In other words, the average shareholder holds onto a specific equity for
less than two years.[8] When someone buys, say, IBM shares, the dollars go not
to the company but to vendors who some time earlier bought the same papers
from previous owners of these shares. Although it is commonly accepted that
corporations exist to enrich their shareholders, many of the latter have no idea
of where their companies are located or what they produce.[9]

In the ordinary course of events, shareholders do not have a direct claim on
any of the assets owned by the company, either tangible or intangible, nor do
they have a say in the decisions taken by management. While they are unques-
tionably the owners of the shares, they are not the owners of the contents of
the company as represented by its assets. Indeed, in large companies, where the
number of shareholders can be many thousands and their turnover relatively
fast, they are invariably anonymous to the corporate managers. What is not often
realized in the corporate world, and is indicative of the distance between the

company and the shareholders, is the fact that in the years between 1987 and 1994, corporations bought back more equity than they issued.

Apart from voting in person or by proxy, usually only once a year at the annual general meeting, shareholders have no way of exercising any additional control over the company. They are, however, protected from losses by their limited liability and they are not held responsible for the debts or possible insolvency of the company. All these things considered, is this a healthy, acceptable relationship, or should it be reassessed?

An influential current thinker, Margaret Blair, suggests that corporate power can be reformed by offering more of it to the labor force, not least by putting employees' representatives on corporate boards (see note 4). Marjorie Kelly supports this position, saying that when a company is said to have done well, it sometimes means that employees are shouldering an outsized workload or are underpaid. She adds that it is rare that rising employee income is regarded as a measure of corporate success (see note 9).

Blair also asserts that a large company is not something that can be owned (see note 4). Rather, she says, companies are human communities, and the people who work there should have a say in their governance and, probably, a stake in the wealth they create. She goes on to spell out what she regards this multiple ownership to be, reminding us that corporations are not simply bundles of physical assets. She also recognizes that although shareholders make the equity investment that enables the mix of inputs that make up the company, there are other important contributors to the company's well-being, including suppliers, lenders, customers, and, especially, employees—all of whom make investments whose value depends on their ongoing relationship with the company. She points particularly to long-term employees, who are likely to have developed specialized skills or ''human capital'' of particular value to the company. And, in a somewhat different context, she refers to suppliers who build a plant to produce and meet the needs of the company. Such specialized investments, she says, are hard to quantify in financial terms, and they present a governance problem to which more attention should be devoted, not least because they cannot easily be measured or relocated or retained by other clients at a comparable return.

With these elements to be taken into account when considering the composition of a corporation, Blair proposes that wealth-creating activity arises from the joint use of the firm-specific physical capital provided by the shareholders and the human capital provided by the employees. She goes on to state that, without the human capital nurtured over the years, the physical capital will be of less value on the market, and that human capital is never owned by the shareholders. This, she suggests, is why not only the shareholders but all those who provide human capital must have their investment rights protected. Where employees are concerned, this end is usually accomplished through fair wages, a fair severance policy, an equitable pension plan, and adequate medical insurance. The protection sometimes also includes profit participation, and its various parts may be periodically renegotiated. In sum, according to her premise, unless their contribution is recognized and rewarded accordingly, working people will be discouraged from investing themselves in the companies that employ them.

Margaret Blair also proposes that employees receive restricted stock that cannot be sold immediately but must be held for some minimum period, such as five years, suggesting that granting such restricted stock to employees would align their interests with those of the shareholders. She predicts that the companies that survive and prosper in the next century will be those that best figure out how to encourage and nourish their human capital, developing a system whereby employees feel reassured that their investment in the company is both appreciated and properly rewarded.

Marjorie Kelly recommends pruning out "old" equity—that is, she believes that, at some point, share rights should expire (see note 9). It seems likely that in the coming years of advanced technological production, equity may have a smaller role than it has had. Instead, human capital may become a far more important and mobile segment of production than it was in the era of heavy industry, and it could well be that measures to recognize labor force interests will take the form of enhanced ownership rights for employees.

The theories of both Blair and Kelly are interesting and thought-provoking. Yet there is little evidence that the trend of events is moving in the direction they map out. In the past decade, as company profits rose gradually and the benefits of senior corporate officers rapidly accelerated, staff benefits increased but little, and yet there is little evidence that the workforce is unhappy with its economic conditions.

Earlier in the century, Britain (and other nations that adopted British corporate law) found it useful to offer redeemable shares as part of the capital structure. These were redeemed by the company under certain conditions or after given periods. Today, with the changing relationship between capital and human resources, the benefits of some similar form of redeemable shares might be studied by corporate structure theorists. Precise details of how and when they are redeemable would be spelled out clearly in the relevant company's prospectus.

THE REAL OWNERS

Until the stock market became such a powerful instrument in the trading of equity, it was common in many companies to differentiate between categories of shares, each with its own voting or dividend rights or other differentials. But when companies began to float their equity in the market, such differences were regarded as discriminatory. Over the years, most companies have converted their traded securities and consolidated them into one class of shares. Both legally and practically, that action brought a sensible conclusion to a class system that had become archaic.

Years ago, it was understood and accepted that corporate officers were basically agents who owed their allegiance to the shareholders and acted on their behalf. The number of shareholders in each company was usually not large, and the board was almost always composed of directors chosen by them, as was the CEO. Today, as the number of shareholders in larger companies has proliferated to many thousands, the individual shareholder's influence on running the company, choosing the management, and electing the board has all but disappeared. He has a minimal sense of ownership in the company. When dissatisfied with its operations, these investors' simplest option is to vote with their feet. It is easier to sell equity than spend many frustrating hours in an attempt to change corporate policy by expressing an opinion at the annual meeting or by attempting to influence the director they could have helped elect. In short, the distance between the shareholder and the company is often so great today that, in practice, the status of shareholders as owners is different from what it used to be.

Since the mid-1980s, institutional investors such as CalPERS have assumed the role of establishing relations with corporations on behalf of their shareholders. Although, as we shall see elsewhere, they have shown that they can have a positive influence on governance, it is too soon to assess how they will influence the market in the coming years. The following observation by John Saul about shareholder relations sums up the situation:

Not only do the large enterprises the managers run not have a close relationship with the shareholders, many of them have large parts of their shares owned by pension funds and their equivalents. These enormous funds are themselves administered by the same sort of managers. . . . This is a domain in which the levels of self-deception are both high and rewarded. The manager has taken on the cloak of capitalism. He lectures the government on risk and incentive, but also pays himself as if he were an owner.[10]

Despite the benefit of the simplification of the share structure, old doubts linger and new ones have arisen as to whether all shareholders should have rights proportionate to their holdings. Should long-term investors have preferred rights over speculators interested only in market changes? Many of the latter have no interest in the company as a viable economic entity; they invest in its equity only to gain and sell quickly.

The opportunity to influence management is key to the involvement of shareholders in a company. Such involvement normally occurs in one of two ways: (1) a material portion of the company is in the hands of a single individual, a family, or a group, and (2) an institutional investor such as CalPERS brings together a significant number of shareholders owning a significant percentage of the stock. In both instances, the involvement may result in significant influence on the owners, management, or boards.

INSTITUTIONAL INVESTORS AND GOVERNANCE

There have been many changes in the world of business since management was separated from ownership. When families owned companies and still had a major stake in their assets, and when the chairman of the board was the head of the family or his appointee, the powers bestowed on the CEO resembled those of today's chief operating officer. It was only with time, as the proportion of family equity declined and the number of shareholders increased, that the shareholders' say in the management of the company lost significance and the concept of the outsider CEO with authoritarian power developed.

In the decades preceding the legislation of the Securities Acts in the early 1930s, Congress paid little attention to the interests of small shareholders and worried little about what today are regarded as the basics of proper corporate governance. Even after these laws were enacted and regulators were content that the level of disclosure was satisfactory, they showed little concern about communication between the shareholders, the CEO, and the board of directors. In recent years, new rules have been introduced relating to how the board should function and how outside directors' independence might better be defined. Few people, however, seem worried by how common it is in public companies for the outside directors to be chosen by the CEO and thus be indebted to him, without any evident involvement or approval by the shareholders.

For most small shareholders, the diminutive nature of their holdings has ensured their distance from management. When a company has shown growth, most have been happy to let management, supported by the board, run it largely unchecked and function with minimum public scrutiny, apparently satisfied with upward changes in the price of stock. Some shareholders, however, dissatisfied by their anonymity, have attempted in recent years to organize themselves into a form of association that would give them a chance to wield power over management.

The CalPERS Model

Since the late 1960s, savings and pension funds have emerged as big investors, increasing and widely diversifying their equity holdings. This change came about when they realized that if they acted together, the individuals would no longer be treated as small fry. Collectively, they had power! The growth and higher profile of these institutions has changed many shareholders' behavior. Once, if the individual mini-shareholder was disappointed with the level of profitability or dividends, he had little choice but to sell his holdings. By contrast, modern institutional investors usually have a significant holding and cannot easily sell their shares and walk away. This situation prompts them to take a stand and try to improve what they regard to be corporate weaknesses. By the mid-1990s, institutional investors owned more than 60 percent of the total U.S. quoted equity market, and their share is expected to grow.[11] Pension funds account for half of these investments. Their share in the market, less than 1 percent in 1950, has passed 30 percent, and their growth has been phenomenal.[12] Not surprisingly, over the past couple of decades they have discovered their power and decided to seek ways to use it.

No matter how constructive the intentions of these institutions, however, they cannot—and they have not attempted to—replace the instruments of corporate governance. Limited in resources but pragmatic in their approach, they at first set themselves modest targets, such as advising companies that seem to be performing poorly to reconsider their operating strategies or protesting apparently exorbitant remuneration of senior officers.[13] As their confidence grew, they became impressively successful by conveying their demands for improved management directly to the boardroom. When they believed it could be helpful, they were not shy about applying media and other pressures in their campaigns for improved governance.

When CalPERS was established in the mid-1980s, few expected its influence to be felt in the market. But CalPERS has been on the cutting edge of corporate governance since 1984, when Jesse Unruh, then California state treasurer, discovered that Texaco had repurchased almost 10 percent of its own stock at a premium of $137 million from the Bass brothers. Texaco management appeared to have paid "greenmail" to avoid loss of their jobs in a takeover (see note 13). Unruh then helped establish the Council of Institutional Investors (CII) to coordinate the fight for corporate governance reform.

A decade later, in 1996, CalPERS had in its control some $100 billion in assets and served one million members. It made a mission of increasing the confidence of its members by simply holding poorly performing CEOs to account and by making it clear that shareholders had an inherent right to discuss corporate matters with the company's officers. Among other accomplishments, CalPERS is especially proud of the fact that:[14]

1. In 1989, following a CalPERS appeal to the SEC for proxy reform, the regulator issued Release Number 31,326, reducing the cost of target mailing to a corporation's 1,000 largest shareholders from $1 million to between $5,000 and $10,000.

2. CalPERS developed an annual list of targeted underperformers. It has been estimated that this corporate governance activism has increased the value of CalPERS holdings considerably.

In May 1994, CalPERS wrote to the largest 200 domestic equity holdings in its portfolio, requesting their boards to perform an analysis of corporate governance issues. It later wrote to an additional 100 companies. CalPERS then issued its famous "report card," which led many corporations to develop and implement corporate governance policy reforms to give shareholders greater voice.

Many board members and chief executive officers at some of the nation's leading corporations were ousted as a result of the CalPERS reform measures listed above. These measures and initiatives by CII and others may signal the end of the separation of ownership and control in public corporations.

The influence of CalPERS and its peers is somewhat curtailed by their means. In a 1996 study, it was noted that the level of institutional ownership and the size of the firm affected the probability of its being targeted by CalPERS.[15] Each year the CalPERS institutional investment committee identifies some dozen poor-performer targets. Often in coordination with other institutional activists, CalPERS calls for the shareholders of such companies to pass resolutions to set up shareholder advisory committees, to change the composition of the board of directors and its committees, and, not least, to restructure executive compensation. One measure of its success has been that in the five years ended in 1993, 72 percent of companies targeted either adopted the proposed governance restructure resolutions or made substantial changes in that direction.

The CalPERS Agenda

As part of its call for better governance, CalPERS has pushed for truly independent directors, for top executive compensation to be correlated with company performance, and for confidential voting in annual shareholders' meetings. In response, some have claimed that CalPERS can be arrogant, but these critics must be reminded of the corporate stonewalling that used to be encountered before companies agreed to hold simple meetings, and the unpleasant and abrasive conduct of company officers when they first met with CalPERS representatives.

It did not take much time for the market to learn how CalPERS and their peers can wield influence through media pressure, by abstaining or voting against management recommendations, and by filing shareholder proposals and resolutions.[16] These measures, especially in the case of negative or low-yield companies, have often been supported by extended press coverage which led, in turn, to public leverage. As corporate management comes to realize that CalPERS and others like it constitute a significant shareholder representation, they begin to treat such groups with great respect.[17] And wisely so, for when they release their list of corporate America's top ten underperformers, the stock market pricks its ears. A Wilshire Associates study of the "CalPERS effect" on corporate governance examined the performance of 53 companies targeted by the group over a five-year period. They found that, while the stock of these companies trailed the Standard & Poor Index by 75.2 percent in the five-year period before CalPERS acted, prices of the same stock exceeded the index by 54.4 percent in the following five years, adding approximately $150 million annually in returns.[18]

In 1986, another group, calling itself the United Shareholders' Association (or USA), organized to provide a conduit through which small shareholders could unite and attempt to influence the governance of large American corporations. Like CalPERS, this organization targeted the underperformers. Among the stated goals of USA were persuading the SEC to ease its rules to enable shareholders to communicate about corporate issues, which the SEC did in 1992. Other aims were to make government friendlier to shareholders' interests and to disseminate its shareholders' rights philosophy. Realizing that its message had been publicly recognized and that other organizations such as CalPERS had similar strategies, USA disbanded in 1993, claiming that in the last three years of its existence, its proposals had increased shareholders' wealth by some $1.3 billion—ample justification of its function.[19]

Although these groups have had successes, the scope of their activities and their resources are too limited to improve the shareholders' lot beyond addressing very obvious corporate shortcomings. They are not able to deal with more recent governance questions concerning, for example, the interests of corporate employees and the environment in which they operate. Even in the arena in which they choose to be active, these groups do not always provide an answer that will ensure substantial upgrading of the level of governance. CalPERS continues to function, however, as do other public pension fund groups throughout the United States. They are present in New York City, Colorado, and Florida, and they include trade union pension funds such as the Teamsters' and Carpenters' and the Investors' Rights Association of America, based in Great Neck, New York.

Agents, Not Principals

Rather ironically, the ever-increasing share of control of equity through institutional investors has, in effect, further reduced direct shareholder ties with America's corporations.[20] As previously mentioned, CalPERS and other institutional investors cannot replace or interfere with the instruments of corporate governance. Nor should they be regarded as shareholders; rather, they are only agents and representatives of shareholders. They have in part filled a vacuum caused by the communications cut-off between directors and shareholders and have offered to become intermediaries as the latter's counsel and representatives. Like the company's management earlier, they have far too little contact with shareholders and they add yet another station in the ever-lengthening distance between the shareholders and the corporation.

In some ways these groups fulfill a role reminiscent of that of the discretionary trust operators, common in Swiss banks and other overseas trust companies but also found in some financial institutions in the United States. Like them, the institutional investors look after the interests of investors. Accordingly, and as mentioned above, their aims are to introduce more sensible policies in management remuneration and to pressure low-performance companies into altering their strategies before crisis hits (see note 17). It would seem wise for students of governance trends to begin considering what the longer-term influence of the institutional investors will be, as they gradually become trustees of an even greater portion of America's corporate equity. One question is whether such a concentration of power will be in the best interests of small shareholders or be a threat to them. A related concern is whether there should be greater regulation of the institutional investor.[21]

INSTITUTIONAL INVESTORS AND PROFITS

In its present form, the attention given to corporate governance is a fairly recent phenomenon. Dating from the late 1970s and early 1980s, it was the result of various facets of dissatisfaction with the operations of companies, one of which was the impression that company officers had become too presumptuous and detached from their principals, showing minimal interest in the shareholders and being preoccupied with their personal well-being. Some shareholders recognized that, in the context of the widening gap between them and corporate management, company officers were becoming far too independent. They also perceived that directors were often close colleagues of senior management, with no real contacts or communications with the shareholders. Unhappy at how little a say they had, they decided to organize and, through institutional investor groups such as CalPERS, to demand a greater say and involvement in corporate matters. Once established, these groups made their presence known, not least by attending annual meetings where they asked questions and made suggestions.

But what has been the result of the efforts by these institutional investors? How effective have they been? Do they merely make themselves heard, or do they actually help improve corporate performance and, especially, contribute to higher profit? There is, in fact, anecdotal support of their claim that they have had an impact on governance. More attention is being focused on the remuneration of senior officers, although it is probably premature to say that CalPERS and similar groups have succeeded in putting a lid on the income of most of this group. Thanks to the institutional investors, there is awareness of the need for outside directors to be more vocal and conscious of their responsibilities. It is generally acknowledged that boards should be smaller, but it is unclear whether this opinion is a result of institutional pressures. And there is a noticeable trend to split the posts of CEO and chairman of the board, although it is far from clear that this would actually be beneficial to the company or its shareholders.

There appears no proof, however, that institutional investors have been effective in helping improve the bottom line and bring about greater profits. According to an article in *The Economist*, institutional activism has no appreciable effect on firm performance.[22] Indeed, the article contends that shareholder activism is little more than window dressing—a public relations ploy rather than a genuine attempt to improve the performance of the firms in which the institutional investors have staked their money. It is clear that institutional investors have more influence on board performance than on company performance; their impact on corporate operations is, at best, only marginal. Perhaps this situation is a reflection of the limited degree of influence the board has on the operations of the company.

THE STAKEHOLDERS

Not least because the corporation and its shareholders are part of society and responsible to it, the subject of corporate governance can be best approached by agreeing on two preliminary hypotheses. First, in complementing a true market economy, it is essential that there be a built-in mechanism of ethics, honesty, and good sense to provide efficient corporate governance. Second, rather than introduce more laws and ordinances, it is probably better to improve governance through education and persuasion of the various actors involved, including the stakeholder.

Despite some critical observations made by the courts and regulatory authorities, corporate management and boards of directors have, in general, recognized or at least paid lip service to their responsibility as agents of the shareholders, with the stakeholders playing a distinctly lesser role. Managerial and board loyalty has been directed more toward shareholders than any other constituency.[23] The leverage of stakeholders in the company, however, is still in an early stage of development. Stakeholders, who have a significant interest in the well-being of the company, include long-term employees, major suppliers, large clients, and sometimes financial institutions. Until recently, little attention has been paid to their role or influence on corporate governance in the United States.

The full range of bodies to which they have a fiduciary duty is not always clear to senior corporate officers. Most continue to maintain that it is to the shareholders, but there are those who assert that they should also serve the interests of the stakeholders. Possibly because the issue was first seriously discussed only in the late 1980s, there continue to be different opinions on this matter. Whether called the "stakeholder," the "stakeholder model," "stakeholder management," or the "stakeholder theory," these ideas are still in the process of being molded.[24]

Essentially, the stakeholder theory establishes the framework for examining the connections between stakeholder management and the achievement of various corporate performance goals. It is assumed that stakeholders are persons (or groups) with legitimate interests in corporate activities, and they are identified by their interest in the corporation, whether or not the corporation has any corresponding interest in them. It is also assumed that the interests of each group of stakeholders merits consideration for its own sake, not merely because of its ability to further the interests of some other group, including the shareholders (see note 24).

Kenneth Goodpaster cautions that a multifiduciary stakeholder approach overlooks the important point that the relationship between management and shareholders is ethically different in kind from the relationship between management and other parties. He agrees that the company's officers have many nonfiduciary duties to various stakeholders, but he insists that they have fiduciary duties to the shareholders alone.[25] Regardless of their fiduciary responsibilities, it is probably not yet fully appreciated that stakeholders—be they employees, suppliers, lenders, or environmentalists—often have a greater influence over corporate results and management than shareholders, especially in a large company where the latter are widely dispersed.

The basic interest of the shareholders is to maximize the net worth of their shares and to receive dividends. Most show little concern about what is happening to the stakeholders. The latter, by contrast, often react to the actions of shareholders, other stakeholders, and the general public, but they have less formal influence over the management of the company. Each party, be they stakeholders, employees, creditors, or environmentalists, observes the corporation from its own vantage point, from which they may wish to acquire certain specific information.

When the shareholders consider the company's state of affairs unsatisfactory, they can react either by making an exit or by voicing their sentiments. In either case, they can press management to take corrective steps. But even before the corporate officers can make a move, the individual stakeholder can transfer material information to others, who might also decide to take action to mend what they see as the shortcomings of management.

Banks and other financial institutions and lenders are among the more important stakeholders. In Britain and even more in the European Union, banking institutions have been a dominant presence on boards of directors and an influential factor in corporate governance for generations. In the United States, they play a more modest role. They maintain a lower profile on the board but have considerable influence over management, especially when the company faces liquidity problems and has to arrange new lines of credit. In these circumstances, the financial institutions prefer to intervene before the firm's condition becomes irreparable. In doing so, they not only look after their own interests but try to help the company survive and ensure that the value of the shareholders' equity is not completely lost.

This complex relationship and interdependence between the corporation, the shareowners, and the stakeholders will no doubt be addressed in the coming years, and there will probably be changes in corporate mores and company laws.

NOTES

1. Harold Williams, "Power and accountability—The changing role of the corporate board of directors," *Corporate Accountability and Corporate Power* (The 1979 Benjamin F. Fairless Memorial Lectures): 28–30.

2. Edward J. Waitzer, chairman of Ontario Securities Commission, in opening remarks to Senate Standing Committee on Banking, Trade and Commerce study of corporate governance (February 22, 1996): CNW, http://www/newswire.ca/releases/February 1996/22/c3262.html.

3. Irving S. Shapiro, "Corporate governance," *Power and Accountability* (The 1979 Benjamin F. Fairless Memorial Lectures).

4. Margaret M. Blair, *Ownership and Control: Rethinking Corporate Governance*

for the Twenty-first Century (Washington, D.C.: The Brookings Institute, 1995). Review by M. E. Sharpe published in *Challenge* (January–February 1996): 62–64.

5. Jonathan Rowe, "Reinventing the corporation," *The Washington Review* (April 1996): 16.

6. Margaret M. Blair, "Ownership and control," anonymous book review, *Harvard Law Review* (March 1996): 1150–1155.

7. Margaret M. Blair, "Corporate ownership," *Brookings Review* (Winter 1995).

8. "Equity trading stock market turnover," *The Economist* (March 15, 1997): 119 (attributing data to Morgan Stanley Capital International).

9. Marjorie Kelly, "Why all the fuss about stockholders?" Co-founder and editor of *Business Ethics*, a newsletter about socially responsible business ethics: http://www.corpgov.net/kellly.html#top.

10. John Ralston Saul, "The unconscious civilization," *Anansi* (1995): 125 (quoted by Edward J. Waitzer, see note 2).

11. "Flow of funds accounts, financial assets and liabilities 1966–88," Federal Reserve Board and *Wall Street Journal* (November 13, 1992): C1.

12. Berret-Koehler Publishers, "Ending the Wall Street Walk: Why corporate governance now?" *At Work*: AtworkNews@aol.com.

13. Joel Chernoff, "UK funds target proxies," *Pensions & Investments* (March 4, 1996): 3.

14. "A conversation with Richard Kopps, retiring CalPERS general counsel," *Corporate Governance Interviews*: http://www/wp.com/CORPGOV/cginterviews.html.

15. Michael P. Smith, "Shareholders activism by institutional investors. Evidence from CalPERS," *Journal of Finance* (March 1996): 227–252.

16. These have been increasing rapidly (265 at the end of 1994, over 400 early in 1996) and are concerned mainly with directors' compensation issues. Vineeta Anand, "Corporate governance shareholders proposals on the rise," *Pensions and Investments* (February 5, 1996): 8. Also, Myron Magnet, "What activist investors want," *Fortune* (March 8, 1993): 59–61; and Judith H. Dobrzynski, "A ground swell builds for 'none of the above': Angry investors' new tactic: Abstaining in corporate board elections," *Business Week* (May 11, 1992): 34–35.

17. Judith H. Dobrzynski, "Small companies, big problems, but CalPERS funds shareholders can still be ignored," *New York Times* (February 6, 1996).

18. "CalPERS announces Top Ten Target Companies," *Bankruptcy News* (February 6, 1996): http://bankrupt.com/news.960206.html#1.

19. Deon Strickland, Kenneth W. Wiles, and Marc Jenner, "A requiem for the USA— Is small shareholder monitoring effective?" *Journal of Financial Economics* (February 1996): 318–338.

20. Jay W. Lorsch, "Real ownership is impossible," *Harvard Business Review* (November 1991): 139.

21. Ada Demb and Brenda Richey, "Defining responsible ownership: Cross-national perspectives," *European Management Journal* (Summer 1994): 287–297.

22. "Awakening the dead," *The Economist* (August 10, 1996): 52.

23. George G. Triantis and Ronald J. Daniels, "The role of debt in interactive corporate governance," *California Law Review* (July 1995): 1073.

24. Thomas Donaldson, School of Business Administration, Georgetown University, and Lee E. Preston, College of Business and Management, University of Maryland, "The

stakeholder theory of the corporation: Concepts, evidence, implications'': http://www/
bmgt/umd/edu/Ciber/wp37.html.

25. John R. Boatright, ''Fiduciary duties and the shareholder-management relation:
Or, what's so special about shareholders?'' (including the quotation by Kenneth Goodpaster), *Business Ethics Quarterly* (October 1994): 393–407.

Chapter 9

The Chief Executive

THE TENURE OF CEOS

Since the mid-1980s, the tenure in office of the average CEO has decreased from roughly 10 years to 5.5 years and it is continuing to drop, says Thomas Kuczmarski, a Chicago consultant.[1] Often in their fifties, CEOs are aware that their current position may well be their last prior to retirement. This accelerated turnover is explained in part by the increased pressure on senior management to produce results quickly. "Executives have to make their numbers each quarter, and the implication is that we continue to focus too much on the short term" he added. There are a number of other reasons why CEOs are spending less time in office, including the greater influence of two different groups on corporate governance: Boards of directors and shareholders. Boards of directors, more than in the past, become impatient with subpar executive performance, are sensitive to negative publicity, and are aware of the possibility of shareholder lawsuits. Shareholders, particularly in large institutions, have become much more demanding of management.

Increased awareness of executive responsibility is emphasized by Kai Lindholst, managing partner in the recruiting firm of Egon Zehnder in Chicago:

With markets and technology changing so rapidly, a company can be irreparably damaged by a CEO who can't realize its full potential. . . . Increased turnover is a result of a revolution in the boardroom. A whole new set of objectives is being used to evaluate CEOs. Boards are now looking for a more participative style of management in extraordinary communicators who can evince trust.

Addressing the qualities needed in the CEO, Hank Conn, vice president at A. T. Kearney, a large management consulting firm, suggests: "You can't tell people what to do anymore. You have to motivate them. Companies are looking for people that have the soft skills to manage and technological skills and leadership traits. They're looking for much more complete people."[2]

Do corporate results really improve when CEO tenure is shorter? Attempts to answer this question have had mixed results. As mentioned elsewhere in this study, companies are not really operated as democratic institutions. Although the heyday of the giants—chiefs such as Harold Geneen of ITT and Lee Iacocca of Chrysler—may be a thing of the past, many present-day CEOs are powerful personalities. Their power is derived from a number of sources, ranging from success in generating revenues to maintaining excellent contacts with power brokers. In large corporations, the CEO can be very much a political person, working closely with the media. The CEO has enough instruments to make his or her rule authoritarian, functioning in a climate that fosters little active opposition. Although boards have become more active, they seldom assume the role of lively opposition, and, unless out to replace him, they support the CEO.

Nevertheless, there is public restlessness about corporate governance and the role of senior management. The voluminous literature on the subject seems not to have explained what truly high quality is or how it can be achieved. Some writers on corporate business have turned to the English language for help, hoping that new words and expressions will enable them to better focus on their aims. The new language includes such terms as reengineering, empowerment, outsourcing, downsizing, increasingly stringent corporate governance, globalization, and fast-paced technological innovation.[3] Have these terms contributed to governance in general, or to clearer strategies on the part of CEOs in particular? They may have enriched the language, but their contribution to better corporate understanding is questionable.

Others believe that the role of the CEO would improve if they were provided with a job description by which they would be measured annually. That was one recommendation made by the National Association of Corporate Directors in July 1994.[4] According to the NACD, this instrument would strengthen boards' control over chief executives and speed their reaction to management failures, but it would also provide CEOs with more security by sketching a clear picture of the yardsticks they would be measured against. A thorough job description would help set performance objectives and establish qualitative measures such as integrity, vision, leadership, and succession planning. In short, it would apply to senior officers rules similar to those applied to ordinary staff. It is of interest to note that there was no vocal opposition to this proposal.

As Harvard business professor Thomas Teal observes, the management role of the CEO is a "supremely human activity." And he adds that one reason for the scarcity of managerial greatness is that in educating and training managers, too much attention is focused on technical proficiency and far too little on the development of character.[5] And he observes that although it has become one of the more common jobs in business, the demands made of CEOs are often im-

possible to meet. Indeed, there is plenty of evidence that CEOs encounter pressures from many directions and that, regardless of the support they receive from
the board, their job (especially when pressures mount) can be very lonely. Maintaining a good sense of balance is an individual ability.

What boards usually are looking for is best enunciated by so-called ''head
hunters'' who search for new CEOs. A group such as Spencer Stuart expects a
viable candidate to have the following qualities:

- a balance of strategic vision and operating experience,
- leadership and team-building capabilities,
- good judgment, balanced by prudent risk-taking,
- financial acumen,
- international (global) experience,
- external focus,
- credibility,
- good communication skills,
- values,
- ability to deal with change, and
- technological knowledge.

Although it is clearly impossible to find a CEO possessing all these qualities
in perfect proportion, all are important attributes.

It is not common to have active supervision by the board, so it is not surprising that many CEOs find their role solitary and stressful. Because they are
somewhat remote and isolated, it is difficult to know when a CEO reaches the
peak of his or her abilities and performance. To strengthen their public image,
many CEOs take it upon themselves to talk periodically with financial analysts,
not just because the latter might help boost the price of the company stock, but
because they know the CEO's business and that of the competition.[6] CEOs find
these exchanges more rewarding than dialogue with their shareholders.

Some CEOs become blinded by their power and affected by dreams of gran-
deur in their isolated environment. The symptoms of such an ''attitude syndrome'' are all too familiar in the corporate world. An executive:

- develops an all-consuming passion for the company airplane,
- feels the urge to redecorate the corner office,
- is chauffeured to work in a stretched limousine,
- joins every organization that is exclusive and expensive,
- talks far more than listens, and
- packs the board with personal friends.[7]

The directors can reduce the likelihood that the CEO will succumb to such a syndrome by doing periodic evaluations of his or her performance, and increasing numbers of companies have adopted this practice. Said Kenneth Macke, CEO of Dayton Hudson: "I don't think this is just in the interest of good governance. As CEO, I want to know where I stand. I can't envision not having a review. Some things in the review I'm not going to like. But what a marvelous opportunity to have that out on the table instead of festering underneath."[8]

THE CEO AND THE BOARD

The opinions of directors about their chief executives range from the total satisfaction of those involved with a successful blue-chip entity whose management is a friendly team headed by a charismatic chief to the skepticism of those who regard their CEO as a high-flying risk-taker supported by a board of yes-people. Most CEOs, in fact, do their best for the company even under adverse conditions; it is rare that one mismanages or wastes the company's resources deliberately.[9] But some resent the notion of corporate governance on the grounds that it interferes with what they do and shackles their entrepreneurial spirit. They do not want to be bothered, but just to be left to do their job.

Some CEOs have begun to complain that criticism of their operations has gone too far. "We've been made out to be freewheeling jetsetters—playboys reliving our adolescent years. Like teenagers, we supposedly resent being told what to do, so we ensure our boards of directors are populated by our buddies or by compliant grandfatherly types," says L. Dennis Kozlowsky.[10] He points out how galling it is for an achiever who has made it to the top to be accused of seeking weak counselors and directors. He maintains that, for example, he wants a strong, competent board. For him, effective governance equates with accountability, which is what he would like his board to provide. In his company, senior management is held to account by the board and the shareholders.

It is common enough to read what various people think of the CEO. Similarly, shareholders, financial analysts, the general public, company management and staff, and, lastly, board members themselves are all ready to air their opinions about the effectiveness of the board, each from his respective viewpoint. Somewhat oddly, it is less common for CEOs to say what they think of their boards and individual directors. At a CEO forum held in Annapolis in July 1995, Albert J. Dunlap, chairman of Scott Paper Co., stated that in many cases directors "are there for the check." Not all attending agreed, and they moved on to the next subject on their agenda.[11]

A brief description of what CEOs think about their directors was published in *Business Week* in 1993.[12] "The tough standards outside directors are demanding for chief executives may cut both ways. A study of 124 large public companies . . . reveals that nearly 40% of the CEOs regard their outside directors as only 'somewhat effective' or 'worse.' " The article also notes that "while most CEOs believe that corporate performance would benefit from more formal reviews by outside directors, some two-thirds of them, for fear of confrontation, would prefer to avoid such encounters.'' It is as if they prefer not to upset an unpleasant standoff they can live with.

Harold Geneen, shortly before he died in the fall of 1997, wrote that ''all too frequently the directors are too subservient to the CEO. Perhaps without realizing it, they lose their impartiality. And even if they don't, how alert will they be when things start going wrong?''[13]

Sometimes, as a result of weak board leadership or because its members are long-winded and underinformed, CEOs feel that there is confusion as to what their board considers to be its governance responsibilities. In other instances there is a lack of clarity as to what the board should concentrate on: Governing or providing advice. Also, there are CEOs who feel that their board does not give them any input on how the company's resources should be used.[14]

The approach of directors to difficult decisions, such as the removal of the CEO, is far from uniform. Most boards are slower and more cautious in their deliberations than hindsight would deem advisable. Even in this age of board activism, there invariably is a certain reluctance to make the decision to dismiss a CEO. Among other factors is the personal contact: Often directors have a long-term social relationship with the CEO, which makes such an assignment even more unpleasant.

Also, these directors—often hand-picked allies of the CEO—worry about the fairness of it all; they are wary of dislodging their chief too soon, especially when there is no obvious internal successor. Uncertain about the possible ensuing shakeup and turbulence that might be caused by inviting an outsider to take over, they agonize over the decision. Board members understandably worry that if they pick the wrong candidate, they will be held accountable for the outcome.[15]

Obviously, there is no such thing as CEO consensus on the performance of directors. Kozlowsky quotes Dennis Carey: ''Few directors serve mainly for money. More typically, they see board service as a way to enhance power, build relationships, and deal with significant issues.''[16] Others assume the contrary: that directors join boards for the honor and economic reward, with little interest in or understanding of the needs of the company. Board members, especially theoreticians and business school academics, do not seem to understand the current corporate criticism of the board. They are confident that the board's performance can be improved with only a slight fine-tuning of procedures.[17] Whatever the case, there is a general sense of increasing tension between the board and the CEO.

Is empowerment ''sweeping corporate boardrooms,'' as Harvard Business School professor Jay Lorsch believes?[18] As he explains it, empowerment means that outside directors have the capability and independence to monitor the performance of top management and to influence it, to change the strategic direction of the company if its performance does not meet the board's expectations, and, when necessary, to change corporate leadership. Lorsch emphasizes that CEOs traditionally regard a powerful, active board as a nuisance, at best, and a force that could improperly interfere in the management of the company, at worst.

No wonder many CEOs view board empowerment with trepidation. But is empowerment truly such a novel idea? Is it not just the manifestation of all the things said in literature in the past 50 years on how the director is expected to perform? Most CEOs do not join this debate, probably because they are too busy managing the firm and are not interested in theorizing and pontificating on the level of the board's contribution, the improvement of which is to them almost hypothetical and of doubtful value.

THE CHAIRMAN AND THE CEO

As we have noted, society expects proper corporate governance but is vague about the price it will pay for it. A free, democratic system would surely favor governance that does not slow down or limit company growth. There are, however, some concepts of government that curb development as well as others that do not necessarily encourage it. Clearly, a concomitant of the call for quality governance is the premise that accountable officers make better executives.

As noted previously, one often-repeated suggestion to improve corporate governance is separation of the office of chief executive officer from that of chairman of the board. The latter, so the theory goes, should be an outside director. "The CEO should not be chairman of the board," said Harold M. Williams when he was chairman of the SEC in the 1970s, because "control of the agenda and pace of the meeting is a powerful control (instrument)." Similarly, Jay Lorsch believes that splitting the functions is "the single most significant thing to do."[19] Indeed, the call to separate the roles was first voiced almost a generation ago. It was reiterated with much conviction by the Cadbury Commission's report, published in Britain in 1992, which strongly recommended improving the balance between board and CEO by assigning the position of the chairman to an outside director. The expected result would be an effective board of directors, under the leadership of an independent chairman, and a capable CEO leading executive management.[20]

But there are those who, although supporting the idea of separation, question whether board chairmanship is a role to be carried out part-time by an outside director. They advocate a full-time chairman, especially in corporations that are large, global, or very diversified. The CEO operates in a world of hard facts and measurables, and usually he does not have time to address such subjective matters as attitudes and perceptions. These advocates encourage the chairman of the board to take responsibility for such conceptual management. For a CEO, having "to contend with tenuous concepts like vision is too much like a public confession" comments New Yorker John Budd.[21]

The logic of this line of thinking is that the nonexecutive chairman would not run the company but, rather, limit himself to managing proper board business. Such an arrangement would ensure more open board proceedings and free discussion, better governance, and improved CEO accountability. But little attention has been given to the qualifications or background of this chairman. Today, the majority of chairmen are ex-CEOs. The experience of recent years shows that the post of CEO is often a temporary assignment lasting only two to three years, after which the incumbent becomes the chairman of the board.[22] In considering this consolidated approach, however, one must keep in mind the original criticism that companies in which the same person discharges both functions perform relatively worse. The proponents of splitting the job pointed, among other things, to the drop in profits or actual losses at the end of the 1980s and early in the 1990s of such major corporations as Westinghouse, Sears, GM, American Express, and IBM. In all of these companies, the same person had filled both roles. They cited Roger Smith, when he was both chairman and CEO of GM, as restricting board oversight and hindering the adoption of strategies appropriate to the changing environment and times, and John Akers, in his dual status at IBM, as responsible for the board's slowness in reaching a critical evaluation and exercising independent judgment of management performance. In contrast to the above-mentioned companies, Compaq Computer kept the two positions distinct. Under the leadership of its nonexecutive chairman Ben Rosen, the board was able to make appropriate strategic responses to a changing competitive environment. Such cases as these gave thrust to shareholder activism to apportion the two responsibilities to different individuals.

Advocates of duality continue to argue that it ensures clearer leadership within the company, in both formulating and implementing strategy. Many CEOs are dissatisfied with this movement and jealous of their prerogatives. They assert that separation of functions would have the following harmful effects:

1. dilute their power to furnish effective leadership,
2. increase the probability of confrontations between management and the board,
3. increase the likelihood of competitive pressures and rivalry between the chairman and the CEO,
4. create confusion in board proceedings and in company policies if the CEO was not fully supported by the chairman, and
5. curb innovation and initiative, if the CEO felt that the board, under the chairman's guidance, had undertaken the role of unfriendly back seat driver.

Those in favor of separating the two roles maintain that when they are combined, it is difficult to keep decision management apart from decision control and awkward for insecure directors to criticize the CEO—in other words, that it limits the independence of the board and curbs its efficacy.

Despite the strong views expressed by supporters of both alternatives, the authors of the study found no proof that the above cases presented more than isolated incidents. Certainly, looking at the *Fortune* 500, one sees little evidence of the role being split; most companies keep the positions of CEO and chairman combined. There are several possible explanations for a lack of change:

1. the traditional influence of management on the board,
2. the reluctance of the board to exercise its governance responsibilities in what appears to them as an inefficient move,
3. board acceptance of the argument that the CEO can fulfill both roles satisfactorily, and that combining the roles is the better organizational structure, and
4. the existence of sufficient control systems to mitigate any abuse of the position(s) when the board is dedicated and wide awake.

The authors found little evidence that separation of the roles improves short-term or long-term performance.[23] Furthermore, they noted that despite the involvement of shareholder activists, both the stock market and analysts regard such matters with indifference. It is reasonable to surmise that, in the long term, success in either approach will depend on the quality of those directors and corporate officers involved and the chemistry between them. Much will also depend on the quality of the CEO's managerial style and the board's culture and capabilities (see note 19).

Some attempt by directors to separate the roles might be seen as scapegoating or as a demonstration by the board that it is exercising its governance role. In the long term, such gambits are regarded as opportunistic and, therefore—if we may risk an observation into the future—the trend will be for the separation movement to dissipate gradually.

SELECTING THE BEST

It is the primary job of the board to replace the chief executive officer with his successor when that is necessary. A wise, open-minded board often identifies a brilliant candidate; it is rare that a mediocre board does better than choose a mediocre CEO. As many directors serve longer than most CEOs, they participate at least once in such a selection. It is often noted that the choice of the next CEO is probably the single most important decision the average director makes, but most come to the board with little or no training for this responsibility. Few boards have members with sufficiently strong judgment and interpersonal skills to choose an outstanding leader. The process of selecting a CEO challenges the board to be a cohesive, efficient unit, with outstanding powers of judgment.[24] Because these qualities are so rare, it is no wonder that boards usually make the safe, rather than the inspired, choice.

Then it usually takes a long time for the board to realize that the new CEO is turning out to be unimpressive. Some boards never discover it. Most mature industries, utilities, banks, or, for that matter, large service groups such as the Big Five accounting firms operate in a staid, uneventful environment. If they succeed in keeping out of trouble and stick to what they know, their CEOs will complete their term of office, perhaps with little glory but also untainted by crisis, debacle, or embarrassment. In a role resembling that of dependable duty officers, they try to prevent upsets, and at best they help improve the position of their company moderately. Soon after they retire, their influence dissipates and they are forgotten. Of course, this is not the scenario in all companies. In rapid-growth companies or those operating in a volatile climate, the challenges CEOs face are much greater, and they have more opportunity to prove their worth. Quite often in such corporations, the quality of the directors is also more impressive and the risks of office are correspondingly greater.

Boards should prepare themselves for the inevitable task of replacing the CEO. One recommended step is to conduct formal annual CEO evaluations, involving all outside directors.[25] If done diligently and in depth, the results will not only highlight the current CEO's strengths and weaknesses but also give the board invaluable information that will guide them when they begin a search for his replacement. Beyond this basic preparation, there are a number of do's and don't's that every board should consider when it comes to selecting the next CEO:

1. Define the needed skills and experience and prioritize them. It is almost impossible to find a candidate with all the desired qualities.
2. Look as far afield as necessary to find candidates with imagination, character, and a gleam in the eye, rather than settling for the solid, duller candidate close to home.
3. Do not be misled by show and bravura. Ask searching questions and seek the clarity of thought so imperative in an emergency.
4. Conclude the search only when the finalists have been subjected to a full due diligence review—a necessary step to avoid most irreversible mistakes.

In other words, the board should see itself as a search committee and prepare a plan of action. Thomas Horton advises the following steps:

1. Prepare a mission statement.
2. Define performance criteria: What will be expected of the new CEO? How will the board assess the success of its choice?
3. Scrutinize the board itself to see whether it includes a suitable person with knowledge of the company.
4. Establish accountability. It will be more effective if not more than three outside directors act as the actual search committee. Their short list should be brought to the full board for consideration and decision.
5. Call for help when time limitations or lack of contacts prevent the board from finding the right candidate. Any outside executive search firm should be given a clear statement of its mission.
6. Be flexible—for example, some excellent potential can be found among younger,

not yet fully tested, executives. Older candidates are often solid and dependable but have a chip on their shoulder or carry baggage that could be an impediment to excellence.

7. Vet any serious candidate carefully. (Horton urges the board not to be impatient when it believes it has found the right candidate. The members should make every effort to understand his or her thought processes and value system, using tests if necessary.)

8. Make sure the candidate understands the company.

9. Make sure there is good chemistry and compatibility between the chosen candidate and the board.

10. And, after all the above is done, intuition can prove to be crucial.

The above are a set of general guidelines; obviously, each board will have its priorities. The board members must remember how crucial their choice will be to the company's future and invest all their talents accordingly.

CEO COMPENSATION IN PERSPECTIVE

It is a matter of public record that the income of many publicly owned companies' CEOs increased annually by one-third in the early 1990s, while that of their corporate staff rose by an average of only 3 percent. In 1996, total compensation for the CEOs of financial companies alone more than doubled, with their median pay package rising from $1.15 million to $2.62 million, according to KPMG.[26] In a report published early in September 1997, the IRS stated that increases in the pay of top corporate executives outpaced corporate revenues and profits significantly between 1980 and 1995. During this period, executive pay (excluding stock options and other deferred compensation plans, which are believed to have grown even more rapidly) increased by 182 percent while taxable corporate income increased by only 127 percent.[27] Even when company income per share declines, CEO remuneration rarely does. Indeed, companies that show hefty losses often continue to provide their corporate chiefs with hefty wages.[28] And even in today's environment of increasing demand for corporate governance and accountability, CEOs continue to compensate themselves at unprecedented levels, with little consideration of the other corporate constituents, observes Robert Monks.[29]

These comparative rewards suggest that CEOs continue to control the one aspect of corporate governance of greatest personal interest to them. But more than that, they highlight a number of other factors to which not enough attention has been given:

1. The ever-increasing distance between shareholder and CEO. The latter usually has no doubts about his worth or the desire of the shareholders to compensate him more.

2. The apparent disregard the CEO has for the company's labor force, who unlike him, have been increasing their annual take-home pay in insignificant amounts.

3. The apparent disappearance of standards, which permits the mushrooming of CEO income without any examination of rewards in the context of social and moral values.

Indeed, little has been published in the world of corporate finance to indicate that anyone is agonizing over the ethical aspects of these ever-increasing rewards. Irving Kristol characterizes the unprecedented size of CEO compensation as mind-boggling.[30] Average compensation in 1996 was $2.3 million, which was an increase of 39 percent over 1995 compensation, which was 30 percent greater than in the previous year. Adding retirement benefits, incentive plans, and gains from stock options, CEOs' average total compensation rose an astounding 54 percent, to close to $5.8 million in 1996.[31] No less striking was the lack of sensitivity of the chief to his staff. The CEO earned an average of 209 times as much as the average factory worker, who garnered a 3 percent raise in 1996. The CEO of a large U.S. corporation earned four times as much as his Japanese counterpart.[32] For many companies, the chief's rewards make news more often than anything else reported about it.

Are such incomes excessive? Do they have any intrinsic relationship to the market? Whatever the answer to these questions, neither Congress nor the regulators can do anything to limit what a CEO earns, because such interference would be an unacceptable intrusion into the market, no matter how conspicuous the salaries are. Any controversy concerning CEO rewards should, of course, be resolved in the corporate boardroom. Ideally, the directors should form a committee composed of truly independent members who have no direct or indirect business ties with the company or personal commitments to the CEO. Even if the CEO is uncomfortable with the decision, this committee should consider retaining outside consultants to advise them on market pay conditions for senior officers. But the record shows that such independent-minded directors and committees are few and far between.

Some will contend that, for the CEO pay system to work perfectly and be related to the market, executive pay should rise whenever the boss delivers the goods to the shareholders but decline when corporate performance shows losses.[33] Also, the CEO's rewards should correspond fairly to the remuneration of the rest of the company staff. Unfortunately, this neat theoretical equation does not work in real life. In most companies, there is no correlation between operating results and the compensation of the chief executive officer. One reason for this situation is the somewhat muddled thinking about the position of the CEO. Until the views of the shareholders and the board on the position of the CEO are clarified, it will be difficult to explain logically how the company head should be rewarded. Is the CEO a glorified employee, or should the chiefs be encouraged to think and act like partners with the shareholders? If the answer is the former, their remuneration should be partially linked to results, whereas if they are considered partners and risk-takers, their rewards should be pegged to the company's profits. Jerre Stead, who in August 1996 became CEO of Ingram Micro Inc., is one of the few who chose the latter track.[34] But few CEOs regard themselves as risk-takers, and many of them will argue that it is not in the interest of the shareholders that they be such.

Even where CEOs are remunerated with stock options, they are often offered flexible terms in the form of repricing the options to reduce the level of their risk. *USA Today* cited Grand Casinos Inc., where the price of the stock dropped close to 75 percent in the nine months following May 1995; the board then reduced the share price of the options of CEO Lyle Berman from $312 to $11. The paper added that Apple Computer repriced options for its top executives eight times in twelve years (through 1996) when its stock prices dropped. Not surprisingly, a study carried out by Virginia Tech and Boston University found that companies that repriced options generally performed poorly against their competitors.[35]

In an attempt to explain the especially high rewards, Irving Kristol shows considerable admiration for the CEO, whom he compares to a baseball team manager. Unlike the latter, who has to negotiate with the team's owners for his compensation, however, the CEO in most large companies in effect negotiates mainly with himself. The corporate chief usually sees little use in consulting the board; in most cases, he is aware that the directors are dependent on him in dealing with important issues and he doubts that there is any separation of powers in corporate leadership.

On the same subject, Robert Monks advises us not to be taken in by what he calls the fiction of independent compensation committees. Do not believe, says he, that they have a real say in how much the senior officer is compensated.[36] It is, at best, difficult for anyone to be independent in the boardroom, where the CEO controls the information and the agenda—and even, to a great extent, the appointment of directors.

Monks further makes the point that many companies are setting aside as much as 10 percent of their stock for options and outright grants for senior officers (three times more than two decades ago). He shows how the equity of the owners and shareholders is being diluted to an unprecedented extent—as is their ability, despite the publicity given institutional investors, to send messages through a shareholder vote. This situation is the result of the CEO's continued power to create the rules and determine the score, with the full acquiescence of his board.

The SEC is concerned with senior officers' remuneration as an aspect of corporate governance. Although the commissioners have not offered any opinion on the size of the rewards, they issued regulations late in 1992 that enable shareholders to be informed as to how the compensation committee of the board reaches its compensation decisions. Harvard professor Joseph Hinsey IV expressed concern about these instructions, suggesting that they could, *inter alia*, intensify (directors') liability exposure (see note 28). Commenting on CEO rewards in general, SEC chairman Arthur Levitt, Jr., cautions that in some instances performance-based pay can encourage managers to assume excessive risks or to pursue short-term strategies that are really not in the best interests of the company or the investors. He goes on to recommend that such pay be tailored to measure long-term effectiveness and take into account both good and poor performance.[37] So far there is no real evidence that companies have taken this advice.

Ralph Ward, who has written at length about corporate governance, observes that high pay combined with staff layoffs looks awful to the general public. He advises that the use of common sense could be helpful in determining these pay packages. Board compensation committees should be sensitive to how their CEO pay plans look in the light of day, and they should be particularly sure that executive performance pay does not reward downsizing as an end in itself.[38] And *The Economist*, tongue in cheek, offers management theorists the following paradox: "Any boss who cannot outmaneuver a system designed to keep him under control is probably not worth having."[39]

Possibly having less respect for its work, Irving Kristol refers to the way the compensation committee performs. Striving to give itself a semblance of responsibility, it usually follows guidelines already established in the business community. Among other things, it must catch up with those companies that have found ways to increase their CEOs' earnings—to avoid losing their own CEO.[40] Kristol believes in enabling the market to determine the rewards of the CEO without interference. He worries, however, that Congress and the regulators might try to regulate these rewards. To offset such a possibility, he suggests that executives be required to hold on to their stock for, say, five years after the options have been exercised and the stock acquired.

A suggestion made by Maura Belliveau and two colleagues, in attempting to explain how pressure to increase CEO rewards can be reduced, is to hand the compensation decision to the upper classes. She alludes to the snobbery so prevalent in the boardroom—a quality she describes as "social capital." According to the results of her study, a lower-class CEO paired with an upper-class compensation committee chairman makes about 20 percent less than an upper-class chief executive paired with a lower-class compensation committee chairman.[41] Thus, she says, social status, unrelated to grit, energy, or the size of the paycheck, remains "incredibly important in the corporate world." If this theory is valid, it could be important to shareholders. They might consider appointing a compensation committee chairman with a higher social status as "better equipped than others to resist CEO influence—a good way to foster accountability."[42]

Appropriate CEO pay has been high on the agenda of corporate governance for years, but little has happened since the *Harvard Business Review* for May–June 1992 asked, "Who should set CEO pay? The press? Congress? Shareholders?" The next issue of the magazine contained a series of angry reactions.[43] There is a public undercurrent of suspicion that CEO rewards are reaching heights which even our materialistic society regards as an ethical problem, and there are signs that these rewards are about to peak. As *Newsweek* recently wrote, "Walt Disney Co. chairman Michael Eisner . . . seems to have been trying out for the role of the little-known eighth dwarf, Greedy."[44] There are other

CEOs like him, and people are asking where it will end. There have been some efforts by institutional investors to reform executive pay, but in sum they have not been effective.

The current assumption seems to be that it is a seller's market, with the CEOs holding most of the cards (see note 31). Much will depend on how the public in general, and the business world in particular, are educated and what their ethical standards are. Concerned about the future, Harvard professor Derek Bok believes that "unless something is done to encourage the growth of stable, long-term investors, giving more power to shareholder-directors and subjecting compensation packages to shareholder approval may only make these problems worse."[45] Irving Kristol is probably right when he calls on the market to determine the size of CEO compensation, but it appears that those in charge should be better versed in the ethical and moral implications.

NOTES

1. Lorri Grube, "CEOs at risk," *Chief Executive* (November 1995): 42.

2. Judith H. Dobrzynski, "In America, soaring demand for executives is good news and bad news: High turnover alarms analysts," *New York Times*, quoted in the *International Herald Tribune* (February 27, 1997).

3. Thomas J. Neff, "Top 12 traits of today's CEO," *Chief Executive* (November 1995): 38.

4. Joann S. Lublin, "Management: How to keep directors' eyes on the CEO," *Wall Street Journal* (July 20, 1994): B1.

5. Thomas Teal, "The human side of management," *Harvard Business Review* (November–December 1996): 35–42.

6. Quote from "Investor capitalism," by Michael Useem, noted in a conversation with Richard Kopps, departing general counsel of CalPERS: http://www/wp.com/CORP-GOV/cginterviews.html.

7. Robert W. Lear, "Attitude adjustment,"*Chief Executive* (November 1995): 14.

8. "CEO evaluation at Dayton Hudson," Harvard Business School Case Study, 9–491–116 (Rev. 10–15/91).

9. "Corporate governance—Watching the boss," a survey of corporate governance, in *The Economist* (January 29, 1994): 3.

10. L. Dennis Kozlowsky, "The vitals of accountability," *Directors and Boards* (Fall 1995): 9. (Tyco International Ltd. is a manufacturer of disposable medical products, packaging materials, flow products, and electronic components, and the world's largest manufacturer and installer of fire protection systems.)

11. Peter Behr, "CEOs debate directors' usefulness," *Washington Post* (July 14, 1995): B1.

12. "What CEOs think about their boards," *Business Week* (November 1, 1993): 43.

13. Harold Geneen, "Baloney: Everything you know is wrong. Well, almost everything," *Across the Board* (September 1997): 25.

14. "In brief, Performance Audit Report, Corporate Governance": http://www.audit.nsw.gov.au/CrpGI-97/inbrief.htm.

15. Joann S. Lublin and Christina Duff, "Management: How do you fire a CEO? Very, very slowly," *Wall Street Journal* (January 20, 1995): B1.

16. Dennis Carey, co-managing director of Spencer Stuart's board practice.

17. Roger M. Kenny, "The changing culture of boards," *Directors and Boards* (Fall 1995): 13.

18. Jay W. Lorsch, "Empowering the board," *Harvard Business Review* (January–February 1995): 107–117.

19. Judith H. Dobrzynski, "Chairman and CEO: One hat too many," *Business Week* (November 18, 1991): 124.

20. Hugh Parker, "The chairman/CEO separation: View one," *Directors and Boards* (Spring 1994): 42–45.

21. John F. Budd, "The chairman/CEO separation: View two," *Directors and Boards* (Spring 1994): 43–46.

22. Ira T. Kay and Diane Lerner, "Paying the separate chairman," *Directors and Boards* (Spring 1994): 47–50.

23. B. Ram Baliga, R. Charles Moyer, and Ramesh S. Rao, "CEO duality and firm performance: What's the fuss?" *Strategic Management Journal* (January 1996): 441–453.

24. Thomas R. Horton, "Selecting the best for the top," *The American Management Review* (January 1996): 20.

25. Walter J. Salmon, "Crisis prevention: How to gear up your board," *Harvard Business Review* (January–February 1993): 68–75.

26. "CEO compensation packages more than double," Reuters (September 10, 1997).

27. "IRS: Executive pay outpaces corporate profits," Reuters (September 3, 1997).

28. Joseph Hinsey IV, "The SEC fix on executive pay: Improved disclosure or intrusion?" *Business Review* (January–February 1993): 77.

29. "The American corporation at the end of the twentieth century," an outline of ownership-based governance in note 27 of speech given by Robert A. G. Monks at Cambridge University (July 1996): http://www.lens-inc.com/info/cambridge.html.

30. Irving Kristol, "What is the CEO worth?" *Wall Street Journal* (June 17, 1996).

31. Jennifer Reingold, "Executive pay—Tying pay to performance is a great idea. But stock-option deals have compensation out of control," *Business Week* cover story (April 21, 1997).

32. "Stopping runaway CEO pay," editorial in *Business Week* (March 30, 1992): 100.

33. John A. Byrne, "Executive pay: The party ain't over yet," *Business Week* (April 26, 1993): 56.

34. Judith H. Dobrzynski, "CEO works for free!" *New York Times/Herald Tribune* (October 5, 1996).

35. "As some stock prices sag, CEOs win, public loses," editorial in *USA Today* (April 29, 1997): 12A.

36. Robert A. G. Monks, "Stock options don't work. If CEOs want shares, let 'em buy some," *Fortune* (September 18, 1995): 230.

37. "Shareholder interests as the director's touchstone," remarks by SEC chairman Arthur Levitt, Jr., at the Directors' College, Stanford, Calif. (March 23, 1995): http://www.sec.gov/news/speeches/ch032.txt.

38. Ralph D. Ward, editor of *The Corporate Board, The Journal of Corporate Governance*, and author of *The 21st Century Corporate Board* (published by John Wiley & Sons), quoted in *News, Corporate Governance Items*: http://www.wp.com/CORPGOV/egitems.html.

39. "Unintended consequences," *The Economist* (August 16, 1997): 55–56.

40. There is little evidence, if any, that anyone has seriously tested the premise that not keeping up with these exorbitant rewards means losing the chief or senior executives. Is there really more demand than supply for CEOs? Surely there are more talented people ready and eager to serve as CEO than companies in search of a chief executive.

41. "You know it makes sense," *The Economist* (March 1, 1997): 79. See also note 42.

42. Jay Mathews, " 'Social Capital' pays off for CEOs," *International Herald Tribune* (January 16, 1997). From the Washington Post Service. Quoting a study co-authored by Maura Belliveau, Charles Reilly III and James Wade published in the December–January issue of the *Academy of Management Journal*.

43. Andrew R. Brownstein and Morris J. Panner, "Who should set CEO pay? The press? Congress? Shareholders?" *Harvard Business Review* (May–June 1992). Also, "CEO pay: How much is enough?" *Harvard Business Review* (July–August 1992).

44. Allan Sloan, "How much is too much—Huge checks make even good CEOs look bad," *Newsweek* (March 17, 1997).

45. Derek Bok, *The Cost of Talent: How Executives and Professionals Are Paid and How It Affects America* (New York: The Free Press, 1993), 116.

Chapter 10

Will Boards Change?

FAMILIES AND DYNASTIES IN CORPORATE AMERICA

Corporate America is ambivalent about its business dynasties. It admires the Rockefellers, the Fords, the Mellons, and the Kelloggs. At the same time, it revels in tattle about gossip-ridden families such as the Hafts of Dart, the Basses, and, in the mid-1990s, the Archer Daniels Midland Co., where almost half the board was composed of Dwayne O. Andreas' family. There is little mention of nepotism in business literature, but there is an ongoing whisper campaign about what an unhealthy situation it is for governance. The lack of open criticism is rather odd, considering the ethical standards cultivated in most Americans from an early age. In companies with revenues below $500 million—the world of private companies—family control is preponderant.[1] This is not to deny that many successful, family-dominated businesses have impressive growth records and contribute to the GNP and to the benefit of their outsider minority investors. A case could be made that it was the entrepreneurs who, with time, grew to head dynasties and lead corporations that made American capitalism the success it is.

The successful family business embodies an unusual mixture of business interests and incentives.[2] No less significant, this form of ownership provides greater stability for its "permanent shareholders." Many a successful initiative by a tough and imaginative entrepreneur continues to develop and thrive under the capable guidance of sons or daughters, often into the third generation. It is rare, however, for a successful business to remain in the family for much longer than that.

Is large size necessarily incompatible with family ownership? The saga of the Cargill family's company, employing more than 70,000 people and with annual sales of over $50 billion, suggests otherwise. Another well-publicized exception is the Rothschild cousins, who operate out of London and Paris. They are into the fifth generation since Nathan Meyer Rothschild left his father's business in Frankfurt late in the eighteenth century. But few families have the good fortune to pass the torch so gracefully and for so long from one generation to the next.[3] (Even the extraordinarily successful run of the Rothschilds may be coming to an end, for in the coming century it will probably no longer be a Rothschild who heads the firm.) The Rothschild family is unique in other ways. It belongs to an exclusive group of capitalists who managed to keep their holdings in a private company and provide minimal financial disclosure. But they are also a very clear example that, without any regulating authority but with talent, integrity, and high ethical standards, businesses can do exceedingly well, not only for themselves but for society in general.

Family firms have advantages. They can avoid the conflict of interest that often arises when management is separated from ownership. They can reinvest more freely in the long-term growth of the company. Families, more than professional management or faraway shareholders, have a greater loyalty to the company as an institution worth preserving, rather than regarding it as a transient instrument of profit maximization (see note 2). The weakness of family leadership is that it does not always know when to step down. Some outstay their capabilities, as did the family owners of Barings Bank. Without knowing it, they lost their business acumen and, with the Leeson roguery in Singapore, their wealth. But when no close relative is willing and able to take over, most families—for example, the Rockefellers and the Fords—bring outsiders into the top management positions.

In addressing the question of continuity, some suggest that each case should be dealt with individually, on its merits. Family firms are often portrayed as little more than the first stage of corporate evolution. It is assumed that the successful corporation will eventually grow beyond the ability of the family to manage and finance it and that gradually it will turn to professional managers and approach the public to raise the additional capital needed for growth.

Some companies prohibit family members from taking any senior position when a relative already works there. For example, Brown Brothers Harriman of New York, a financial institution, bars partners' children. The common argument is that there are plenty of talented people outside the company who should be encouraged to join, compete, and climb the rungs of the business, and that the children of top executives should prove their worth objectively in an independent environment rather than under the tutelage of their protective elders. This is a sound argument, but one cannot help wonder whether some talent is not wasted in this quest for equal opportunity.

When scrutinizing a business, the general public and shareholders usually do not attach special significance to the fact that it is family-run; rather, they judge by results. It is only in rare cases, such as when a regulator opens an inquiry into a company's operations, that there is public interest in the extent to which family patronage might affect governance or management. In October 1995, for example, when questions arose concerning the corporate governance procedures of Archer Daniels Midland Co., CEO Dwayne Andreas asked a group of outside directors to review the company's performance. In January 1996 they recommended that the number of company executives sitting on the board be reduced and a smaller, more independent board be installed, with the lead director having nearly as much power as the chairman. They also suggested developing a plan for choosing successors to top management.[4]

ANNUAL MEETINGS: AN ANACHRONISM?

Most states have laws concerning the kind of corporate information that must be given to shareholders, as well as what should be presented at the annual meeting. This information is fairly limited and does not provide the small shareholder with much opportunity to influence the conduct of the company's affairs. The only operative contact point of shareholders and management is the annual meeting. Apart from that event, there is no official way for shareholders to communicate with management. Clearly, except for holding the annual meeting and providing financial reports, the company's officers and directors have no obligation to communicate with the shareholders. But shareholders do have a limited number of rights, summarized here by the SEC[5] and including the right in most states to:

1. vote on questions that affect the company as a whole,
2. hold a proportionate ownership in the assets of the company,
3. transfer ownership of shares,
4. receive dividends when they are declared by the board of directors,
5. inspect the corporate books and records,
6. sue the corporation for wrongful acts, and
7. share in the proceeds of a corporate liquidation.

In connection with the first item on this list, the annual meeting as originally conceived was thought of as an experience in democracy, resembling the form of direct democracy that exists in some cantons of central and eastern Switzerland. There, once a year, the townspeople who have the vote gather in the open for *Landsgemeinde*, a custom dating back to 1378 that enables them to elect their *Landammann*, or top official, and deal with whatever else is on the agenda. In fact, however, there is a lack of ongoing communication between the shareholder and the large corporation. Although this situation has been the cause of increasing dissatisfaction, little has been done to make contacts more effective. Today, the individual shareholder who prefers not to be served by an institutional investor has, in effect, no say in the company's operation or management even at the annual meeting.

Many shareholders, however, have chosen to participate in the most publicized development of the past decade: They have joined institutional investors,
such as CalPERS. These investing organizations have experienced such extraordinary growth that they have become the largest single shareholder in many
companies, and they have had some success in influencing corporate governance. Because they study the company carefully and do their homework, they
have been able to produce achievements at annual meetings, compelling managers to examine publicly their business strategy, review performance, and quantify the value they are creating for investors.[6]

When companies took the legal form they have today, it was clearly established that the shareholder would have an opportunity to express himself or
herself at the annual meeting. There, management would present the past year's
financial statements, directors would be elected to the board, and shareholders
could ask their questions. In practice, however, the annual meeting has become
the most anachronistic instrument of corporate governance. In its present form
it is of little use to either shareholders or management. Reminiscent of a nine-
teenth-century town meeting, it no longer can be regarded as a practical instrument in the modern business world. As John Wilcox suggested, "Annual
meetings have become little more than a costly, time-consuming, embarrassing
anachronism, useless to both corporations and shareholders" (see note 6). As
an alternative, he proposed the Japanese model of efficiency—meetings that can
be telescoped into as little as twelve minutes. Although annual meetings remain
a symbolic safeguard of constituent rights, in practice—to quote a 1994 editorial
co-authored by former SEC commissioner Philip Lochner and Richard Kopps,
at the time general counsel of CalPERS—the meeting has become an "empty
ritual" and (possibly exaggerating somewhat) a "monumental waste of time
and energy," indeed a magnet for disorder and inefficiency (see note 6).

The 1992 proxy rule amendments, enabling the SEC to encourage greater
flexibility in the proxy process, contributed significantly to the strength of institutional investors. Their influence today is a result not only of their size but
of the fact that they devised a strategy and invested a considerable amount of
time in meetings and public relations gambits designed to influence companies.
Their activism is a year-round affair, not just for annual meetings.

In view of the foregoing, should the structure of annual meetings be modified
and, if so, how? John Wilcox has a number of very different suggestions:

1. a "get-tough" model, which would basically reduce the activity to a minimum,

2. a "love-fest" model, which would be a publicity happening with the aim of ever-
   better public relations and goodwill,

3. a model with high-tech features and add-ons, which would be somewhat more intellectual than the love-fest and, probably, more businesslike, and

4. an analyst meeting model, which would encourage the sophisticated, in-depth pres-

entation of business strategy attuned to the demands of institutional investors, security analysts, and other financial professionals.

If the latter approach were properly institutionalized in the code of governance and if the meetings actually took place for the benefit of the shareholders each quarter, more meaningful relations between management and shareholders might be achieved. Another essential provision, however, should be added to enable individual shareholders to contact the company directly, on a year-round basis. Management, of course, might feel uncomfortable with such a possibility. To avoid resistance by management, there should be written guidelines for the dialogue allowed in such exchanges.

WHY CEOS JOIN OTHER BOARDS

Many shareholders and stakeholders believe that CEOs should invest all their working day in the company and they are suspicious if they discover that the company chief has time to spare from the company he heads. The company principals may argue that if their CEO is a board member of another company, he is wasting time that should rightfully be invested in the company that employs him. They may resent his absence from what they believe to be his full-time occupation—running their company.

Still, many CEOs do join other boards, recognizing the fact that this responsibility will demand as much as two full days, or at least twelve hours per month. They do not believe that they are neglecting their corporate responsibility; on the contrary, almost all are confident that they take their main assignment seriously and devote all the time necessary to help ensure their company's well-being. But, for what purpose do they join another board? There are two main reasons why they do so: recognition and collegiality. Being invited to join a board, especially that of a prestige company, is an honor that CEOs are rarely able to resist. Indeed, being human, they enjoy it. In the second instance, CEOs are often invited to join the board by a personal acquaintance, and they regard the invitation as an act of friendship.

There are, of course, more practical reasons for CEOs to accept invitations to join other boards. According to a study by James Booth and Daniel Deli, company chiefs believe that such participation will bring the following benefits:[7]

1. It enables them to assess how policies, programs, and practices similar to their own are carried out in other companies and, thus, to build standards of comparison.

2. It exposes them to innovation by enabling them to learn how new ideas are adopted and activated by other companies.

3. It broadens their insight, giving them valuable information on macroeconomic and other market issues.

4. It exposes them to different management styles by revealing how other CEOs operate.

5. It serves as a source of counsel, for although at times the board is regarded as a clubby retreat, it is, in most cases, a forum in which CEOs can compare notes, exchange advice, and gain moral support.

Booth and Deli showed that the number of outside directorships held by CEOs is influenced by the nature of their firms. Where the contribution of the CEO is relatively high and the firm's value is made up of growth opportunities, it is less common for him or her to hold an outside directorship, for in such growth companies it is particularly costly for the CEO to be away. Where a CEO has held the position for longer, or where the post of board chairman is separate from that of CEO, the frequency with which he holds one or more outside directorships is greater. In other words, the number of outside directorships held by CEOs is linked to the value of the time they devote to their companies.

Whereas CEOs are quite specific in considering the main benefits of joining other companies' boards, they seldom consider the possibility that the other companies will run into difficulties and that such an event will test their sense of fiduciary responsibility and force them to make difficult decisions. CEOs may be powerful, determined, and courageous leaders on their home turf, where they know precisely what their responsibilities are, but they are often reticent and less inquisitive as directors. Clearly, a CEO would refuse to join an outside board if he knew that it faced troubles and uncertainty. After all, why would he be willing to risk the goodwill he has built up over the years to join in a confrontation where he does not have a dominant voice?

There is, in fact, evidence that CEOs have realized that real threats to their well-being exist outside, and they may be becoming less enthusiastic about joining other boards. The 1993 annual Korn Ferry study of 348 corporate boards showed that 65 percent of all CEOs surveyed, as well as 76 percent of CEOs at companies with more than $1 billion in revenues, declined invitations to join other boards. In 1988, according to the report, only one quarter of CEOs had turned down board invitations.[8]

It should be mentioned that the benefits arising from a CEO sitting on another company's board travel a two-way street. In larger companies, having other CEOs on the board provides added prestige and varied experience. In smaller firms, the outside CEOs are often invited to the board for their specific talent and knowledge.[9]

But what happens when a CEO is ousted from his or her job? The clear pattern is that these individuals are in danger of being removed from the boards on which they serve as outside directors. Until, say, the end of the 1980s, companies seemed to believe that dethroned executives could still contribute much—sometimes even more than when they were engrossed by their office. But by 1995, with directors increasingly becoming targets of shareholder criticism, close to one-third of companies insisted that board members resign when they left their senior post. This philosophy seems to be that "CEOs who fail in running their own companies should not be on other boards. If you can't run your own company, why should you be on another company's board?"[10]

THE DIRECTOR IN THE AGE OF HIGH TECHNOLOGY

Directors should, of course, be intelligent, knowledgeable, and experienced in the ways of the business world, and they should have a reputation for high ethics. But are these qualities enough to serve modern high-tech companies in a competitive growth market in which many or most of the company's assets are intangibles and income is derived from services rather than products? If not, directors must find ways to adapt to modern needs. As mass production operations have evolved into far leaner and more specialized production systems, industry has entered an age in which such factors as the spread and diversification of technology, global economics, the demand for speed, and more sophisticated customers are forcing companies to compete to survive in a fast, often sharply focused arena.[11]

Intellectual Capital

High-tech companies are frequently alone in their market. Often the first-generation result of an ingenious innovation, they face little immediate competition. But unlike the monopolies of the past that were often perceived to be fat, lazy, and ugly, they are still in their mean and lean period and keenly aware of the need to remain ahead of the field. Because these companies operate in what may soon become a very competitive market, they must be able to move quickly. Such pressure sometimes requires decision making in a short time frame that most boards of directors cannot deal with.[12]

In this context, quantifying intellectual capital is not yet a common criterion. Indeed, many involved in corporate governance are unaware of the need to address these resources in modern business, and they do not know how to evaluate their contribution to economic growth. It is still rare for management and directors to appreciate the intellectual capital available in the company, let alone to know how to measure it or take it into consideration when making decisions. Yet, intellectual capital has become a major, if intangible, corporate asset. The business aspects of intellectual capital require special attention and knowledge not only from senior management but also from directors. It is, however, increasingly apparent that there are few people sufficiently well versed in the intricacies of high-tech to perform properly as directors of such companies.

There are a number of basic differences between intangible intellectual capital and tangible fixed assets. A fixed asset usually has a market price, influenced by its expected productive lifespan, the existence of replacements, and the extent of competition. Its value is affected by the size and length of time it or its product is expected to go on being in demand. The value—and, therefore, the market price—of intellectual capital is far more difficult to determine. Often, the know-how it represents has no previous sales record, nor is there any form of measurement to help establish its price. Intellectual capital cannot be compared to material products or conventional services. When attempts are made to set a price on it, usually it is found to be unique, in contrast to tangible assets such as cars, sweaters, and real estate. Its value is in the profits it will generate in the future, but there are few data on which to base estimates and projections of future benefits. Understandably, generally accepted accounting principles, one of the basic tenets of which is the existence of a market and hence comparability, have been unable to provide guidelines to help decide the worth of intellectual capital.

Turning ideas into innovations and then into revenue-producing business to "make knowledge productive," as professor Peter Drucker wrote some decades ago, is one of the great adventures of our age. How do directors of high-tech companies address themselves to the challenges offered in this field and the need to understand the new language of innovation? High-tech companies, of course, operate in a world of unknowns and challenges. Entrepreneurs thrive on it when founding companies, but once they establish boards with outside directors and go public, they must adjust their innovative policies to the discipline expected from public companies. They and the board must be aware that their shareholders will hold them accountable for their strategic growth plans and their operating results. Although the corporate officers are almost invariably knowledgeable about the company's operations, can the same be said of the directors?

Guidelines for treating intellectual capital are still in their early stages. Some corporations—especially large ones—have arrived at temporary technical solutions. For example, companies such as Dow Chemical Co., with a portfolio of over 30,000 patents, have instituted an "intellectual asset management" unit. Dow has developed a methodology for classifying, assessing, and investing in such assets. Some medium-sized companies do the same, if somewhat less formally. Both these groups can describe their intellectual assets to the shareholders and the general public in fairly simple language, somewhat as other companies describe their tangible assets. But it is not practical for small start-up companies, still in their development stages and early marketing period, to treat their untested innovative achievements as commodities available for trading on the market. Choosing the best time to make the initial stock offering requires market expertise. Certainly, not least among the requirements is finding qualified candidates to sit on the board; individuals, willing to be accountable, who are capable of addressing the specific governance needs of a young high-tech company.[13]

Only when the company's founders have been able to evaluate the intellectual capital available to them, and have made a reasonable estimate of their potential client market and what they can produce, can they make credible projections for the venture's growth. Even more important, they must assess the pace of innovation and what their company will have to do to keep pace with the state of the art before they can draw up a realistic business plan. It is rare to find an outside director conversant enough with such specialized matters and the changing pace of the related technology to be able to participate and advise on policymaking or to evaluate the intangible asset in the crucible.

Missing Qualifications?

"High-tech" is a broad category embracing a rapidly increasing number of products. Growing daily in volume, variety, and share of the gross national product, this business segment has certain characteristics of its own that will, in coming years, have even greater influence on the nation's economy than they do today. Unlike the more conventional sectors of the economy, in which directors can be expected to know their roles as participants in proper corporate governance, some time will pass before there will be an assortment of high-tech company directors sufficiently well instructed to fulfill their roles.

In its spring 1997 issue, *The Economist* provided an admiring, in-depth survey of Silicon Valley, concluding that the region's "ability to create wealth depends on its single-mindedness and leanness." But nowhere did the article consider the contribution of the different boards of directors.[14] The wisdom of keeping expectations for directors in high-tech companies relatively low and of giving them only a modest role in governance applies also to other operations in which change is rapid and information specialized. The world of derivatives provides an example. Although directors could at some stage have asked questions about the operating results of Barings and what made the trading in Singapore so profitable, it would not have been realistic to expect these individuals to be knowledgeable about this often off-balance-sheet expertise.

Although it is generally urged that, for the purposes of governance, directors should be knowledgeable about their brief, there are companies that succeed without such a presence. For example, in 1996, AT&T, the global telecommunications giant, had no independent board member with experience in high technology.[15] Somewhat similarly, Coca-Cola was not bothered by the fact that on its thirteen-person board there was no outside director who had any experience in consumer marketing. Such examples do not necessarily indicate a diminished role for the director, but they do suggest certain limits on his ability to contribute.

CORPORATE GOVERNANCE IN REAL TIME

It is still probably too soon to attempt a definitive description of the impact of the Internet, cellular phones, the personal computer, and other forms of instant communication on day-to-day business. Gone are the days when weeks or months passed before the public learned of a meeting of heads of government, a decisive military battle, or a new sports record. Today, events are reported in real time. It is difficult to envisage how George Washington or Thomas Jefferson would have performed and how the America of then would have been governed under the scrutinizing lens of television.

Certainly, television now has a major influence on public opinion. It even supports or opposes the way governments wage military campaigns or conduct themselves in crisis situations—for example, in the Los Angeles Rodney King affair. Television news is also having an influence on the corporate world. When the concept of full disclosure was introduced with the birth of the SEC over 60 years ago, nobody anticipated that communications, as we witness them today, were going to have an impact that might be described as "instant" or "full real-time disclosure." Richard Nathan says that in the future, major public companies will conduct an ongoing dialogue with their shareholders.[16] In these exchanges, directors and senior management will review and participate in public discussions on major issues facing the company.

Some of the effects of recent communications developments can already be discerned. In the first post–World War II generation, for instance, it was almost unheard of for shareholders to attempt to make contact with the company outside the annual meeting. This situation changed in the 1980s with the decision of the mutual and pension funds to assert themselves, informing management and directors alike that henceforth they expected their voices to be heard. Possibly CalPERS is the best known of the institutions established at that time to represent the small shareholder. These institutions called for a dialogue with the corporate heads and, where they believed performance was substandard, put pressure on management for new strategy or other changes. Many of the companies began to respond by arranging meetings for their representatives with senior management. To explain what they had in mind, others developed the practice of holding press conferences to provide additional information and to state points of view. For their part, the institutional investors made conference and direct calls to tens—sometimes hundreds—of analysts and investors to describe what they expected in the realm of "information liquidity," and there is anecdotal evidence that the timeliness of corporate disclosure provided to the marketplace has improved significantly. Today, more than ever before, investor relations are a high priority for many publicly traded companies. Moreover, new techniques are being developed to further improve these lines of communications.

Richard Nathan suggests that, as information liquidity increases, shareholders will become more powerful. In their planning and behavior, companies will be pressured to consider shareholder interests and expectations. As an example, he cites the almost instantaneous moves made when a takeover bid is announced. Those responsible for the decision are fully aware of the chain reaction that will follow the announcement, and they prepare for the event accordingly. The market will move more quickly because more shareholders have better information sooner. It follows that information liquidity may be expected to continue to increase. Shareholders may soon express individual and collective opinions on a growing number of corporate decisions closer to when they take place and expect management to respond. Nathan assumes that the competitive nature of the market for corporate information will drive companies to provide better and more interactive communications with their shareholders.

From the companies' viewpoint, there will be a significantly wider choice in managing the delivery of all kinds of corporate news. Company officers and directors will be able to measure the support of their shareholders more frequently and accurately. Nathan ventures to guess that directors will be able to assess shareholder preferences and draw operative conclusions somewhat in the way politicians currently react to opinion polls. He emphasizes "real-time" relations between the company and the shareholders. Although obviously shareholders will be even closer to the sources of information, how this will affect relations with the stakeholders, including suppliers, bankers, and employees, is not as predictable.

Last but not least, thanks to PCs and laptops, directors will be asking the CEO to allow them to communicate directly with the company's managers, be they in manufacturing, in accounting, or in other corporate divisions. Such directors will have the opportunity to gather information directly from its sources within the company without bothering the corporate officers. It is still premature to predict how all concerned will adjust to these new lines of communication.

If officers and directors do not properly consider the impact of these modern means of communication, shareholders, stakeholders, and analysts may well become noisy kibitzers and back-seat drivers. One thing is certain: The era of glass-house decision making and management will have far-reaching effects on the relations between owners and management. Like that of society as a whole, we may anticipate a stimulating, challenging future for the corporate world.

ADVISORY BOARDS

As discussed at some length, many directors are chosen to serve on boards because they are believed to have some expertise and knowledge that can support senior management in the conduct of the company's business. Some boards of directors, aware that they cannot individually master all the data they need to fulfill their mission, have begun to use consultants—both individuals and groups—to provide advice upon request. The perception that such services are important has grown in recent years, creating a new corporate structure, the advisory board.

In the beginning, the advisory board was not a fully thought-out concept. The initial suggestion was that boards should retain consulting staff of their own, independent from the company, but this idea was resisted by many corporate executives. The alternative proposal of advisory boards set up on an ad hoc basis to provide essential but otherwise unavailable resources seemed less threatening. It was thought that they would perform until they were no longer required or, alternatively, that the contributions of their members would be significant enough for them to be invited to join the staff of the company.

Who first thought of establishing such a body? Was it some insecure board member or was it a business school pundit? In any case, advisory boards have become something of a fad. They are expected to give the main board additional corporate intelligence and to assist both it and management in making decisions.[17] Advisory boards are of various types and sizes. Small companies, with limited human and financial resources, find advisory boards an excellent source of expertise for strengthening both their boards and management. Larger corporations, less formal and more flexible in their structure, prefer to include individual specialists, advisors, and consultants on the board itself.

There are newer reasons why the role of this advisory structure may grow. With increased awareness that conflicts of interest can exist between board members' fiduciary responsibilities to shareholders and the consulting needs of management, it could be that future boards will be formally split: Consultants will serve management on the advisory board, and fiduciarily responsible directors will be the only truly independent board directors. Such advisory groups could become an important factor in corporate governance.

A no less intriguing question is: What will be the format of the board of directors of tomorrow? The author suggests that it be composed of fewer members—say, three to five. Their sole responsibility will be to act as agents and fiduciaries of the shareholders. Spending anywhere from one-third to half their time on the company's affairs, they will be fully conversant with its business. To ensure their independence, they would be appointed and remunerated by an organization financed by all quoted companies and others in which the public has an interest. As mentioned in the introduction to this book, this organization, in consultation with the individual company's management, would appoint the directors on a staggered basis for, say, a five-year renewable period. Although they should have an open line of communication with the company staff, their activities will have to be kept clearly distinct from those of the executive staff. The internal audit unit should report to them and be their main information resource.

NOTES

1. Richard Narva, "Corporate governance in family-controlled businesses" (Genus Resources, Inc.): http://www.corpgov.ne:80/family.html.

2. "In praise of the family firm," *The Economist* (March 9, 1996): 16.

3. George Graham, "The Rothschilds and the decline of relative values," *Sunday Times* (July 13, 1996).

4. Sharon Walsh, "Battling bloodlines on ADM's board," *Washington Post* (January 21, 1996): Section H, 1.

5. Shareholders' rights: ftp://ftp.fedworld.gov/pub/sec-inv/ii004.txt.

6. John C. Wilcox, "Rethinking the annual meeting": http://www.georgeson.com/greport/1.html.

7. James R. Booth and Daniel N. Deli, "Factors affecting the number of outside directorships held by CEOs," *Journal of Financial Economics* (January 1996): 81.

8. "Companies use incentives to attract board members; CEOs don't take the bait," *HR Focus* (August 1994): 14.

9. Todd Hyten, "Above board: Directors get back to business," *Boston Business Journal* (August 1994): 14.

10. Joann S. Lublin, "Management: Ousted CEOs less welcome on some boards," *Wall Street Journal* (November 24, 1995): B1.

11. Timothy R. Carpenter, "Corporate anorexia, a dangerous epidemic," *USA Today* (July 1996): 36–38.

12. "Gentle giants," *The Economist* (December 21, 1996): 15–16.

13. "The rush to knowledge," *Industry Week* (February 19, 1996): 53–56.

14. "A survey of Silicon Valley: Future perfect?" *The Economist* (March 29, 1997): 24.

15. John A. Byrne with Richard A. Melcher, "The best and worst boards: Our new report card on corporate governance," *Business Week* cover story (November 25, 1996).

16. Richard Nathan, "Corporate governance at the speed of light," Osler, Hoskin and Harcourt, Toronto (April 1996): http://www.io.org/~logic/papers/rn-corpgov.html.

17. Nathalie Borris Carlyle, "Expert advice: A look at advisory boards," *Canadian Business Review* (Autumn 1995): 27.

Chapter 11

The Future for Auditors

DIMINISHED RESPONSIBILITY

A generation ago, when a company went under with little advance warning, it was common enough to hear the question, "Where were the auditors?" In more recent collapses, however, it was rarer to hear this query. Accountants have managed to convince at least part of the general public that it is not their responsibility to discover inherent weaknesses, and it is unusual for them to anticipate or warn of the possible breakdown of the company they have just audited. Some—certainly not all—will concede that the traditional audit opinion, with its central assertion concerning the truth and fairness of the accounts, has not stood up well to the test of financial scandals and corporate shenanigans. One example: Of the 30 Californian savings and loan companies that failed in 1985 and 1986, 28 had a clean audit the year before collapsing.[1] Even those who would prefer to rely on the auditors' opinions are increasingly skeptical of them. As William Seidman suggested, it is no longer assumed that "acquirers of companies should be able to rely on an audit of the firms they buy as much as an investor who seeks assurance from audits of companies whose stock he purchases."[2]

In 1984, Chief Justice Warren Burger gave it as his opinion that "the independent public accountant . . . owes ultimate allegiance to the company's creditors and stockholders, as well as to (the) investing public. This 'public watchdog' function demands that the accountant maintain total independence from the client at all times and requires complete fidelity to the public trust."[3] Repeatedly, over the years, the courts have expressed a similar view that auditors must act in the interests of external users of financial statements and also assumed that it is possible for them to do so. The authors of an article entitled

"The Impossibility of Auditor Independence" note that in recent years there have been increasing doubts whether the profession can deliver the quality service its leaders aim to provide. In other words, questions have arisen as to how realistic the assumption is that an auditor of even the highest integrity can provide such impartial judgment.[4]

The profession of CPA is just over a century old. Until well after World War II, it provided services for the governance of a business community caught up in turbulent political times and a rapidly changing society. And, for a time, the business world regarded the profession and its endeavors with respect. But in the past generation, as business greatly diversified and became ever more specialized, and as the areas of comparability between the company and its peers contracted, the auditor found fewer yardsticks on which to base his opinion. Furthermore, as business became global in nature and as the firm's labor and service costs grew, the profession found itself in a competitive, often cannibalistic, climate. No wonder that underbidding ultimately impaired the already defensive practices.

It is many years since the courts confirmed that the auditor is no bloodhound. With smaller expectations to meet, firms have reduced the extent of their audit and have given more attention to fulfilling the demands for greater disclosure; consequently, CPAs do not perform the functions required to make them dependable watchdogs. There is no record of the number of instances of embezzlement, gross negligence, or other misdeeds left undiscovered by the profession. What is clear is that auditors (like board members) are usually among the last to learn that crooks and high flyers have caused sometimes irreparable damage to audited companies, as mentioned earlier in these pages.

A major factor in the professional weakness of present-day auditors is the very limited time they devote to the actual audit. Because of the constraints on audit fees, the amount of real time devoted to an audit has been continuously declining. Auditors know it, and they hide behind rationales such as the safety net of statistical sampling—a procedure that will not deter clients who set out to be dishonest. Although most criminal clients do not worry about an audit unearthing their crimes, auditors have rarely taken steps to widen the scope of their work.

Because they carry out only minimal audit procedures and most of the company's accounts often remain unreviewed, and because there have been an increasing number of instances in which auditors are sued for negligence by shareholders or third parties, audit partners—especially among the Big Five—cannot sign their opinions before having their working papers reviewed by peers, sometimes residing in another city. In other words, guardians are guarding the guards. Some auditors wonder uncomfortably whether their working procedures have become unwieldy. Not surprisingly, auditors seem to have lost their sense of direction.

A PROFESSION IN TURMOIL

Since the Kingston Cotton Mill ruling of 1896, the business community has become reconciled to the fact that the accountant cannot be expected to find every fraud and error in the course of an audit. Over the years, professionals have also made efforts to convince the public not to hold them responsible for failure to find ingenious, carefully laid-out schemes of client fraud. But with time, these explanations have led the public to ask questions. Why did the outside auditors fail to warn of many of the recent corporate collapses? Are they sufficiently independent of their clients? And, most to the point, what are accountants good for?

There do not appear to be satisfactory answers to these questions. Some professionals try to explain the problem by means of a new term they are marketing. It is, they claim, the "expectation gap" that causes so much misunderstanding between the public and the auditor. Firms are forced to defend themselves against lawsuits based more on mistaken expectations than on actual malpractice, said Nashville accountant William Blaufuss, and he added that an audit is not designed to determine whether the information is true—a common misconception.[5]

In any case, there is disenchantment with the accounting profession, as evidenced by the rapid increase in legal claims, among other things. In Britain alone, claims grew from the three filed in 1982 to 627 in 1992. In the United States, litigation began earlier and the absolute growth in suits has been significantly larger. Indeed, few developments in the past generation have been more aggravating to the auditing profession than the ease with which litigation has become such a common and frequent process. Scores of lawyers seem eager to file suits, and accountants have become both very sensitive and fatalistic as to their inevitable cost in time, money, and nuisance.

To these difficulties may be added other professional problems, such as increasing competition and the irritating reluctance of clients to pay audit fees. In the past, as medium-sized and large companies attracted better-trained professionals into their own accounting and financial departments, outside auditors began to meet corporate opposition to their fee quotations and their proposals to provide further services. The company, now having competent, intelligent, and knowledgeable staff of its own, was able to fulfill its expected needs at a cost clearly indicating that the auditors' demands were unreasonable. Consequently, companies began demanding that auditors reduce their fees to be commensurate with the reduced scope of services they now provided.

Although market economists invariably regard competition as an essential ingredient in the accounting profession, experience does not necessarily prove this so. As Richard Morris, then Cipra's deputy chief executive, stated in 1994, "In the accountancy profession, the impression we have of competition is that it can drive down standards because of the urgent desire to increase financial resources and to raise the number of students. Training requirements become more relaxed, the granting of exemptions becomes more liberal . . . and so on."[6]

All these developments are not only annoying but menacing to the profession. Numerous auditors feel that they fall short of public expectations owing to a misunderstanding of their role. Embittered and worried by the debilitating costs of litigation, they seek ways to improve their standing with their clients and the potential market, aware that the threat of court action remains the biggest bogey. Not only auditors but also those close to the profession are worried about the turmoil being caused by litigation. Some fear that it is the beginning of the end of the profession as heretofore practiced, and many wonder how they can calm public concern about the perceived failure of auditors to provide investors and creditors with adequate warning of corporate failure.

Especially discomforting to a number of leading accountants are instances where certain companies receive clean audit reports just a short time before collapsing. These fiascoes have led to calls for closer financial accounting and auditing regulations, some of which could involve radical change. They include the following:[7]

- a general tightening of accounting standards;
- replacement of the arms-length, self-regulatory relationship with public sector regulations;
- a ban on accountants performing consultancy work for audit clients and on other practices such as lowballing;
- limits on auditor tenure; and
- toughening the treatment of deviant auditors by the courts, including increased penalties.

It is fairly safe to assume that these recommendations will be met by considerable opposition, and one might question the chances of their being adopted.

There is little evidence that the profession's leaders have yet found an effective way to defend themselves. In statements with overtones of despair, they reemphasize how diligent they are. Typical was the rebuttal of the president of the AICPA, Philip Chenok, to the above proposals. In a letter to the editor of the *Wall Street Journal* in 1993, he explained that auditing standards require the auditor to "design the audit to provide reasonable assurance of detecting errors and irregularities that are material to the financial statements."[8] The auditors' report says, "We plan and perform our audit to obtain reasonable assurance about whether the financial statements are free of material misstatement." That, observes Chenok, is a clear statement of the auditor's responsibility. He goes on to add that the concept of reasonable assurance recognizes that an audit should be cost-effective and that the cost of auditing all transactions would be prohibitive. Therefore, audits are ordinarily performed on a test basis, and it is on this basis that the professional's judgment is examined.

The eight largest British firms were hardly more convincing than their American counterparts in their report of February 1994 to the Department of Trade and Industry (DTI). In it, they claimed that "the annual audit, with its robust challenge to management's performance, is a major contributor to the underlying investors' willingness to entrust their funds to U.K. business in the British tradition of good corporate stewardship. The global business and political world finds the case made by the auditing profession weak, to say the least."

The authors of an article in *Economic Policy* approach the predicament from a different viewpoint.[9] They argue that part of the problem is that the auditors base their findings on hard, quantifiable information, which is an imperfect guide to the prospects of the company; subjective and nonquantifiable factors are likely to be at least as important. Merely because subjective information cannot be recorded directly in the accounts, they contend, does not mean that auditors should ignore it. Indeed, they assert, making decisions on the basis of subjective information is the right approach to exercising "professional judgment." Not least because many lack the tools to do so, far too few auditors apply their judgment today.

In fact, the profession has not taken advantage of the opportunities it was offered. When, in the mid-1980s, it was suggested that auditors cooperate with regulators in stamping out fraud, they preferred not to participate. Instead, most hid behind the requirement for them to remain independent and attributed their poor image to the expectations gap theory. Sadly, they continue to rationalize the reasons for nonreporting of suspected illegalities to the client's board or audit committee. Time and again, they assert that it is not their task to detect fraud. This diffident approach possibly explains why auditors failed to expose the suspicious situation that led to the most notorious debacle of recent years, the collapse of BCCI.

Indeed, in the aftermath of the BCCI collapse, the senior partner of a second-tier firm suggested that the profession was in a mess and that "we are moving close to needing the independence of a separate regulatory authority."[10] Had it been more seriously studied, the BCCI affair could have been a watershed in the proper distribution of responsibility between the regulator, the Bank of England, and the auditors, Price Waterhouse (which has since merged with Coopers & Lybrand to become PriceWaterhouseCoopers). Instead, it led to a tirade of recriminations and litigation. Despite having evidence of fraudulent transactions, the firm attested to the bank's financial statements as being "true and fair" as late as April 1990. Yet when the bank was seized by the Bank of England, Ian Brindle, Price Waterhouse senior partner, explained in an interview that his firm had maintained "prompt, regular and full" contact with regulators from before the time it took over the audit in 1988 (see note 10). Without being specific, he acknowledged that Price Waterhouse had become aware of serious irregularities at BCCI long before the firm was asked by the Bank of England to investigate the bank's affairs under Section 41 of the Banking Act. (It was the result of that investigation that led to the closure of BCCI in July 1991.)

Price Waterhouse staunchly defended itself further, stating, "common sense dictates . . . that even the best planned and executed audit will not necessarily discover a sophisticated fraud, especially one where there is collusion at the highest level of management and with third parties." The statement continued, "While evidence of certain false and deceitful transactions had been discovered, we believed the extent of these transactions to be limited."[11] Ian Brindle went on to address what some believe is the heart of the problem: that it is impossible to give an explicit warning in the audit opinion because it might lead to a run on the bank. Would the same reasoning apply to all banks, or only the larger ones? Would it apply to large insurance companies and other financial institutions? And, not least, is the possibility of a run on the bank reason enough for the auditors to suppress a qualification of their opinion? The fact that auditors on both sides of the Atlantic failed to rise to the challenges posed by the BCCI debacle, the S&Ls scandal, and similar collapses should worry all those looking for ways to enhance the profession.

If, as suggested above, the final responsibility for qualifying an audit report rests not with the auditor but with the regulatory authority, what service, exactly, does the CPA render? If auditors cannot qualify their opinions without coordination with regulatory authority, must not all interested parties be warned of that fact? How can the profession protect its independence, and how should this independence be measured? Under what circumstances can auditors state that their opinion is true and fair and independent? These and other questions must be answered if the profession is to perform in the public interest.

NO ROLE IN ECONOMIC GROWTH

Although many leading voices in the English-speaking world, from SEC's Arthur Levitt, Jr., to the British *The Economist*, laud the accounting profession and stress its importance for full disclosure which, they believe, contributes to healthy growth, many economies that do not share this culture have grown as rapidly as the American and British. Among the major economies, the standing of the profession is influenced to a large degree by how it is regarded under the law. U.S., British, Canadian, and Australian corporate laws give much prominence to the CPA (and the CA). In the non-English-speaking world, however, including Germany, France, Italy, and Switzerland, both the principles of full disclosure and the profession have a more modest standing. In these countries, outside auditors are not expected to act as the shareholders' guardians; their audited opinions carry less weight, they have fewer legal responsibilities concerning financial statements. Even though the volume and influence of the stock exchange in these countries is less than in the English-speaking world, their economic growth in the past generation has at least matched—often outpaced— that of the United States, Canada, and the United Kingdom. Accordingly, there is no obvious correlation between economic growth and affluence and the prestige of auditors. Could it be that their importance is exaggerated by the regulators and the media in the United States?

ETHICS, SKEPTICISM, AND JUDGMENT

A healthy skepticism, based on independent thought and sound judgment, is essential on the part of those in whom corporate governance controls are vested. Although such an attitude will not enable them to provide absolute protection, it will reduce the likelihood of crime, help prevent mishaps, and improve the chances of discovering problems while still in the bud. The alternative is to apply routine programmed systems that may appear to be adequate, like those in place when the Singapore roguery came to light at Barings Bank early in 1995, and run the risk that they will turn out to be completely unsatisfactory. Constant assessment and reassessment of controls is essential to the survival of corporate culture and should be an integral part of it.[12]

Healthy skepticism cannot carry the day without ensuring that ethical standards prevail. The tenets of the accounting profession include moral considerations, although, unfortunately, not enough attention is paid to them in practice. How many accountants remember that most codes of professional conduct, including the AICPA's, contain general ethical principles that are aspirational in character and represent the objectives toward which every member of the profession should strive? Or that the high level of conduct toward which CPAs should strive is embodied in philosophical principles that call for an unswerving commitment to honorable behavior, even at the sacrifice of personal advantage? According to the ''Principles of the Code of Professional Conduct'':

Integrity is an element of character fundamental to professional recognition. It is the quality from which the public trust derives and the benchmark against which a member must ultimately test all decisions. . . . Integrity also requires a member to observe the principles of objectivity and independence and of care.

Objectivity is a state of mind, a quality that lends value to a member's services. It is a distinguishing feature of the profession. The principle of objectivity imposes the obligation to be impartial, intellectually honest, and free of conflicts of interest. Independence precludes relationships that may appear to impair a member's objectivity in rendering attestation services.[13]

But the above rules depend on ethical mores being deeply imbedded in the practitioner. Professional literature informs us that many people today have little awareness of or concern about ethics. Why have ethics, once recognized as basic to business activities, in general, and the education of the CPA, in particular, become so neglected? Certainly, it has much to do with the need for continuing education, from early childhood and on to college and the business community. If properly instilled from early youth, ethical behavior should become second nature, like driving a car—as, indeed, it often is, but not often enough.

Psychology professor Stephen Davis says that cheating by high school students has increased from about 20 percent in the 1940s to 75 percent today, and he adds, "Students say cheating in high school is for grades, cheating in college is for a career."[14] He notes that the accounting students sampled (at a major university) strongly believe that ethics is a major issue in business and accounting; they think the lack of ethics hurts the accounting profession; and they feel the need for more ethical and moral direction. He sums up by saying, "Ethics is a critical sense in accounting practice and, consequently, to accounting education. Heightened public concern regarding business ethics, along with the declining influence of social institutions has increased the role educators must play in forming students' ethical attitudes and beliefs." But recourse to present-day educators may not be enough, for how can we be sure that the virus has not infected the teachers, as well?

Another article concludes that the current public expectation is that accountants should demonstrate a high standard of ethics and integrity; and that the accounting profession must follow ethical principles.[15] The writer does not, however, describe how to put these standards into practice or how senior staff and young partners can be encouraged to think ethically.

Ethics tests often come at the least convenient moment, when the auditor is under pressure—but is that not just when he or she should be tested? Applying ethics, after all, is not a purely theoretical or abstract exercise; it addresses very practical matters. The ethical questions crop up, for example, when the professional is expected to complete the assignment forthwith, even though at the last minute a problem is detected that could change the substance of the opinion. The client may be pressing for an immediate report or exerting pressure on the professional to help find a technical solution which, neither believes, will be substantially true. There are many such difficult situations where ethical judgment is called for.

Theoretical case studies, of course, are not the same as real-time confrontations with clients. Courage and curiosity in real time can be far more important than knowing the solution offered in a school case study. Often there is a very thin line between what is right and what might be wrong, and it is then that the inquisitive mind that has gathered all available information and become aware of the risk involved is challenged to apply ethical judgment. An ethical question carries the risk of offending or aggravating the client to the extent that the professional will be fired or, worse, sued for damages. Making a decision under these circumstances demands commitment and understanding and the resolve to distinguish and make a judgment. It is not a situation that can be taken lightly. The ethical aspects of issues that come up for decision are often not considered in the business world. Instead, mercenary and economic considerations create pressure for selective ethical behavior that somehow helps improve financial returns. The truth is that, without a thorough commitment to ethical standards, professional judgment will be made in a flawed climate.

Ethics is not, of course, solely a concern of the auditing profession but is the responsibility of society in general and the whole of the business world. Nevertheless, ethical conduct is probably more closely linked to auditors' decisions than to those of some of the other members of the community. If ethical studies are given a higher priority and more attention is given to the ethical aspects of the practice, the odds in favor of the survival of the profession will be greater.

FIRMS WITH PROBLEMS

Although the profession prides itself on being an assembly of independently thinking people, in fact the individual's scope for original thinking—especially in the larger firms—is close to nonexistent. A young partner has as much leeway to make judgment decisions as a medium-ranking officer in the army. And yet, owing to the anachronistic partnership concept based on a law that leaves CPAs hardly any mode of self-defense apart from timely retirement, they continue to carry unlimited liability for damages caused by a colleague—perhaps someone in a remote location whom they have never even met. At best, the partners may be regarded as somewhat glorified profit-loss-sharing employees.

The only real assets professionals have are their skills, motivation, and judgment, but these are qualities of which the managing partners of the larger firms are suspicious. In firms beyond a certain size, any synergy among accountants on a service-providing team is often more than offset by the firm's bureaucracy and overhead and by the defensive posture of its head. It would seem reasonable to expect the small- to medium-sized firms to be able to avoid this pitfall, providing the personal, creative type of service to which clients believe they are entitled and which larger firms cannot or dare not supply. These firms should be able to preserve their sense of duty and involvement and keep their clients satisfied at a reasonable fee. Their structure, however, presents an almost insurmountable hurdle when they presume to service a large, publicly quoted company. Overdependence on a single client will raise the question of independence.

No wonder young practitioners find themselves in a quandary. When they are employed by the larger firms, they know that their promotion depends on how those clients that they look after personally evaluate them and how much revenue they bring in. If a partner's client changes auditors (even through no fault of his own) and even if the loss in revenue is not significant, his chances of further climbing the rungs of the organization will slow down or come to a complete halt. Joining second-tier or even lesser firms whose clients are often correspondingly smaller—perhaps family-owned—can give young accountants more independence, but the scope of practice is far more limited. Unless they specialize in matters such as tax planning and become proficient in tax avoidance, their chores are generally anything but inspiring.

Auditors would like to believe that although they do not have any explicit reporting duty to the regulators, their opinion on the financial statements and other related documents is valuable to them. Although their advice does not carry the force of law and is, at times, ignored by the board and management, auditors do, in fact, have some impact on how the public reads the financial and accounting information published. At the same time, despite professional requirements and public expectations, CPAs prefer to avoid conflict with their clients. They take all possible steps to avoid applying SAS (Statement on Accounting Standards) 53, which states that the external auditors should withdraw from the audit engagement if irregularities that they have identified and reported to the audit committee remain unresolved.[16]

AUDITORS' INDEPENDENCE

How dependent are auditors on their clients? Although medium-sized and larger auditing firms repeatedly assert their independence from their clients, the question may be expected to remain open for discussion. Accounting institutes and regulatory authorities have set up what they consider strict criteria to ensure the CPA's independence from his client, including:

• Audit fees from any one client should not exceed a certain percentage of the aggregate income of the firm.
• The CPA should not own any equity of his client.
• The CPA should not perform any work that might turn him or her into a de facto employee of the client.

These are but three of the rules that help answer the question of whether an accountant is independent of the client. Another measure, discussed in the following pages, is whether to forbid the involvement of the CPA in the client's consulting or trustee services.

The Big Five support the yardsticks established by the accounting institutes and regulatory authorities. Notwithstanding the wide range of the consulting services they provide, they have always maintained emphatically that their independence is unquestionable. That tone of confidence, however, is not totally convincing in the current business climate. Indeed, client shareholders have been suggesting hat these mega-sized auditing and service firms are tampering with the concept of independence. As examples, they cite underbidding as a means to acquire a client and, what some suspect are the consequences of this competition, lower audit standards. Are these not the result of dubious concepts of independence?

There are other questions, such as whether an individual partner in an ostensibly independent firm can be regarded as independent and is really identified fully with the partnership. The Big Five may declare that a $200,000 audit fee from an individual client is insignificant compared with their multibillion-dollar fee income in the United States alone. But what about the individual partner who loses such an account assigned to him? Let's assume that he lives in a medium-sized city in the Midwest, grew up with his client, and has a personal relationship with the CEO; perhaps he was made partner largely because he grew with the client or persuaded this company to choose his firm as auditor. He is well aware that his chances of increasing the number of "units" with which he is credited each year are dependent on retaining this client and ensuring regular and continually larger fees from him. One day, perhaps, the client is faced with a complex problem that requires an imaginative but possibly borderline audit decision. Although the auditor knows that the conservative approach is the right answer, he is also aware that, should this course be taken, the client might look elsewhere for auditing services. Against his professional judgment, the audit partner may accommodate the client.

A case in point was that of the investors who sued Coopers & Lybrand (now part of PriceWaterhouseCoopers), contending that Gregory Finerty, partner in charge of the Phar-Mor audit, was "hungry for business because he had been passed over for additional profit-sharing in 1988 for failing to sell enough of the firm's services." Reports were that Finerty had become too close to the client to maintain the professional skepticism necessary to conducting an independent audit (see note 4).

Can such a partner be regarded as truly independent? When auditors are influenced by the threat of dismissal, is there not a question concerning their independence? And, finally, are not a substantial number of the Big Five audit partners affected by such worries when making audit judgments? (see note 7).

Both the professionals and the regulators are aware of these pressures and have developed some defense mechanisms to deter the wavering partner from making the wrong judgment, but these measures are not always timely or good enough. On the more positive side, however, when the accounts of small companies are audited (and the fee is insignificant), it is possible to work without active pressures between auditor and client. Also, auditors are more likely to resist client pressure if the client may be exposed to public criticism that could implicate them.

When negotiating with their client, just as when scrutinizing the facts and figures, auditors are expected to use their professional judgment to weigh subjective, nonquantifiable information. It is inconceivable that, in such ongoing discussions and relationships, one side would always be right, while the other should always give in.

There may be a number of legitimate solutions to problems that arise in the course of an audit. All call for careful examination in which, not least, the interests of the client should be considered. In the larger audit firms, there are professionals with special expertise who may be called in to advise on preferred treatment. When the consequences could be material, the client may consult with other professionals to get their opinion, or to confirm the one in process. Many professionals are disdainful of "opinion shopping," some regulators oppose it and, indeed, it is sometimes misused. Experienced professional consultants realize that they are being used, but if they have access to the relevant details before offering their opinion, not only is it impossible to prevent the practice but, in fact, it can prove helpful. The final opinion is frequently the result of a process of compromise, although it is sometimes not easy to state whether the concessions made by the CPA are the result of good judgment or of yielding to the client.

No number of professional audit standard pronouncements will persuade the market to trust figures unless there is confidence that the auditors who provide the opinions have no interest in pandering to their clients. It is an industry in which the companies, themselves, hire the auditing firms. This situation can be compared to that of artists, actors, or musicians who hire their own critics and reviewers. In an article that appeared in 1990, *The Economist* stressed that "the key is to be impartial. No sport allows the scorer to be paid by the players . . . or always to preside over the same matches. Yet that is what the business world does with its referees—the accountancy profession."[17] And the publication adds that, coincidentally or not, annual reports have rarely been less clear. As long as auditors are chosen and paid by the board of directors, almost invariably at the recommendation of the CEO or his management, true independence will not be achieved.

The financial ties of the CPA with his client have wider implications than the size of the audit fee alone. Because audit fees have become far too competitive for comfort, many professionals have been seeking to enhance their income by providing additional services, such as consulting work. All major and most mid-size accounting firms have developed consulting services focused on wealthy individuals, executives, and groups of employees in large companies. These services include tax planning and tax return preparation, estate planning, and insurance advice. It is difficult to believe that provision of such services to the audit client does not create a flaw in the firm's status of independence. Sharing investment advice incidental to the tax services they provide, however, is a somewhat different matter. When registering with the SEC, for example, the CPA might well suggest to his clients how to allocate the assets in their port-folios, or the kind of investments to choose.[18] So, there is no simple answer to the question of when and whether consulting services impair professional in-dependence. Nor it is clear whether and, if so, at what stage the auditing firm that is willing to underquote actually loses its independence from the client.[19] And as this section of the industry has grown, the profession has realized that, while it might increase gross revenues, it also creates new problems. One is that the basis according to which clients are charged is different for auditors, on the one hand, and consultants, on the other. Consultants often bring in more money, but in most firms they are expected to share their income and negligence exposure with auditors and tax partners.[20] Linked to the different types of services provided and the eagerness with which the CPA tries to market his consulting partner to his client, there is the question of whether professional independence is impaired when the auditing firm also provides consulting services to the same client.

Another question is whether a long-term relationship between client and au-ditor reduces the alertness of the latter and, hence, possibly brings his inde-pendence into question. It has been recommended that periodically rotating audit assignments might produce a healthier climate, but the idea does not seem to have generated much enthusiasm. Despite the moderate, sometimes low esteem in which outside auditors are held, rotation of auditors is far less common than it is believed to be. There is general agreement that turning rotation into an obligatory practice would be rather costly, would not strengthen the practice, and would not improve governance. As the Cohen commission reported in the late 1970s, "It would considerably increase the cost of audits because of the frequent duplication of the start-up and the learning time."

In sum, the accounting profession may continue performing in its present mode for some time to come. Auditors may not be completely independent, but many of them will use good judgment and caution in attempting to recognize what is right and ethical. Possibly, the fact that their professional authority is not automatically accepted generates positive discussion and contributes to the open debate on corporate matters. Somewhat paradoxically, it may also result in more attention to and better understanding of the analysis of companies' financial data.

A Matter of Judgment

Early in 1994, then chief accountant of the SEC Walter Schuetze severely criticized independent auditors for not measuring up to the high standards of integrity and objectivity expected from them. He concluded his remarks by questioning the profession's very independence: "If public companies are pressuring their outside auditors and the Accounting Standards Executive Committee of the AICPA to take particular positions on financial accounting and reporting issues, and outside auditors are subordinating their views to their clients' views, can the outside auditors' community continue to claim to be independent?"[21] He went on to say, "Auditors, by not standing up to their clients, take a position that is, at best, not supported in the accounting literature or, at worst, directly contrary to existing accounting pronouncements. This raises a nasty issue about independence both in appearance and in fact."

In the wake of his strictures, the Public Oversight Board (POB) and the American Institute of CPAs SEC Practice Section (SECPS) appointed a three-member advisory panel to determine whether "the SECPS, the accounting profession, or the SEC should take steps to better ensure the independence of auditors and the integrity and objectivity of their judgments."[22] Recognizing the need to prove that the profession was up to par by producing its report quickly, the POB came out with a series of recommendations within nine months, on September 16, 1994.[23] The report emphasized the importance of maintaining professional independence. Citing a Supreme Court opinion that described the independent audit as a public watchdog function, it noted:

If investors were to view the auditor as an advocate for the corporate client, the value of the audit might well be lost . . . [the independent public accountant] . . . owes ultimate allegiance to the corporation's creditors and stockholders, as well as the investing public. This "public watchdog" function demands that the accountant maintain total independence from the client at all times and requires complete fidelity to the public trust.[24]

The report itself went on to state that firms need to emphasize to all concerned that auditing is special, involving a *"public* responsibility transcending any employment relationship with the client."

The members of the panel were clearly worried when they stated that independent auditing firms need to focus on how the audit function can be enhanced and not submerged in the other activities of large, multiline public accounting/ management consulting firms. Like many other professional publications, this defensive report devoted much space to "what not to" expect from the practitioner. But it also stressed that good performance depends on tough decisions just as much as on precautions. It went on to say that it is key to the firm's processes that those decisions be insulated from undue pressure from, or on behalf of, clients.

Walter Schuetze also directed criticism at corporate directors, whom he charged with failure to act as guardians of the corporation and its shareholders and being passive supporters of management. This major topic was addressed by the panel in its report which stressed the need for strengthening the relationship between the board of directors and the independent auditor. The panel called for stronger boards with a sharper sense of accountability as a means of strengthening the professionalism of the outside auditor. It recommended that the profession expand its thinking to recognize the board of directors as its client, part of a corporate governance approach to improved financial reporting.

The panel's central recommendation was that, rather than legislate how they should function, corporate boards and audit committees should expect independent auditors to communicate forthrightly and in a timely fashion their views on the quality—not just the acceptability—of a company's financial reporting. The panel placed the initial burden of judging the appropriateness of the company's accounting principles and taking the initiative to present other pertinent data concerning the company's activities on the auditor rather than on the audit committee. Its report called for quality assessment to encompass judgments of the appropriateness—whether aggressive or conservative—of estimates and elective accounting principles, description of methods used, and evaluation of the clarity of disclosures.

The panel seemed to recognize that the public should not be satisfied solely with adjectives such as "appropriate" or "aggressive" but should expect greater emphasis on the most important aspect of the profession: good judgment. The authors of the report explained that the circumstances surrounding the accounting and disclosure choices made by a client might, at times, be case-specific and differ subtly from the seemingly similar circumstances of other companies. They quoted the panel as stating that the auditor should not only evaluate the company's compliance with generally accepted accounting principles but also express to the audit committee and the board of directors a qualitative judgment about the company's choice of principles, disclosures, and estimates. Further, the authors of the report emphasized that high-quality financial reporting does not result from mere compliance with rules; rather, it calls for an open and inquiring mind and the auditor's sense of security in exercising personal judgment. In assessing the quality of the client's financial reporting, the individual auditor needs to apply his experience, competence, and judgment, not merely a set of intransigent rules. All of this constitutes no small demand from today's professionals. There is no evidence that the distant relations between CPAs and their clients have improved in the wake of this report.

This was reiterated by a series of events toward the close of 1997, and included a stern warning by top SEC enforcement official William McLucas. He urged accounting professionals not to compromise their work as independent auditors when they expand into new lines of business. "It is imperative that the market's perception as independent in fact and in appearance not be compromised by the transformation of auditing firms into full service entities," he said, adding that he was worried that the independence requirement of accounting firms is "being treated as an obstacle" now that firms are profiting by other services.[25] An illustration of what he meant came in January 1998, with the reports of a class action, settled out of court, in which the accounting firm of KPMG was blamed for ignoring signs that its independence was not as complete as it should be, partly due to its entanglements with the real estate Teachers Management and Investment Corporation. KPMG had allowed the corporation to run up an inordinate sum in unpaid fees; some of its leading partners had taken jobs with the client and others had been overly keen to solicit consulting work from it. Having lost about $100 million and collapsed, Teachers Management and Investment Corporation sued its auditors, who agreed to pay them "something less than $10 million."[26]

There is still public criticism of auditors' independence and, given the complexity of today's economy, there is perhaps no satisfactory answer. The subject never quite dies down, but from time to time events bring it into sharper focus. Everybody is in favor, in theory, but obstacles often make it hard to achieve or keep the ideal degree of objectivity and aloofness. No wonder there are those who believe that current independence standards are outmoded and should not only include the formally accepted measurements but should also look at the interests of the relevant partner. Thus, although the Big Five who audit almost all the *Fortune* 500 and similar giant firms claim to be independent in their professional relations, that can sometimes be shown to be not exactly so. Although under certain circumstances and in what is clearly a show of independence, they will be willing to meet a small client up to halfway, they will be more flexible and ready to bend to the wishes of a mega-company. Independence is relative to the customer's size and prestige and an auditor is willing to accept a considerable amount of pressure if it ensures his reappointment to a prize client, rather than dig in his heels over a tricky borderline case of judgment.

AUDITORS AND THEIR CLIENTS

The public does not regard accountants as creative entrepreneurs or romantic visionaries, and rightly so. Most are straightforward and unimaginative, and no matter how ably they perform their jobs, it is rare that clients are impressed by the services they receive from them.[27] Auditing firms are chosen for the qualities they are perceived to have—for example, their relations with the IRS or their client's bank—and not necessarily because they are perceived as talented professionals with auditing abilities. If auditors dream at all, it is that one day a client will consult them as company advisors rather than as mere number crunchers.[28] My impression, gained over several decades in the practice, is that partners in auditing firms are not a happy lot. It is not only that they do not usually feel appreciated or respected by their clients, but most have little respect for the business sense or performance of many of the senior officers in the companies they audit. They feel frustrated that their clients rarely ask for, let alone take, their advice. Somewhat like art or music critics, they tend to believe that they could do a far better job than their clients, sadly knowing that they never will.

A Growing Chasm

One indication of the marked deterioration in the auditor–client relationship is the lack of management respect for auditors. This is far more pronounced in the larger accounting firms than in the smaller ones. Few CEOs of firms whose shares are traded on the stock exchange maintain personal or social relationships with their CPAs. They rarely regard the external accountants as a resource on audited financial data, or discuss strategic corporate strategy with them. The CEO is confident that there are other people—far closer, better qualified, and more knowledgeable—on hand to provide such expert assistance.

Although for a time they hoped otherwise, outside auditors are now aware that if they fail in their endeavors to create continuous personal links with the corporate officers, they cannot rely on the audit committee when they need objective umpires. They know that unless the CEO is blatantly wrong (and sometimes not even then), the audit committee will support the company's position rather than the CPA's. Accountants are aware that they cannot afford to be repeatedly timid in their relations with the client, but they are also careful not to present too tough a posture contrary to the position management prefers.

Many auditors are alert to the decline in their clients' regard for them, but with few exceptions they have done very little to prevent it or, better still, to try to create a turnaround. From their research, they know that most of their clients believe they do not get good enough value for the money they spend on the auditing services they receive (see note 28). Many feel they can do little more than pray that the links will not weaken further, seemingly having lost any confidence that they could convince their clients to use them more effectively. "What a splendid profession we could be, if only we could make do without our clients!" seems to be a common lament.

As mentioned above and with an eye to strengthening their practice, the Big Five (and some of their competitors) have developed consulting arms. In recent years these have become multibillion dollar businesses—an apparently growing and diversifying part of the company. KPMG, for example, is considering the addition of legal services to its international operations. And in widening the scope of its activities, the firm also believes it can charge fees to clients that require KPMG business ethics services, for which it has established a special group.[29]

It is, however, rare for an audit client to call the auditor with a request for consulting support. Almost to the contrary, there is increasing evidence that both the regulatory authorities and potential clients prefer someone other than the auditing firm to provide them with consulting services. Corporations that seek consulting services in addition to the annual auditing demanded by law prefer to retain a different group for that purpose. Consultants can best make progress when they gently nudge their client, rather than stating matters by the book. The risks, the composition of staff, and, indeed, the profitability patterns are so different from one type of service to another that the professional firms have reason to establish independent profit centers for each service.

Unlike their accounting associates, who are professionally expected to disclose much of what they produce, consultants remain a secretive lot, and, understandably, these are very different disciplines. Consulting has no agreed standards or self-established regulatory system similar to Generally Accepted Accounting Principles (GAAP). Anybody can call himself a consultant and dispense management wisdom.[30] This posture, some believe, has allowed ethical standards among consultants to slip, although it is difficult to ascertain how seriously. Nor is it practical even to hazard a guess as to when the consultants' ethical mystique will be punctured and whether they should be regulated (see note 30).

As the consulting arms of CPA firms grew and became more profitable, some of the consultants began to feel that they were subsidizing the accountants and that it would be more equitable to separate their income kitty from that of the auditors. The first to do so was Arthur Andersen, in 1989; the other large firms are expected to follow. Once that happens, it is probable that there will be full legal separation between the two services within a few years. In fact, early in 1998 it became clear that the Andersen operating arrangement was coming to an end. The gulf between the two arms seemed to be growing wider with Andersen Consulting contending that Arthur Andersen was in direct competition with them. As they approached an arbitrator, it appeared that it was only a question of time before the consulting firm, where on average each partner generated $8 million annually, would be going its own way.[31]

Choosing to enter the consulting industry in their quest for greater financial security, auditors took on not only competition within the profession but also specialists in other industries, ranging from banks and financial institutions to insurance companies and independent consulting firms, some with revenues matching those of the Big Five. Most of these specialists have confidence in their abilities, and many feel that competing with the large and medium-sized auditing firms is fair game. When, in March 1997, American Express Co.'s tax and business services subsidiary acquired Checkers, Simon and Rosner LP, the tax and business division of one of Chicago's largest accounting firms, Bob Basten, the CEO of the American Express subsidiary, observed that "the marketplace is becoming increasingly demanding and competitive for accounting firms."[32] The extent to which services extending beyond auditing, accounting, and tax preparation contribute to the strength and substance of the profession is still unclear.

The Auditors under Siege

Possibly because of their defensive posture, the professional organizations have found it even more difficult to address the need for a close auditor–client relationship. Altogether, the profession is in the doldrums; it usually avoids the burning professional issues, preferring to stress those that are of secondary importance. Not atypical was a summary of issues presented by Philip B. Chenok, one of the CPAs most respected by his colleagues in recent years.[33] He wrote in 1995 of the need to attract the best and brightest talent to raise the standards of accounting education and the performance of the practitioner, and he enumerated other challenges: the professional knowledge of CPAs working in industry, finance, and other services; supporting management accounting programs; nurturing the development of specialized services; and helping to create more relevant standards and services. In every case, he delved into considerable technical detail, and he advised professionals to make their voices heard in Washington and to handle their legal liability with more confidence. One may speculate on Chenok's belief that if all these points were taken seriously, relations with clients would become better and the level of respect shown by the latter would improve. His summary did not, however, suggest how relations between auditors and clients could be uplifted, and little has happened since to instill optimism for the future of the profession.

The widening gap between CPAs and the public is also of concern to SEC chairman Arthur Levitt, Jr., who has come out strongly and repeatedly to emphasize the importance of CPA services as protectors of the truth, without which the American economy would be crippled. And, although he realizes that they have not captured the popular imagination, he views accountants as "highly sophisticated, knowledgeable professionals . . . they serve one of the most valuable functions in the capitalist society.''[34] But he, too, cautions the professionals not to exceed their brief by expanding their business beyond their traditional services into investment banking, franchising the use of the firm's name, and providing outsourcing for a variety of services.

When Clients Fire Auditors

In the generation following World War II, the economy and the business world enjoyed steady growth. It was a time in which the accounting profession was acknowledged to have expertise unmatched by the corporate financial executive and was held in esteem by senior company officers. Unless an outside auditor made a professional blunder or fell afoul of the CEO, reappointment was secure—almost like tenure. But this state of relations has gradually changed. Today, most corporate financial officers know as much about the theory of the profession as do the outside auditors, and they are invariably far more conversant with the immediate financial reporting needs of the company. The auditor lacks the personal touch of his predecessors a generation earlier in working with the CEO and senior officers, who appreciated the latter's professional know-how, consulting capabilities, and support.

The particular business links of the CPA with the client's CEO have weakened, without compensatory increase in prestige with its board. This deterioration in relationships is a primary factor contributing to the acceleration in the turnover of outside auditors. The outside auditor is regarded not as an intimate or a friendly consultant but as a regulatory necessity. Executive management, which wants to present its financial information in the best possible light, hires, fires, and pays them for what is to them a burden and very technical service.[35]

For their part, clients state that after a "honeymoon" with newly appointed auditors, during which they are provided with same-day service, the professional attention tends to fizzle out. The quality of auditing personnel drops and their turnover rises. Inexperienced staff are sent to them and they spend hours learning how to fill forms rather than carrying out even part of the audit. Small and medium-sized clients often feel that the larger auditing firms tend to focus their resources on their larger clients, leaving smaller ones neglected and feeling like second-class citizens, yet they are obliged to pay the same high fees. Disenchanted with the attention they receive, many clients leave for other, hopefully more personal, sometimes smaller firms. Those who remain often do so because they believe that the goodwill they get from the financial institutions they work with or from the stock exchange analysts more than offsets the ordinary service they receive from the larger firms.[36] A survey of 400 small business owners conducted in 1993 showed that, whereas in 1987 the big accounting firms had ranked first, this time they ranked ninth in twelve industry groups in responsiveness to small business needs.[37] In a 1995 study, some 200 firms all over the world were asked why they had not reappointed their outside accountants. The most frequently given reasons were:

1. lack of communication, including lack of timeliness and responsiveness;

2. lack of perceived value by the clients of the services they received;

3. the perception by the client that their business was not appreciated; and

4. a sense among clients that their auditors could not provide them with the additional services they required.

Other studies showed different disappointments, such as:

1. core service failures, including service mistakes, billing errors, and damage-causing mistakes;

2. failure in personal interactions, brought about by the attitude of staff or partners who were uncaring, impolite, unresponsive, or unknowledgeable; and

3. dissatisfaction with fees, which were perceived to be too high and unexplained or unacceptable price increases, unfair pricing practices, and deceptive pricing practices.

It is probable that if all the Big Five and second-tier firms carried out such studies, the findings would be similar. It is presumed that all larger firms spend many hours attempting to understand the threats facing them and considering ways to deal with them. As one consultant observed, the bigger firms will attempt to maintain their business-as-usual marketing posture, but this will be done at a price, not the least of it being that the partners will be stretched in so many directions that they cannot develop the essential rapport vital to maintaining friendly, on-call relations with clients (see note 37). It all leads to the impression that auditors today have a bunker mentality and find it difficult to make their performance more attractive.

A Problem of Image

There are numerous jokes about the nonhero posture of the accountant. Can auditors be stereotyped? Those who come into contact with the larger accounting firms see quite clearly that they prefer solid, meticulous staff to adventurous, imaginative professionals. When evaluating these mammoth organizations and assessing their operations, it can easily be surmised that the individual partner rarely is the galloping entrepreneurial type. Not even in the tax planning divisions should one expect to meet a really open mind, imaginative and sensitive to the client's needs. Any sparkling young enthusiast seeking an auditor's career soon discovers that the larger firms regard originality and zest with suspicion. These outfits discourage original zeal in favor of commitment to long hours and solid dependability. It is less clear whether they seek gravitas or unassuming grayness in a partner. A creative professional can provide impressive services and demand high fees but might take gambles that would turn out to be costly.

Indeed, the management of the Big Five firms realized long ago that they cannot afford to have free-spirited professionals at work in the far reaches of their practice, serving their clients with creative accounting. The risk of litigation is just too great. The heads of large firms therefore seek dependable staff who might not be entrepreneurs but who will, hopefully, prove reliable. Possibly because they are discouraged from being innovative or intellectually independent, auditors usually do not have personalities of the kind that gain one prominence in public life. There are far fewer trained CPAs on Capitol Hill than qualified lawyers. William Seidman, who served presidents Ford, Reagan, and Bush and headed the FDIC, was one of those exceptional CPAs who reached a high position in government. But presidents and businessmen alike expect originality from their legal consultants and dry, fastidious services from their accountants.

Although they believe it vital to improve their public image, accountants seem to have very little to contribute in general or conceptual discussion. Joe Queenan, a writer for Barron's, noted that although there are some accountants who do interesting things, these activities are far away from their practice. "Personally, I hold no brief for accountants as a unit and would be loath to argue that they are, collectively or individually, electrifying fireballs."[38] As if waiting to prove the point, Michael Henning, chairman of Ernst & Young, stated in an interview, "We want to be seen by our clients as one firm worldwide and we want them to see our services as more seamless. That, I think, is the challenge everybody has in the accounting profession.[39] Ernst & Young may have attempted to undergo considerable change in a bid to become more competitive, but it is not realistic to expect any of the firm's clients to remember this statement, still less to be stimulated by it. In general, accountants take a cautious, serious approach, and it is for this that they deserve respect.

Can Auditors Face Reality?

There are many signs that the auditing profession has either lost touch with what the public expects or has not learned how to provide satisfactory service in this age of increased diversification and specialization. The failure to come to grips with the situation is clear when one reads the various professional publications. Two Colorado professors, for example, wrote an article on the code of professional conduct, explaining that the accounting profession should operate for the benefit of the public and that CPAs are obliged to consider the public good when executing their duties.[40] They quote A. Briloff's Talmudic explanation of the concept of the client "versus" the public:

While management may be signing the check, they're not really paying our fee; instead, we should know that the major portion of the fee is paid by the government through the tax deduction; the rest of it is paid by the shareholders and/or customers for the entity's goods and services. In short, the corporation's management is doing nothing more than acting as an intermediary in behalf of the whole world of third parties to whom we are responsible.[41]

Is this rather far-fetched? Possibly, but then it would appear that, in their way, the British are just as remote from reality. After its council meeting of November 1995, the British Institute of Chartered Accountants set out a list of ten principal initiatives for the profession in 1996:[42]

1. putting the management accountant merger proposals to members;

2. continuing to promote the title "Chartered Accountant";

3. enhancing the technical reputation of the institute;

4. contributing to the development of better corporate governance;

5. implementing proposals on regulation of members;

6. taking a leading role in the debate on financial reporting in the European Union;

7. influencing European Union initiatives concerning the statutory auditor;

8. continuing to promote training in smaller firms;

9. continuing to implement the education and training strategy developed in 1993, including the new intermediate exam syllabuses and new-style fellowship schemes; and

10. providing constructive help to those who serve small and medium-sized enterprises.

Note that there is no apparent agonizing about how to enhance professional credibility or sensitivity to client needs or third-party expectations. Is there a connection between the state of siege the profession finds itself in and the fact that its leadership is so inward-looking?

STRIVING FOR IMPROVEMENT

If the average partner is on the defensive, the senior partners and staff of the major auditing organizations appear to be in a state of permanent uncertainty. No wonder. Called upon in no uncertain terms to improve, to perform better, to redeem their long-lost credibility, they are under fire from all directions. Some wonder whether they have lost their sense of direction. In recent years, the firms' elders have set up committees, both ad hoc and permanent, to convince the public that they are helping the profession to improve. There are no indications that these measures were helpful.

Some segments of the profession believe that what they lack is better public relations. In the early autumn of 1995, the AICPA launched a $3 million advertising campaign to enhance the image of accountants. Supporters of this program noted that "too many associate accountants with death, tax, and bad news, and question our integrity," and therefore that better public exposure "is sorely needed."[43] Not surprisingly, there is no evidence that the standing of the profession improved because of this campaign.

OTHER WAYS TO STRENGTHEN THE PROFESSION

Not as effectively as it would wish, the accounting profession is struggling to put theory into practice and is seeking ways to adjust to the demanding business practices of today's market. According to *Accounting Today*, the inflation-adjusted accounting and auditing revenues of the 60 largest firms (half their total revenue) have been stagnant since the beginning of the decade. Accounting firms are therefore trying to develop new products that will meet potential market needs.[44] Aware that their core service—auditing—is no longer a basic client need but mainly a regulatory requirement, CPAs know that to survive they must consider the decision-making needs of those who retain their services. As larger clients nurture in-house accounting services to supply the expertise that used to be provided by the outside auditor, and as the cost of similar services by independent professionals rises to unacceptable levels, the marketplace appears to be cautioning that the audit is no longer an attractive value-added service and that its scope should be kept to the minimum required by law.

In their defensive ways, auditors are usually a cautious lot, and they realize how crucial it is for their well-being to modernize and streamline audit procedures. Clients have usually accepted their work as a basic essential of the due diligence required for management to fulfill its responsibilities. Thus, the minimal audit program became a common practice for the Big Five and most second-tier auditing firms.

In essence, the minimal audit program is audit by sampling. Some auditors call it "auditing by review of risks and objectives." Others explain that they assess the inherent risk and the different strengths and weaknesses they encounter to determine the client's risk profile. The public accepts the minimal audit program and reputable statisticians confirm that it ensures standards sufficiently high for proper audits. This approach enabled them, not least, to reduce auditing work to the bare essentials and gave them the opportunity to charge what their clients regarded as reasonable audit fees. Unfortunately, however, not all auditors show the discipline required for such procedures or apply them with the necessary conscientiousness, caution, and judgment. Behind many recent embarrassments, such as that caused Phar-Mor by an Indiana Coopers & Lybrand partner, lies the fact that some auditors shortchanged the procedures.

But improved audit procedures alone are not enough, and the professionals would like to provide other services, including:

1. dealing with financial and nonfinancial data;
2. dealing not only with the reliability of information but also with its relevance;
3. reporting on data or systems that produce or interpret data; and
4. offering assurance on client-prepared data and also providing their own comments or analysis.

They are also guardedly optimistic that developments in information technology will help them develop other new services.

These ideas might contain some wishful thinking. First, it is doubtful how much more educated and astute a CPA partner can become. He or she is already required to be conversant with almost endless bits of knowledge relating to regulations, laws, ordinances, and professional practices. Gaining the additional insight to fully comprehend the above subjects is no mean task, nor will it be easy to convince clients and potential clients to turn to their CPAs for these services.

There is also a psychological aspect that puts in doubt the ability of auditors to widen the scope of their activities. As already mentioned, most clients expect them to maintain a low profile. They prefer their auditors to stick to their professional assignments and, unless asked, refrain from offering advice. Growth based on the various services noted above would require greater involvement and a more aggressive approach. It is far from certain that most professionals have that trait and, as mentioned elsewhere, it could threaten their independence.

NOTES

1. William Sternberg, "Cooked books," *Atlantic Monthly* (January 1992): 20.

2. Lee Berton and Stephen J. Adler, "CPA's nightmare: How the audit of a bank cost Price Waterhouse a $338 million judgment," *Wall Street Journal* (August 14, 1992): A1 (quoting William Seidman, former head of the FDIC and consultant to BDO Seidman).

3. Quoted in *United States v. Arthur Young & Co.*, U.S. Supreme Court Reports 79, 2nd edition (26 April 1984): 826–838 L. Ed.

4. Max H. Bazeman, Kimberly P. Morgan, and George F. Loewenstein, "The Impossibility of auditor independence," *Sloan Management Review* (Summer 1997): 89–94.

5. Gwen Moritz, "Standards, expectations of CPA field rise," *Nashville Business Journal* (January 11, 1993): 29.

6. "Profession faces troubled times," editorial news, *Accountancy* (December 14, 1994): 16.

7. Paul Grant, Ian Jewitt, and Geoff Whittington, "Auditor professional judgment: Implications for regulation and the law," *Economic Policy* (October 1994): 324.

8. Philip B. Chenok, "Letters to the editor: Auditors sniff out most cooked books," *Wall Street Journal* (April 23, 1993): A15.

9. "Bringing auditors to book: Britain's accountants can help curb financial crimes," editorial in *The Economist* (May 31, 1986): 16. Also, "Auditing the auditors," editorial in *The Economist* (November 28, 1992).

10. *The Financial Times* (July 12, 1991 and August 16, 1991).

11. Ken Wells, "Auditor in U.K. defends role in BCCI report," *Wall Street Journal* (February 6, 1992): A11.

12. David Brilliant, "Tone at the top," *Banker* (November 1995): 26.

13. "Auditing Standards and Professional Conduct,"*The AICPA Code of Professional Conduct*, 50–51.

14. David S. Kerr and L. Murphy Smith, "Importance of approaches to incorporating ethics into the accounting classroom," *Journal of Business Ethics* (December 1995): 987.

15. James Poon Teng Fatt, "Ethics and the accountant," *Journal of Business Ethics* (December 1995): 997.

16. *Defining the Roles of Accountants, Bankers and Regulators in the United States: A Study Group Report*, by the Group of Thirty (1994): 21–22.

17. "Blowing the whistle on accountancy," *The Economist* (December 22, 1990): 15.

18. Ellen E. Schultz, "Big accounting firms to offer investors advice," *Wall Street Journal* (February 9, 1995): C1.

19. Note that in 1991 such lowballing was outlawed in Texas.

20. Lee Berton, "Corporate focus: Big Six's shift to consulting accelerates," *Wall Street Journal* (September 1, 1995): B1.

21. Walter P. Schuetze, "A mountain or a molehill," Twenty-First Annual National Conference of the AICPA (January 11, 1994): 8. (Quoted in "The American corporation at the end of the twentieth century," an outline of ownership-based governance in a speech given by Robert A. G. Monks at Cambridge University (July 1996): http://www.lens-inc.com/info/cambridge.html).

22. Donald J. Kirk and Arthur Siegel, "How directors and auditors can improve corporate governance," *Journal of Accountancy* (January 1996): 53.

23. "Strengthening the professionalism of the independent auditor," report to the Public Oversight Board of the SEC Practice Section, AICPA, from the Advisory Panel on Auditor Independence (September 13, 1994).

24. *United States v. Arthur Young & Co.*, U.S. 805 (1984).

25. Joanne Morrison, "SEC enforcement chief issues warning to auditors," Reuters (December 9, 1997): Yahoo.

26. Melody Petersen, "Auditors varied duties said to create conflicts," *The New York Times on the Web*, Business Section (January 7, 1998) and, by the same author, "KPMG settling suit by California Teachers," *The New York Times on the Web*, Business Section (January 21, 1998).

27. Neasa MacErlean, "Entrants line up for a beauty contest," *Accountancy* (May 1993): 42–43.

28. "A glimmer of hope," *The Economist* (April 1, 1995): 74.

29. Thomas Petzinger, Jr., "This auditing team wants you to create a moral organization," *Wall Street Journal* (January 19, 1996): B1.

30. "Management consultancy—The advice business," *The Economist* (March 22, 1997): 3–22.

31. Melody Petersen, "Andersen Worldwide's civil war heats up," *The New York Times on the Web*, Business Section (December 18, 1997).

32. "American Express acquires accounting divisions," Reuters (March 19, 1997).

33. Philip B. Chenok, "Fifteen years of meeting challenges, strategies in action 1980–1995: Creating a measure of excellence for the accounting profession," *Journal of Accountancy* (June 1995): 66.

34. "A glimmer of hope," *The Economist* (April 1, 1995): 74.

35. Andrew Jack, "No accounting for standards," *Financial Times* (September 21, 1994).

36. Lee Berton, "Booked up: Big accounting firms, striving to cut costs, irritate small clients; many companies say service has slipped badly, hurt in part by staff turnover," *Wall Street Journal* (April 21, 1994): A1.

37. Ibid. (Quotes a survey of 400 small-business owners by Cicco & Associates, a Murraysville, Pa., consulting firm.)

38. Joe Queenan, "I married an accountant," *Newsweek* (November 14, 1988): 12.

39. Michael Henning interviewed by Ciar'an Hancock, "All change for the way ahead," *International Accounting Bulletin* (June 17, 1996): 10.

40. Allison Collins and Norm Schultz, "A critical examination of the AICPA Code of Professional Conduct," *Journal of Business Ethics* (January 1995): 31–41.

41. A. J. Briloff, *Unaccountable Accounting* (New York: Harper and Row, 1972), 283–284.

42. Michael Groom, "The year ahead," *Accountancy* (January 1996): 90.

43. Lee Berton, "Accountants group to spend $3 million on ad hoc campaign, organization aims to enhance image of profession hurt by audit failures, lawsuits," *Wall Street Journal* (September 27, 1995): C21. (The quote in the article is of Michael Klein, partner in the New York City accounting firm of Fasman, Klein & Feldstein.)

44. Don M. Pallais, "Positioning the audit function for growth," *Journal of Accountancy* (July 1995): 14.

Chapter 12

What Role for the Big Five?

THE AUDITING OLIGOPOLY

In a pattern reminiscent of other maturing industries, the auditing profession is becoming concentrated in an ever-smaller number of firms. The term "mature" is used here to describe an industry whose sales do not expand more rapidly than the economy it serves—exactly what has happened to this profession in the past generation.[1] The Big Eight organized as such in the 1960s, when they significantly outdistanced in revenue the far more numerous second-tier group to become the largest auditing firms in the country. The number of second-tier firms has since declined, some through merger and others through liquidation. Meanwhile, as a result of two mergers in the late 1980s, the Big Eight were reduced to the Big Six. In 1996 the Big Six had a gross income of close to $44.0 billion, representing some 87 percent of the top 19 international firms. Their share in the audit of publicly quoted companies was even higher—nearly 95 percent. Indeed, the number of major firms has shrunk steadily in the past 60 years.

When Ernst and Whinney merged with Arthur Young Co. and Deloitte Haskins & Sells with Touche Ross & Co. in the late 1980s, the respective senior partners explained the benefits their clients would enjoy as a result. Ten years later there was little evidence that these advantages have, in fact, come about. There are no signs that the services provided by the Big Five are any better than were those of the Big Eight. And, within the firms themselves, there are indications that the overhead has increased and decision making has become more cumbersome.

Not long after these mergers took place, I ventured to predict that, by the middle of the twenty-first century, the certified public accountant could become

extinct. Although few will acknowledge it, they are already an endangered species. While many accountants are worried about what is happening to their
profession and are dissatisfied with the defensive posture of their leaders, there
are few, if any, innovative thinkers who have begun charting new trails to guide
auditors toward survival in the complex, diversified economy of tomorrow.

Then, in the fall of 1997, came the announcement of two more impending
mergers; the first, in September, between Coopers & Lybrand and Price Waterhouse, which together had $11.8 billion in revenues in 1996 and over 8,500
partners.[2] A month later the even larger firms of KPMG and Ernst & Young,
with joint revenues of $15.3 billion and some 11,700 partners, announced similar
plans.[3] Echoing the pronouncements of a decade earlier, Nicholas G. Moore,
slated to become chairman of the new Coopers Lybrand Price Waterhouse
group, explained that the merger was driven ''by the recognition that our clients
require seamless global support and unprecedented levels of expertise that, until
now, were simply not available from any one organization.''[4] The then Big Six
have claimed to be proud of their different corporate cultures but, in fact, these
individual characteristics were similar enough to pose no obstacle to merger.
James J. Schiro, soon to be the CEO of PriceWaterhouseCoopers, added that
''We have been struck by the compatibility of our cultures and our shared
vision.''[5] But Richard C. Breeden, a former chairman of the SEC, seemed to
question the benefits of such mergers, saying that ''Whether these mergers make
sense for the country, given the high degree of concentration, is another question. It would certainly force the antitrust authorities to take a look.''[6]

The first proposed merger was soon consummated under the name of
PriceWaterhouseCoopers, but in mid-February, four months after they declared
their intention to merge, Ernst & Young and KPMG announced that they had
abandoned the plan. As Melody Petersen of the *New York Times* observed, it
was a startling and embarrassing turnabout after they had taken such significant
steps toward establishing the new mega-firm, insisting to their clients and the
general public that it was crucial for their long-term survival.[7] Disregarding the
advice they say they give to clients, they had not done their market research
before signing the merger agreement and did not anticipate the difficulties regulators could cause in Europe, Canada, Australia, and possibly the United States.
Nor did they realize how unimpressed their clients would be by the merger
prospect. Not least, there was significant opposition to the move from partners
outside the United States.[8]

With the noted exception of Arthur Andersen, the other Big Five and second-
tier accounting organizations are basically associations of independent firms acting under a trade name, very much like a franchise system. It is quite striking
how dominant the Big Five—only recently the Big Eight—have remained. The
second-tier firms have hardly made a dent in their client bases. Although they
are just as proud of their standards as the Big Five and often charge less, the
second-tier firms simply do not get the message across that they can provide
the security and comfort potential clients expect. Like the Big Five, their num-

bers, too, are shrinking as their members either cease to exist or merge upstream, usually with one of the Big Five. Since the late 1980s both Laventhol & Horwath and Oppenheim, Dixon and Appel have disintegrated, and Binder's in the United Kingdom has merged with Arthur Andersen. It is even more common for partners in the local practices of second-tier firms to become, with age, pessimistic about the future and, opting out of their responsibilities, sell their practice to a willing Big Five buyer. In other words, the number of big and second-tier firms has halved in less than a decade. The general public does not seem concerned about this trend. Although strategic meetings among second-tier firms are much concerned with the Big Five, they have never established a working plan for drawing significant numbers of clients away from the latter.

Not surprisingly, there are professional pundits who believe that this reduction in numbers of the larger and second-tier firms will change the whole modus operandi of the profession, not least its relations with clients. Questions may be raised as to whether the remaining five giant firms conform with the various antitrust laws of the United States, and the European Community. Examination of this issue is not likely to be completed soon. Another question will be what such mega-firms can contribute to economic growth. Maybe the biggest change in audit responsibilities will be to boost the responsibilities and prestige of the internal auditors. In any case, the image of the profession will change—far more quickly than expected only recently.

Together, at the end of 1996, the then Big Six employed 460,000 partners and staff around the world.[9] Arthur Andersen led these firms with gross income of $9.1 billion (17 percent of the income of the 19 largest firms). The smallest was Price Waterhouse, which reported income of close to $5 billion (9.4 percent). Revenues of the two leaders of the second tier, BDO and Grant Thornton, were approximately 2.7 percent each of this tier's total, while those of number 9 (Moors Rowland) to 15 (HLB) were each between 1 and 2 percent. The income of number 19, Kreston International, was just over 0.5 percent. It should be emphasized, however, that not only the smaller firms but also five of the Big Six (with the exception of Arthur Andersen) have numerous independent income centers and are not full partnerships in the strictly legal sense.

Are the Big Five a cartel? Some of their activities could lead one to the conclusion that they are. Certainly, the banks and underwriters of companies registering with the SEC to make an initial public offering (IPO) in the capital markets are well aware of the need to be audited by a member of the Big Five. A cartel, of course, is an economic body in which members agree to some form of joint action; rather than being directed by a central management, they retain control of their own affairs. Often these bodies are international trade organizations, and the agreements they reach—at times orally—concern production restrictions, removal of competition, or price-fixing. In this vein, it has been alleged that the Big Five work in concert to keep second-tier and other auditing firms out of what they regard as their backyard. Through their senior partners, they have a dominant influence on accounting institutes and other self-regulating professional bodies such as the Financial Accounting Standards Board in the United States and the Accounting Standards Board in the United Kingdom.

In Britain, the senior partners of the Big Six meet at least four times a year over a dinner hosted and chaired by each of them, in turn.[10] No agenda or minutes are committed to writing. Officially, they discuss only issues of general interest to the profession. More conscious of the antitrust laws, their American counterparts still keep an ongoing line of communication open. In it they address matters of common concern, ranging from the cost of litigation to forming what the business world perceives as self-serving accounting statements.

Are audit services improved thanks to this cooperation? Does it encourage talented, imaginative people to join their ranks? Does it fulfill a function in striving for a professional sense of direction? And not least, to what extent do these firms contribute to better corporate governance and accountability? There is, in fact, little evidence that they help promote standards.

THE BIG FIVE UNDER FIRE

Until not too long ago, a partner in a Big Five accounting firm was assured of secure and lucrative tenure until retirement. That is no longer so. Not only are partners apparently dispensable, but, as repeated in the previous section's discussion of the profession, there is doubt as to whether all the Five will still be in business in the next generation. Competition has become rough and frustrating, and fee-cutting is commonplace. Audit and tax services are often zero-sum games: Get a client, lose a client.

The Big Five, like the second-tier and almost all other accounting firms, are formal, legal partnerships in which each partner has an unlimited liability. That is how they market and present themselves to their clients and the public. If one investigates how they are managed, however, one soon understands that they actually are run like a corporation. The partners do not really have more say in management than senior and medium-level staff in incorporated companies. Once they have elected the executive partner and the executive management committee, they function as mid-level corporate executives who only meet their superiors periodically—for instance, at the annual retreat and general meeting. Their responsibilities are limited to their own assignments, and they have little information or knowledge as to what is happening in other sections of the firm. They have no effective voice in such matters as their position in the pecking order, their annual rewards, and their share in the partnership's equity. These decisions are made by a select committee headed by the managing partner, who assesses the value of each partner's performance. This mechanism also controls whether they are promoted or—in a few but increasing number of cases—shown the way out of the firm. After decades of growth, accounting firms have, since the 1980s, seen their auditing divisions stagnate—an uncomfortable development and one believed to require harsh corrective measures. Aware that they must cut the fat, KPMG, Ernst & Young, and Coopers & Lybrand collectively released more than 800 partners in the early 1990s. "It was a sobering, frightening experience," noted one then Big Six partner.[11]

THE CLOUD OF LITIGATION

Probably the single most irritating aspect of litigation is its cost. Many class actions and other legal initiatives do not reach the courts, but the average cost of addressing them is approximately $1 million. At an average of at least 12 percent of the total accounting and audit revenue of the Big Six, the cost of litigation has become hazardous to the continued professional existence of some of these firms.

Among the possibilities recently considered by some CPAs are countersuits against their clients (or ex-clients). For example, in the Phar-Mor case, Coopers & Lybrand countersued management; BDO Seidman charged the outside directors and the audit committee of Leslie Fay Companies, Inc., for not having asked the necessary questions concerning the company's borrowings to buy inventory when sales were declining.[12] Had they done so, the board might have identified the overstatement of inventory in 1992 and the overall manipulation of the financial statements. It is too soon to assess whether such countersuits will convince those who are considering a lawsuit against an accounting firm to resist the urge.

Are all the lawsuits unfair? Not necessarily. Samples of over 150 firms that were audited in the 40 years ending in 1994 show that auditors were more likely to be named as defendants when client firms were relatively large, suffered from financial difficulties and poor price performance, and received qualified audit reports. Lawsuits were more common if the auditor employed unstructured audit technology and the client represented a relatively larger proportion of its revenues. Indeed, there is evidence that these suits were often associated with both misleading financial statements and audit failures.[13]

Not least because of their fear of litigation, large and medium-sized firms publicize that they do not automatically take on new clients, and they have developed procedures to dump risky ones. Some issue a policy of not taking new clients unless they are "squeaky clean." But the record shows that even if they are willing to forego business, their precautionary steps are still not foolproof, and they still take gambles as they inevitably accept clients who turn out to be hazardous and costly.[14]

One of the characteristics of the profession today is that, in most cases where damages are claimed against one firm of CPAs, the claimant retains another auditing group as supporting specialist. It is more than a little ironic that, while the managing partners of the major firms call for a limit on their legal liability in lawsuits, the heads of their own insolvency practices are busy filing against each others' firms for negligent auditing—a rather weird round-robin syndrome to which most of the Big Five, from Arthur Andersen to KPMG, are party.[15]

The collapse of the savings and loan industry brought several dozen suits against auditing firms in general and the then Big Six in particular—more than any previous other single economic breakdown. Although the amount of money paid as damages (mainly by the Big Six) reached many hundreds of millions of dollars, the Resolution Trust Corporation (RTC) continued to award audit contracts to the Big Six, for substantial fees. Aware that there are cases in which the performance of their colleagues is substandard, auditors do not always argue that the charges against them are biased or unfair. They contend, however, that in total they are exaggerated, giving two arguments: First, they say that imposing total punishment for partial blame is vindictive; second, they point out that the present system harms everyone and that ultimately the increased costs of insurance and legal fees are transferred, through higher audit fees, to the clients.

Some of the Big Five believe that if the courts would recognize the principle of proportional liability, their lives would be far simpler and less threatened and that legal judgments would be much fairer. Although some members of Congress support the auditors' call to limit their liability, it appears that the majority will not, at least for the foreseeable future. In a typical comment, made when legislation that would set new federal rules for product liability was killed in the Senate at the end of June 1994, Senator Paul Wellstone (D-Minn.) commented, "We need more corporate accountability, not less."[16] If direct legislation is not enacted, one way the Big Five may attempt to find protection would be by turning into limited liability partnerships. This form of organization provides a legal shield that protects the personal assets of those partners not directly involved in litigation. This approach may, however, have only limited value, for it is far from certain that it will afford protection from the type of liability suits usually filed against professional partnerships.[17]

Some practitioners—especially in the United Kingdom—suggest that accounting firms move offshore. But the efficacy of doing so is dubious. Even though they can relocate to the Channel Islands, for example, they will still be practicing for clients in the City of London, and it will be possible to sue them there. Then there is the school that wants permission for partnerships to incorporate, thus enabling them to limit their liability. Others advocate limiting the damages claimed from professionals to a proportion of the total damage caused by all involved, including management and others; thus, each party would pay a part of the damages apportioned according to its degree of culpability.[18] Measuring responsibility to this end would be no mean feat.

There are politicians on either side of the Atlantic who are at least willing to listen to such proposals, but despite the discomfort of recent years, little progress has been made, not least because there are counterarguments against reducing the cost to the professionals. One is that proportional liability would allow accountants to bear only part of the cost of failing, thereby encouraging them to take fewer precautions and risk more fraud. It is unfortunate, but inevitable, that some clients will attempt to cook their books. Making auditors consider the full cost of their efforts, however, encourages them to approach every audit "with a healthy sense of terror," and many believe that the threat of litigation is the best way to convince auditors to conduct a proper audit and attempt to expose fraud. It is a viewpoint that should not be dismissed as long as the profession remains so vague about its ethical and professional obligations.[19] At the same time, however, we must consider the effectiveness of litigation in an age in which auditors simply cannot be in control of all the facts that should be at their disposal.

Can Conditions Be Improved?

The Economist made a strong statement of auditors' responsibilities late in the 1980s: "Auditors are capitalism's handmaidens. Unless they provide, and are seen to provide, accurate, honest, and impartial information on companies, the whole structure of market economies will be threatened. There is therefore a strong public interest in ensuring that accountancy firms themselves are in good health." The writer went on to comment that there was no apparent benefit to the public in larger accounting firms becoming even larger, and he appeared worried that the firms that had recently merged to become the Big Six would not necessarily be more efficient or offer better choices to clients.[20]

Since the Big Six emerged at the end of the 1980s, their members have been criticized for missing too many bad cases, even long after the alarm had been raised. In self-defense, the professionals alluded to an "expectations gap," and tried to explain that their role was limited to expressing an opinion on the financial statements, after employing Generally Accepted Accounting Standards; they disclaimed the broader role of corporate behavior watchdog. The public, however, expects the external auditor to play a greater role in ensuring that the corporate value is stated accurately and in detecting and exposing fraud and mismanagement (see note 20). Evidently, the profession is in a state of siege, suffering from too many class actions and too much destructive interfirm competition. The average partner senses almost continuous pressures from his clients.

Partners and principals in the consulting wing of auditing firms usually address the needs of new clients, whose core accounting needs are served by other firms of CPAs. Because their per capita income is often considerably higher than that of the practicing auditors, there have been efforts to separate the two profit centers, but implementing this change is problematic. Not only might the split not really ease the difficulties of the accounting arm, but it could also create conflicts of interest and personality issues, and there are other criticisms. First, how can an auditor in a firm providing both services to the same client retain his independence? Second, such consulting services may detract from auditing professionalism. In response, Philip Laskawy, chairman of Ernst & Young, says that through consulting, clients are given good advice on how they can be more efficient or better at what they are doing. "That's not additional consulting service. That's part of the audit," he says.

The concept that cross-fertilization between the auditor and the consultant improves the auditing services provided to individual clients has not, however, proved itself, and most consulting fees come from clients not audited by the firm. Although there are only partial data on the subject and although the leaders of the Big Five would be hesitant to admit failure, there is reason to believe that the synergy they were hoping for from their consulting arms has not materialized. Some of them, notably Andersen Consulting, have performed impressively, but most of their consulting income still comes from companies not audited by the firm. Similarly, their success in convincing their clients to have their auditing carried out by their accounting arm has, at best, been moderate. This has not deterred the accounting firms from continuing to nurture their consulting divisions, taking this to be their major thrust toward economic growth.

In the fall of 1997, the leaders of four of the Big Six announced their intention to merge, which would have reduced their number to the Big Four. The resolve was duly approved by the U.S. and U.K. partners. But the public and American and European regulators soon began to ask whether a group of four might not restrict competition and therefore not be in the public interest. The regulators in Washington appeared relatively willing to accept the mergers, but the European Commission's top antitrust official, Commissioner Karel van Miert, expressed "serious concerns," saying that the two proposed mergers could damage competition and perhaps undermine the integrity of the independent auditors.

Most of those who tried to guess what the regulators would decide doubted that they would veto the planned mergers themselves, although there was some speculation that, in order to prevent conflicts of interest from proliferating, they might require the merging firms to separate their consulting arms from their auditing business. Many believe that it is the combination of auditing and consulting that clients and financial regulators find least appealing in the profession.[21]

Early in 1998, opposition to these mergers became more focused. A "global survey on attitudes toward consolidation within the accounting profession" conducted by the London-based RI found that seven out of ten of the world's top business executives were opposed to reducing the Big Six to four, and thought that it would be harmful to competition.[22] The Economist supported this view, pointing out that "the accountancy firms have offered no concessions to ease concerns about diminished competition. . . . That leaves competition authorities with no choice but to say no." [23] This criticism will surely be considered by the regulators, on both sides of the Atlantic.

If relations between the Big Five and their clients are so uneasy and unsatisfactory, how can they be improved? Today's oligopolistic conditions, in which a handful of firms audit more than 90 percent of all the thousands of traded companies and banks, insurance companies, and utilities whose shares are not quoted, do not encourage the sensible pricing of accounting services. This situation can change only if and when the clients' actual needs, rather than those spelled out by the regulator, gain a greater influence on the profession.

Meanwhile, however, many companies retain one of the Big Five for convenience, because it is a regulatory necessity and because they do not give a high priority to the selection of a new CPA. This lack of action, whether owing to inertia or otherwise, also reduces the number of inconvenient questions that might be asked by the audit committee, often dominated by outside directors who, unable or unwilling to invest the time needed to penetrate deeply into the company's affairs, prefer the apparent security of commissioning a recognized brand name to perform the audit. Likewise, senior company officers usually feel more comfortable with members of the Big Five, for they are less likely to poke their noses into the corporate structure and come up with unexpected, potentially embarrassing questions.

In short, there is no magic strategy that will lift the profession out of the doldrums, but the following guidelines could reduce CPA anxiety:

1. Make sure that the auditor genuinely understands the client and the industrial environment involved.
2. Make sure that the public knows that the auditors are not certifying the truth of financial statements but, rather, simply affirming that those statements are presented in accordance with Generally Accepted Accounting Principles.
3. Press more strongly on the FASB and other regulators to change the very nature of the financial statements to reflect more realistically how companies operate today.

And, suggests Richard Measelle of Arthur Andersen, "Measure a company's performance not only against itself, period to period, but against other companies within the industry.... Focus on best practices ... value intangible assets, which are increasingly the real value of the company. They say you cannot value intellectual capital, but maybe you can value some of the external signs of it through R&D spending, the number of Ph.D.s on staff, or how much training the company provides." All these things are easier said than done. The ideas have been familiar to the profession for years, but individual CPAs have not managed to get their message across to their clients. Apparently, it will take years for these ideas to mature into an integrated program and much training and tactics will be required to streamline the marketing capabilities of CPAs and improve their specialized knowledge. Meanwhile, it looks as though they will just continue to maintain their defensive posture. Sooner or later, a call to reassess relations between auditor and client will surely come. In such an examination, the question will arise of whether the profession as practiced today is truly necessary or whether it should change radically, as in the example shown in the next chapter.

NOTES

1. "The fountain of youth," *The Economist*, Focus (January 16, 1993): 65.
2. Andrew Young, "Coopers & Lybrand, Price Waterhouse to merge," Reuters (September 18, 1997).

3. "KPMG, Ernst & Young tipped for merger-paper," Reuters (October 17, 1997); and "KPMG, Ernst & Young set for mega merger," Reuters (October 18, 1997).

4. Martha M. Hamilton, "Two accounting firms to form world's biggest," *The Washington Post* (September 19, 1997): GO1.

5. "Coopers Lybrand, Price Waterhouse to merge, vision to create global professional services powerhouse": http://www.coopers.co.za/mrege/intpress.htm'.

6. "Big accounting firms may merge," AP (October 18, 1997).

7. Melody Petersen, "Plans to create world's largest accounting and consulting firm abandoned," *The New York Times on the Web*, Business Section (February 14, 1998).

8. Amy Yuhn, "KPMG, Ernst & Young call off merger," Reuters (February 13, 1998).

9. See also the schedule below, taken from *Accountancy* (January 1997): 13.

Firm	Fee Income U.S. billion 1996	Fee Income U.S. billion 1995	% Change	Partners	Total Staff	Offices
Andersen Worldwide	9.5	8.1	17.0	2,777	91,572	371
KPMG	8.1	7.5	8.0	6,250	77,000	812
Ernst & Young	7.8	6.9	13.0	5,500	72,000	660
Coopers & Lybrand Intl.	6.8	6.2	9.0	5,250	74,000	760
Deloitte Touche	6.5	5.9	9.5	4,749	63,440	692
Price Waterhouse	5.0	4.5	13.0	3,246*	55,000	420
	43.7	39.1		27,772	433,012	

* 1995 figure

10. City People, "Nick Land rocks the dinner table," *Financial Times* (March 4, 1996).

11. Richard and Katherine Barret, "Auditing the accounting firms: Under heavy fire the Big Six are finally changing how they do business," *Financial World* (September 27, 1995): 30.

12. *United States District Court, Southern District of New York, in re Leslie Fay Companies, Inc.*, Securities Litigation, Third-Party Complaint of BDO Seidman, 92 Civ. 8036 (WCC).

13. Thomas Lys and Ross L. Watts, "Lawsuits against auditors," *Journal of Accounting Research* (Supplement 1994): 95–102.

14. John Schwartz, "Large CPA firms shed 'iffy' audits," *Phoenix & Valley of the Sun* (business journal) (July 7, 1995): 1.

15. "The liabilities of auditors," *Financial Times* (May 23, 1994).

16. "Product liability bill killed again," *Chemical Marketing Reporter* (July 4, 1994): 4.

17. Bart Ziegler, "Top accountants to shield partners from lawsuits," *Wall Street Journal* (n.d.): C14.

18. "Quaking in their books," *The Economist* (December 16, 1995).

19. "The Big Six PLC," *The Economist* (October 7, 1995): 109.

20. "Who will audit the auditors? Ever bigger partnerships of accountants aren't much use to anyone," editorial in *The Economist* (July 15, 1989): 18.

21. Alexander Smith, "Focus—U.K. gives Europe views on accountancy mergers," Reuters (January 13, 1998), London. http://biz.yahoo.com/financ/980113/britain-ac-2.html.

See also "Double entries—accountancy mergers," *The Economist* (December 13, 1997): 68; and Edmund L. Andrews, "European inquiry on accounting mergers," *The New York Times on the Web*, Business Section (January 21, 1998).

22. "Business leaders oppose accountancy mergers—survey," Reuters (January 28, 1998).

23. "Too few accountants," *The Economist* (January 31, 1998): 18.

Chapter 13

The Rise of
the Audit Committee

AUDITORS AND INTERNAL CONTROLS

In theory, auditors are in a unique position to advise audit committees—and, for that matter, management—on the quality of the company's internal controls. It is reasonable to expect them to be skilled in evaluating such systems, although, of course, they must have regular and unrestricted access to all employees, including those in the company's internal audit department.[1] Many CPAs believe, however, that evaluating audit controls forces them to assume too much responsibility and poses too many questions and uncertainties for a comfortable relationship with the client. Consequently, even though there has been little public notice of this fact, auditors in the United States—and more so in Britain—often withhold their opinion on the effectiveness of internal controls.

This practice is a change from that of a generation ago, when outside auditors regarded the review of internal controls as an integral part of their work, essential to a proper audit. But as the size of their clients and the scale of their paperwork increased they often supported the suggestion—and sometimes actively encouraged it—that the company set up an internal audit team to carry out tasks they had previously undertaken themselves. At first, when such teams were formed, they followed closely a program designed by the audit firm. Gradually, however, the internal auditors became more and more independent from the influence and supervision of the outside auditors and later from the direct authority of executive management. Today, many boards of directors, which previously had discovered the use of audit committees, have learned how to benefit from the internal audit team's input; and often it is the latter, rather than the outside auditors, who perform the function of senior accounting consultants and act as a resource for the audit committee and the board.

The story has not yet been told in detail of how, without fully realizing what it was doing, the accounting profession abdicated its traditional responsibility for internal controls. Suddenly, there seemed to be no public call or professional requirement for outside auditors to offer an opinion on the effectiveness of the internal controls. It seems now as if the traditional auditing services have been split in two, with the CPAs quite comfortable in ignoring the internal audit team, and it is unclear who should evaluate the performance of the latter. When they finally realized how this service had been usurped, auditors could only rationalize the benefits resulting from its transfer outside their brief. Observers trying to understand how this split in assignments occurred, however, may find the professional explanation unconvincing, for surely this change has reduced the effectiveness, the use, and some of the meaning of the outside audit. Indeed, when a professional now sets out to report on the level of competence of internal control, such reporting, rather than being an integral part of the audit, becomes an objective in its own right, independent from the regular audit. British auditors, for example, are now advised that appropriate criteria for the purpose of evaluating the adequacy of internal controls must be established separately; until this is done, they must refrain from expressing any opinion on the standards and efficiency of the controls.

When U.S. CPAs follow the U.K. trend, as they sometimes do, and reserve their opinion on the client's internal control system, their business colleagues have even less need for (or appreciation of) the services they provide. Already it is clear that external auditors have less information about the firm than the internal audit team, and they often find that collecting it is more costly to the client than leaving the whole matter to the in-house auditor. The board now often perceives the value of information provided by external auditors over and above that provided by the internal auditors as of secondary importance.[2] How the position of the internal auditor has become more central to governance is amplified in the following pages.

A SHIFT OF RESPONSIBILITY

As noted above, a quiet, almost unnoticed and bloodless revolution has been taking place in the auditing discipline. The internal auditors of large companies today are rapidly assuming responsibilities that, until recently, the outside independent auditors claimed as theirs. The development gathered momentum in the 1970s, when companies were growing and diversifying, and outside auditors were finding it difficult, relatively costly, to carry out comprehensive, in-depth audits that included reviews of internal controls. A far more sophisticated in-house accounting staff was part of this corporate growth, as was the introduction of electronic data processing (EDP) systems, and a competitive market deterred accountants from exaggerated billings. It was an era when the independent CPA learned to be far more cautious in dealing with clients.

In the course of this evolution, outside auditors began to delegate some of their work to what they thought was an unassuming, moderately sized internal audit department. Early on, they believed they would monitor and use the internal audit as a resource for their overall work, not anticipating that the internal auditor would become a power in his own right—one that gradually established considerable influence. Clearly, these outside CPAs failed to anticipate the increasing knowledge and professionalism of internal control units, nor did they foresee that giving up some of their traditional responsibilities would reduce their overall attractiveness to clients. The internal auditor has become an important and well-informed corporate officer. By encouraging the rise of the internal auditor, CPAs divested themselves not only of direct responsibility but also of influence in matters concerning internal controls. This shift has become especially apparent in their relationships with their boards of directors and with the increasingly influential audit committees. Through the audit committee the internal auditor began to be heard in the boardroom. Indeed, today, most directors are more interested in internal reporting than that of the independent auditor.

Boards and, especially, audit committees have discovered that the internal auditor is a far more knowledgeable resource, at less cost, than the outside auditor. Internal auditors have learned to provide a wider range of services than outside auditors, and they are always on call. They have also accepted the challenge of providing relevant information and training to audit committee members. In addition, they have tacitly undertaken to review the extent to which the reporting system is satisfactory, knowing that if data presented to the board are "materially misstated" they should say so. Most importantly, they have acquired considerable independence from management by convincing the officers and directors that it is in everyone's best interests that they report directly to the audit committee.[3] This arrangement, of course, implies a responsibility, for the corporate officers and board members are aware that if the audit committee fails to act, the internal controller may report his findings to the regulators.[4]

The British Auditing Practices Board recognized the importance of the internal audit unit when Philip Ashton, chairman of its Internal Control Working Party, observed "it may well be that an internal audit group is best placed to understand business risks and how they are controlled, and they could probably look beyond internal financial controls."[5] And yet, although both the function and the prestige of the internal control departments of large and medium-sized companies have been continuously growing, their role has not yet been fully defined. It is, indeed, still unclear to some that they cannot be effective in the dual capacity of watchdog of controls and business advisor, as some boards of directors expect of them.[6] That is to say, one cannot be a fully accountable auditor while also being responsible for executive activities, for there is a built-in conflict between the roles. If, as seems increasingly likely and as many expect, the internal auditor becomes the "corporate conscience," it will be the responsibility of senior management and the audit committee to ensure that this function is not sullied by asking auditors to provide counsel on operations and strategy.

Of course, it is understandable that corporations want the internal auditor to be a superman, advising and helping to reduce costs and deliver better returns while operating within the confines of a closely scrutinized control environment. But the audit duties should be considered the more important function, for it is here that the internal auditor can provide protection for the directors. They look to him for relevant information and security in carrying out their fiduciary responsibility—something they increasingly no longer expect from their outside auditors.

As we have seen, one of the ancillary changes brought about by the emergence of the audit committee was a major shift in the culture of corporate governance: upgrading of the role of the internal auditor at the expense of the external CPA. The veteran external auditors were far more concerned with what the CFO reported and about his relationship with the committee. Although part of the original mission of audit committees was to meet with the external auditors to discuss the performance of the internal auditors, the committees came to realize that the input of the internal auditors is considerably more valuable. Even more embarrassing to the external auditors, in many cases the director of internal auditing has in recent years been given the responsibility of coordinating the audit of the outside auditors.

It did not take long for directors of internal auditing to realize the opportunities available to them in becoming a dependable resource for the audit committee. They saw that they increased their stature by reporting to the audit committee and that a good working relationship between them and the committee could assist the latter in fulfilling its responsibility to the board of directors, shareholders, and other parties. The internal auditors have also been strengthened in many instances when audit committees have been given responsibility for appointment and removal of heads of their bureaus. Unlike an external auditor, the director of internal auditing attends nearly 90 percent of audit committee meetings and fairly frequently meets separately with the head of the committee.[7]

Thus, in far less than a generation, a major change in professional standing has taken place. Today the audit committees of many boards expect the company's internal audit office, as part of its assignments, to be responsible for all the external auditing activity of the corporation—and this procedure is accepted by the outside auditors. Accordingly, internal auditors are expected to advise the audit committee on objectives and scope of the external audit prior to its start. Upon completion of the audit the internal auditors are then expected to participate in the exit meetings with the outside auditors, to discuss the latter's findings and recommendations, to advise the audit committee on management's responsiveness to them.

One indication of how far expectations have advanced is the fact that the internal audit department sometimes outsources work. Internal audit heads have become cost-conscious and have found that at least some of their work can be performed more cost-effectively if outsourced. Often, the first candidate for such work is an outside firm of independent CPAs. Whereas, only a generation ago, these functions were assumed to be the responsibility of the latter, the questions that have arisen about the shift in responsibility have led Michael H. Sutton, the SEC's chief accountant, to state "It is not the staff's goal to preclude auditors from providing internal audit outsourcing. Rather, if auditors provide those services to their audit clients, we believe that the impact of those arrangements on auditors' independence should be carefully considered in each situation."[8]

One development that may be expected in the next few years is full recognition of the important contribution of the internal auditor to corporate governance. One step further is envisaged by some experts who urge that, rather than outsourcing, the internal auditors team up with the outside auditors to provide an attractive blend of resources. Such a joint undertaking would increase staff flexibility, enable the acquisition of outside technical expertise, and reduce costs without sacrificing control. Although the final outcome is still undecided, some auditors worry that outsourcing could have a bearing on their professional independence (a topic addressed at the end of this chapter.)

THE ROLE OF THE AUDIT COMMITTEE

Audit committees in publicly owned companies, composed of outside directors, first came into being in 1978 at the insistence of the New York Stock Exchange. Their role is still expanding, but it is too early to assess their contribution (see note 3). Once considered the wimps of corporate governance, they are coming under increased scrutiny amid the proliferation of shareholder suits and boardroom upheavals over poor top management.[9] But when they do their job well, they gain respect and prestige.

The call a generation ago for the establishment of audit committees arose when it was recognized that the board of directors was too cumbersome and often ill-equipped to deal with auditing and accounting matters. The boards believed that they had higher priorities they were more competent to address. (In many cases, of course, they were proved wrong. Among the more infamous shortcomings of boards was the failure to anticipate the collapse of the huge Penn Central conglomerate or the aggressively growing Equity Funding, a financial and insurance group. Also, the boards of some of the companies engaged in foreign trade at that time took no steps to prevent the bribery of foreign officials, which came to public notice in the mid-1970s.) Today audit committees are expected to review management's financial actions and controls, in addition to keeping tabs on internal and outside auditors.

All involved regulators, ranging from the SEC to the AICPA and the Institute of Internal Auditors, welcomed the NYSE initiative of 1977 and 1978 that brought about the ruling mentioned above. Especially receptive was the AICPA. When it first adopted the concept, this institute encouraged all public companies to establish audit committees with at least the following mandates:

* approve the selection of the independent auditor;

* review the arrangement and scope of the audit;

* consider the comments of the independent auditor with respect to weaknesses in internal control and the consideration given to corrective action taken by management;

* discuss matters of concern to the audit committee, the auditor, or management relating to the company's financial statement or other results of the audit;

* review internal accounting controls with the company's financial and accounting staff; and

* review the activities and recommendations of the company's internal auditor.

The institute added that there will, with time, be other chores that this committee should undertake.[10]

In the following years, the creation of an audit committee became common practice in all major companies. It was soon made clear by these committees that they regarded their tasks as being oversight rather than management. They recognized that if they were to interfere with management prerogatives, they would be encroaching and, worse, taking on more than they could handle.[11] Of course, a smoothly functioning audit committee will keep management staff on their toes. When management knows that it may be asked pointed questions, it may take action on problems that it might otherwise let slide.

Both the standing and the accountability of the audit committee were enhanced as a result of the proposals of the Treadway Commission in 1987 and the Public Oversight Board of the SEC Practice Section of the AICPA, which suggested that annual financial statements should be accompanied by a statement from the audit committee. According to the POB formulation published in 1994, the statement would attest that the members of the committee had reviewed the audited financial statements, conferred with management and the external auditors, and come to the conclusion that the financial statements were complete and reflected appropriate accounting principles.[12]

Boards of directors often assign audit committees diverse tasks, including overseeing financial activities, reporting on the internal controls of the company, and maintaining direct lines of communication between the board, financial managers, independent auditors, and internal auditors. Other duties range from review of corporate policies to dealing with litigation and regulatory proceedings, as well as performing or supervising special investigations.[13] Professor P. W. Wolnizer quotes paragraph 4.8 of the Macdonald Commission report, which states, "We believe the audit committee . . . should develop its own financial disclosure philosophy . . . (and) vigorously present this philosophy to both the auditor and management to ensure the best disclosure is made."[14]

Indeed, audit committees seem to be wielding considerable oversight power today. A Coopers & Lybrand survey (published early in 1995) of 250 audit committees at large companies found that 75 percent require management to

explain financial statement disparities and a full 86 percent demand that management explain financial statement accounting changes, up from 11 and 43
percent, respectively, in 1981 (see note 9).

The auditing profession was especially enthusiastic about the establishment
of audit committees. By the 1970s, auditors realized that although periodically
they had what they believed were important messages for those responsible for
the company's governance, their contacts with the boards of directors were minimal and unsatisfactory. Although outside auditors did meet with the corporate
officers, they rarely met with the directors and thus failed to establish an ongoing
dialogue with them. Accordingly, they actively encouraged all involved, from
the SEC downwards, first to consider and then to structure audit committees.
Especially enthusiastic were the second-tier firms, which were worried about
being encircled by the (then) Big Eight. They felt that if such committees came
into being, they would get a fairer hearing and, hopefully, protection in dealing
with matters they brought to the attention of the board. Soon, however, they
discovered that the audit committee had little more time for them than had the
full board previously. And one of the early steps often taken by an audit committee (without going too deeply into the qualifications or level of performance
of the serving firm, but as a matter of comfort and cautionary diligence) was to
recommend that the audit of their company be transferred to one of the Big
Eight.

Nevertheless, although they do not always receive the respect they expect
from the board, outside auditors strongly continue to support closer ties with
the audit committee. Thus, in a 1994 report, the POB recommended that the
audit committee:[15]

1. Expect the auditor, as a professional expert, to express independent judgment about
   not just the acceptability but the appropriateness of the accounting principles and the
   clarity of the financial disclosure practices used or proposed to be adopted by the
   company.

2. Hear directly from the auditors their opinion on whether management's choices of
   accounting principles are conservative, moderate, or extreme.

3. Be informed of the auditor's reasoning in determining the appropriateness of changes
   in accounting principles and disclosure practices (as well as new transactions or
   events).

4. Be informed of the auditor's reasoning in accepting or questioning significant estimates made by management.

5. Be informed of and discuss the appropriateness of all new accounting principles and
   disclosure practices on a timely basis, and discuss with the auditor how the company's
   choices of accounting principles and disclosure practices may affect shareholders and
   public views and attitudes about the company.

6. Review the auditors' fees to ensure that they are appropriate for the services they
   render.

In *Statement of Auditing Standards No. 61*, entitled "Communication with Audit Committees," the AICPA Auditing Standards Board in 1988 recognized the increased responsibility of audit committees as a necessary link with the external auditors. According to that statement, auditors are required to communicate to the committee information not specifically addressed in professional pronouncements that may assist the committee in overseeing the financial reporting and disclosure process for which management is responsible. Although many audit committees conform to the above working prescription, few regard the outside auditors as a prime source of intelligence. When they need information, they usually look to the internal auditors.

The audit committee is still in its formative years, but its record of contribution to governance thus far is encouraging, and many of those close to corporate issues will be advocating further responsibilities and assignments for it.[16] But others caution that unless the performance of audit committees is accompanied by reform of accounting and auditing practices, such that the elements of financial statements can be authenticated by recourse to reliable or public evidence, the confidence engendered by the presence of audit committees may only last until the next spate of unheralded company failures (see note 12).

However important it is to have vigorous audit committees, they may still fail to uncover financial misdeeds. One basic reason is that audit committees often lack the necessary training to perform their role. Also, they deal with past events and are (even with the support received from the internal auditors) still very dependent on the corporate information they receive. This fact became evident in the aftermath of the collapse of the savings and loan institutions, when the General Accounting Office (GAO) (the investigative arm of Congress) found that the audit committees of these thrifts had "lacked expertise in banking and related financial management" (see note 9). To enhance the standing of the audit committee, ways will have to be established to ensure that those who join have the thorough, vigorous training their fiduciary responsibilities require and that they recognize the need to spend far more time than past committee members.

Although it is difficult to predict how auditing will evolve, it is reasonable to assume that there will be considerable changes from the way it was conducted in the past. The diminution in the number of major firms, the advent of internal corporate audit divisions, the growing power of the audit committee and the difficulty—if not impossibility—of ensuring independence are all factors that will influence the direction this discipline will take. Not least, the proliferation of products and the weakening of "comparability," that basic professional tool during the era of accountancy growth, makes the application of sound professional judgment more difficult.

Not least because of the increasingly burdensome overhead that is inevitable as a result of the size of the multibillion-dollar mega-firm members of the Big Five, auditors have become far too expensive for their clients. The shareholders and stakeholders of the average medium-sized company in the United States, the United Kingdom, or anywhere else know that they should not be expected to support such a fee structure. If and when an acceptable alternative auditing system can be worked out, more attuned to clients' needs and less costly, it should be encouraged.

One of several options worth studying consists of a truly independent board supported by the internal auditing staff, strengthened as the need arises by an outside firm of independent auditors. Internal and external auditors alike would be accountable directly to the revamped auditing committee and general board, which in turn would be accountable to a public body.

It has long been evident that when the CEO is responsible for the remuneration of the auditors of his company, their independence is impaired. A possible solution would be to set up a public corporation, funded by all publicly quoted companies, whose responsibility would be to look after the remuneration of auditors.[17] It could be the same public body as envisaged above to appoint the members of the board. Not the least of the advantages of such a proposal would be the accountability of auditors in real time to an independent controlling body.

Another option that would also enhance the workings of this modernized board would be to give it a budget and responsibility for appointing the outside auditors, who would report directly to the proposed board and be remunerated by them. In this way the auditors would be independent of management and insulated from any conflict of interest.

A little further into the future, as the tasks of the various accounting bodies evolve, we may hear a call for stronger links between outside and internal auditors. Perhaps some of their staff will be structured into one team, assigned to serve the audit committee. In such a setup the internal auditors would provide the core audit staff while the external auditor would support the team by providing specialized expertise. Such a group would replace the current structure of outside auditors whose independence may be questioned, and a board that spends far too little time on its brief to become sufficiently knowledgeable about it. Headed by the audit committee, this group could be of considerable benefit to the board and could enhance governance. It could also form a body more accountable to the shareholders and the public.

NOTES

1. Steven Leonard, "The internal control debate," *Accountancy* (June 1995): 74.

2. Fred Kofman and Jacques Lawarree, "Collusion in hierarchical agency," *Econometria* (May 1993): 630–631.

3. Rocco R. Vanasco, "The audit committee: An international perspective," *Managerial Auditing Journal*: http://www.mcb.co.uk/services/articles/liblinkpubartui/maj/vanasco.htm.

4. Lee Berton, "Accounting: Code may force CPAs to inform on employers," *Wall Street Journal* (August 4, 1995): B1.

5. Christy Chapman, "Auditors seek period to test the waters," *Internal Auditor* (April 1996): 11.

6. "Championing internal auditors," editorial in *World Accounting Report* (March 1996).

7. C. C. Verschoor, "Internal auditing interactions with the audit committee," *Internal Auditing* (Spring 1992): 20–23.

8. Christy Chapman, ed., "SEC chief accountant expressed concern over independence and outsourcing," *Internal Auditor* (February 1996): 8.

9. Lee Berton, "Corporate woes put the board audit panels in the spotlight," *Wall Street Journal* (April 7, 1995): B4.

10. Report of the Special Committee on Audit Committees, AICPA (New York, N.Y., 1979).

11. L. B. Sawyer, "Internal auditing" (Altamonte Springs, Fla.: The Institute of Internal Auditors, 1978).

12. A Study Group Report: Defining the Roles of Accountants, Bankers, and Regulators in the United States, by the Group of Thirty (1994).

13. R. Bromak and R. Hoffman, "An audit committee for dynamic times," *Directors and Boards* (Spring 1992): 51–60.

14. P. W. Wolnizer, "Are audit committees red herrings?" *Abacus* (March 1995): 45–66.

15. "Strengthening the professionalism of the independent auditor," report to the Public Oversight Board of the SEC Practice Section, AICPA, from the Advisory Panel on Auditor Independence (September 13, 1994): 16–17.

16. Arthur L. Ruffing, Jr., "The future role of the audit committee," *Directors and Boards* (Spring 1994): 51–54.

17. William Sternberg, "Cooked books," *The Atlantic Monthly* (January 1992): 38.

Selected Bibliography

Adams, James Ring, and Douglas Franz. *A Full Service Bank: How BCCI Stole Billions Around the World*. Pocket Books, 1993.

Barth, James R. *The Great Savings and Loan Debacle*. The AEI Press, 1991.

Beaty, Jonathan, and S. C. Gwynne. *The Outlaw Bank: A Wild Ride into the Secret Heart of BCCI*. Random House, 1993.

Berle, Adolph, Jr., and Gardiner C. Means. *The Modern Corporation and Private Property*. Macmillan, 1932.

Blair, Margaret M. *Ownership and Control: Rethinking Corporate Governance for the Twenty-First Century*. Brookings Institute, 1995.

Blasi, Joseph Raphael, and Douglas Lynn. *The New Owners: The Mass Emergence of Employee Ownership in Public Companies and What It Means to American Business*. HarperBusiness, 1991.

Bok, Derek. *The Cost of Talent: How Executives and Professionals Are Paid and How It Affects America*. The Free Press, 1993.

Bowen, William G. *Inside the Boardroom: Governance by Directors and Trustees*. John Wiley & Sons, 1994.

Cottell, Philip G., Jr., and Terry M Perlin. *Accounting Ethics: A Practical Guide for Professionals*. Quorum Books, 1990.

Cullinane, John J. *The Entrepreneur's Survival Guide: 101 Tips for Managing in Good Times and Bad*. Business One Irwin, 1993.

Defining the Roles of Accountants, Bankers and Regulators in the United States: A Study Group Report. Group of Thirty, 1994.

Drucker, Peter F. *The Bored Board: Towards the Next Economics and Other Essays*. Heinemann, 1981.

———. *The Changing World of the Executive*. Times Books, 1982.

Eichler, Ned. *The Thrift Debacle*. University of California Press, 1989.

Hampden-Turner, Charles. *Corporate Culture, from Vicious to Virtuous Circles*. The Economist Books, Hutchinson, 1990.

Hansen, Charles. *A Guide to the American Law Institute Corporate Governance Project.* The National Legal Center for the Public Interest, 1995.

Keasey, Kevin, and Mike Wright, eds. *Corporate Governance: Responsibilities, Risks and Remuneration.* John Wiley & Sons, 1997.

Light, Paul C. *Monitoring Government: Inspectors General and the Search for Accountability.* The Brookings Institute, 1993.

———. *Thickening Government: Federal Hierarchy and the Diffusion of Accountability.* Published jointly by the Brookings Institute and the Governance Institute, 1995.

Long, Robert Emmet. *Banking Scandals: The S&Ls and BCCI.* H. W. Wilson, 1993.

Lorsch, J. W., and E. MacIver. *Pawns or Potentates: The Reality of America's Corporate Boards.* Harvard Business School Press, 1989.

Loss, Louis. *Securities Regulation: 1955 Supplement.* Little, Brown, 1955.

Mace, Miles. *Directors: Myth and Reality.* Division of Business Administration, Harvard University, 1971.

Monks, Robert A. G., and Nell Minow. *Corporate Governance.* Blackwell Business, 1995.

Naylor, R. T. *Hot Money and the Politics of Debt.* Unwin Hyman, 1987.

Picket, K. H. Spencer, and Gerald Vinten. *The Internal Auditing Handbook.* John Wiley & Sons, 1997.

Pratt, John W., and Richard J. Zeckhauser, eds. *Principals and Agents: The Structure of Business.* Harvard Business School Press, 1991.

Ratliff, Richard L., Wanda A. Wallace, James K. Loebbecke, and William G. McFarlane. *Internal Auditing: Principles and Techniques.* Institute of Internal Auditors, 1996.

Renton, Nick. *Company Directors: Masters or Servants.* Wrightbooks Pty Ltd., 1994.

Roe, Mark J. *Strong Managers, Weak Owners: The Political Roots of American Corporate Finance.* Princeton University Press, 1994.

Stoner, James A., and Frank Werner. "Internal audit and innovation." *Financial Executives* (August 1995).

Tricker, Robert I. *International Corporate Governance: Text, Readings and Cases.* Prentice-Hall, 1995.

Truell, Peter, and Larry Gurwin. *False Profits: The Inside Story of BCCI and the World's Most Corrupt Financial Empire.* Houghton Mifflin, 1992.

Useem, Michael. *Executive Defense: Shareholder Power and Corporate Reorganization.* Harvard University Press, 1993.

Ward, Ralph D. *The 21st Century Corporate Board.* John Wiley & Sons, 1996.

Index

AICPA (American Institute of Chartered Public Accountants), 10, 22, 68, 73, 75, 76, 182; Accounting Standards Executive Committee, 72–73, 173; and audit committees, 203; Auditing Standards Board, 72, 190; POB (Public Oversight Board of), 173; POB and views on audit committees, 204, 205; president Philip Chenok, 164, 178; SECPS (SEC Practice Section), 173; and *Statement of Auditing Standards No. 61*, 206

Alberta, Canada, definition of accountability, 8

Altman, Robert, and BCCI, 44

America First, and Clark Clifford, 36

American Express Co., 2, 36, 105, 110, 137; Bob Basten, CEO of, 178; tax and business services subsidiary, 178

American Life and Casualty, and S&Ls, 30

Amoco Oil Company, 28

Andreas, Dwayne O. (CEO of Archer Daniels Midland Co.): nepotism on board of directors, 147; oversize board, 149

Apple Computer, and options for top executives, 142

Archer, William (Chairman, House Ways and Means Committee), 20 new protections for taxpayers, 24

Argentina, inability to repay sovereign debt, 35

Arthur Andersen, 177, 188, 191; Andersen Consulting, 177, 194; Binder's merged with, 189; leader of Big Six, 189; Richard Measelle, 195. *See also* Big Five

Arthur Young Co., merger with Ernst and Whinney, 187

AT&T, 76, 110, 155

Bank America, 106

Bank for International Settlements, 60

Bank of America, unwieldiness of annual reports, 76

Bank of England, 37, 38, 39, 42, 44, 165

Barings Bank, 38, 39, 41–43, 47, 148, 166; chairman Peter Baring, 47; Future Singapore, 42

Bass brothers, 122, 147

BCCI (Bank of Credit and Commerce International), 23, 28, 36, 37, 40, 44, 46; and Andrew Young, former mayor of Atlanta, 44; President Agha Hasan Abedi, 44; U.S. Senate report, 37

About the Author

DAN A. BAVLY has been a senior audit executive, director, and board member of several not-for-profit corporations, mainly in centers of higher learning, and a journalist. He is a recent Fellow at the Center for Business and Government at Harvard University's John F. Kennedy School of Government and the author of numerous books and articles, including *The Subterranean Economy.*